TEXAS GUN OWNER'S Guide

Who
can bear arms?

❖

Where
are guns forbidden?

❖

When
can you shoot to kill?

by *Alan Korwin*
and *Georgene Lockwood*
illustrations by Gregg Myers and Ralph Richardson

BLOOMFIELD PRESS
Phoenix, Arizona

BLOOMFIELD PRESS

12629 N. Tatum #440X
Phoenix, AZ 85032
(602) 996-4020 in Arizona
1-800-707-4020

ISBN: 0-9621958-5-5
Library of Congress Catalog Card Number: 95-77340

ATTENTION

Firearms Training Instructors, Clubs, Organizations,
Educators and all other interested parties:
Call us for information on quantity discounts!

To Order: For single copies or for wholesale shipments, call
1-800-707-4020, or write to us at the address above.

For Updates: Send us a self-addressed stamped envelope.

Every gun owner needs this book—
"It doesn't make sense to own a gun and not know the rules."

Printed and bound in the United States of America
at Griffin Printing of Sacramento, Calif.

10 9 8 7 6 5 4 3 2

TABLE OF CONTENTS

ILLUSTRATIONS

ACKNOWLEDGMENTS

This book is really the result of all the help we received, great and small, from the good people who shared their thoughts and resources with us. Thank you.

Ron Bertsch, Deputy, National Forests and Grasslands

Dr. James T. "Doc" Brown, Texas State Rifle Association

Susan Carley, Research and Support

Bill Clede, Sysop, Firearms Forum, CompuServe, along with Jeff Halapin, M. Scott Hammon, Kelley Hughes, John Rich and Mark Thompson

Larry Cooper, Marksman Indoor Range, Inc.

Candice M. DeBarr, Research and Support

Tom Gresham, Contributing Editor, Sports Afield

Steve Hall, Conservation Ed. Dir., Texas Parks & Wildlife Dept.

Gary Kansteiner, Attorney, Texas Legislative Council

Fred Knot, Research and Support

Marshall Kummel, Research and Support

Cheryl and Tyler Korwin

Jim Lockwood

Jeff Long, Information Coordinator, Texas General Land Office

Joe McBride, President, McBride's Guns, Inc.

John Molleston, Texas General Land Office

Harold D. Oates, Captain, Texas Parks & Wildlife Dept.

Karl N. Olson, Security Officer, Texas Parks & Wildlife Dept.

The Honorable Senator Jerry Patterson

Linda Paulson, CompuServe Journalism Forum

Terrence Plas, The Pensus Group

E.B. Reddoch, III, Exec. Dir., Texas State Rifle Association

Richard Shaw, The Pensus Group

David Smith, Alpine Range

Texas Arms Rights Coalition, Neil Atkins

Texas Gun Dealers Association
Gabriel Torre, Sportsman Shooting Center
Carlos Vaca, Asst. Commander, Texas Parks & Wildlife Dept.
Paul Velte IV, Attorney at Law
Charles Wallace, Coordinator, TSRA Grass Roots
W.L. Don Welch, Chief Ranger, Lower Colorado River Authority
James C. "Jimmy" Williams, Attorney
Karen Ziegler, Red's Indoor Range

The Texas State Rifle Association
allowed the use of information in their pamphlet,
"Know Your Texas Firearm Laws."

The National Rifle Association Institute
allowed the use of material in their pamphlet,
"Your State Firearms Laws."

In their dealings with us we found the Texas Dept. of Public Safety
to be cooperative, professional, hard-working and dedicated to fair
implementation of the complex 1995 Right-to-Carry law.

The Texas River Authorities' cooperation was greatly appreciated.
Special thanks to Phoenix trial lawyer Michael P. Anthony
Cover design by Ralph Richardson

PREFACE

Texas has strict gun laws. You have to obey the laws. There are serious penalties for breaking the rules.

Many gun owners don't know all the rules. Some have the wrong idea of what the rules are. It doesn't make sense to own a gun and not know the rules.

Here at last is a comprehensive book, in plain English, about the laws and regulations which control firearms in Texas.

The One-Glaring-Error theory says there's at least one glaring error hidden in any complex piece of work. This book is no different. Watch out for it.

FOREWORD • WARNING! • DON'T MISS THIS!

This book is not a substitute for the law. You are fully accountable under the exact wording and current interpretations of all applicable laws and regulations when you deal with firearms under any circumstances.

Many people find laws hard to understand, and gathering all the relevant ones is a lot of work. This book helps you with these chores. Collected in one volume are the principal state laws controlling gun use in Texas.

In addition, the laws and other regulations are expressed in regular conversational terms for your convenience. While great care has been taken to accomplish this with a high degree of accuracy, **no guarantee of accuracy is expressed or implied, and the explanatory sections of this book are not to be considered as legal advice or a restatement of law.** In explaining the general meanings of the laws, using plain English, differences inevitably arise, so **you must always check the actual laws.** The authors and publisher expressly disclaim any liability whatsoever arising out of reliance on information found in this book. New laws and regulations may be enacted at any time by the authorities. **The authors and publisher make no representation that this book includes all requirements and prohibitions which may exist.**

This book concerns the gun laws as they apply to law-abiding private residents in the state of Texas only. It is not intended to and does not describe most situations relating to licensed gun dealers, museums or educational institutions, local or federal military personnel, American Indians, foreign nationals, the police or other peace officers, any person summoned by a peace officer to help in the performance of official duties, persons with special licenses (including collectors), non-residents, persons with special permits or authorizations, bequests or intestate succession, persons under indictment, felons, prisoners, escapees, dangerous or repetitive offenders, criminal street gang members, delinquent, incorrigible or unsupervised juveniles, government employees, or any other people restricted or prohibited from firearm possession.

While this book discusses possible criminal consequences of improper gun use, it avoids most issues related to deliberate gun crimes. This means that certain laws are excluded, or not explained in the text. Some examples are: criminally negligent homicide and capital murder; manslaughter; concealment of stolen firearms; enhanced penalties for commission of crimes with firearms, including armed robbery, burglary, theft, kidnapping, drug offenses and assault; smuggling firearms into public aircraft; taking a weapon from a peace officer; possession of contraband; possession of a firearm in a prison by a prisoner; false application for a firearm; removal of a body after a shooting; drive by shootings; and this is only a partial list.

The main relevant parts of Texas state laws which relate to private gun ownership and use are reproduced in Appendix D. These are formally known as *Texas Revised Statutes,* and includes the *Penal Code* and *Code of Criminal Procedure.* Other state laws which may apply, such as Hunting Laws and official agency regulations, are discussed, but these laws are *not* reproduced. Key federal laws are discussed, but the laws themselves are *not* reproduced. Case law decisions, which affect the interpretation of the statutes, are *not* included.

FIREARMS LAWS ARE SUBJECT TO CHANGE WITHOUT NOTICE. You are strongly urged to consult with a qualified attorney and local authorities to determine the current status and applicability of the law to specific situations which you may encounter. The proper authorities are in Appendix C.

Guns are serious business and require the highest level of responsibility from you. **What the law says and what the authorities and courts do aren't always an exact match.** You must remember that each legal case is different and frequently lacks prior court precedents. A decision to prosecute a case and the charges brought may involve a degree of discretion from the authorities involved. Sometimes, there just isn't a plain, clear-cut answer you can rely upon. **ALWAYS ERR ON THE SIDE OF SAFETY.**

Special Note on Pending Legislation

Bills have been proposed by law makers nationally who would:

- Outlaw specific or classes of firearms by name, by operating characteristics, or by appearance
- Restrict the amount of ammunition a gun can hold and the devices for feeding ammunition
- Restrict the number of firearms and the amount of ammunition a citizen may buy or own
- Require proficiency testing and periodic licensing
- Register firearms and owners nationally
- Use taxes to limit firearm and ammunition ownership
- Create new liabilities for firearm owners, manufacturers, dealers, parents and persons involved in firearms accidents
- Outlaw keeping firearms loaded or not locked away
- Censor classified ads for firearms and eliminate firearms publications and outlaw any dangerous speech or publication
- Melt down firearms that are confiscated by police
- Prohibit gun shows and abolish hunting
- Deny or criminalize civil rights for government-promised security
- Repeal the Second Amendment to the Constitution

In contrast, less attention has been paid to laws that would:

- Mandate school-based safety training
- Provide general self-defense awareness and training
- Encourage personal responsibility in resisting crime
- Protect citizens who stand up and act against crime
- Guarantee citizens' right to travel legally armed for personal safety
- Fix the conditions which generate hard-core criminals
- Assure sentencing of serious criminals, increase the percentage of sentences actually served, provide more prison space and permanently remove habitual criminals from society
- Improve rehabilitation and reduce repeat offenses
- Reduce plea bargaining and parole abuses
- Close legal loopholes and reform criminal justice malpractice
- Reform the juvenile justice system
- Improve law enforcement quality and efficiency
- Establish and strengthen victims' rights and protection
- Hold the rights of all American citizens in unassailable esteem
- Provide for the common defense and buttress the Constitution

Some experts have noted that easy-to-enact but ineffectual "feel good" laws are sometimes pursued instead of the much tougher course of laws and social changes that would reduce crime and its root causes. Many laws aim at disarming citizens while ignoring the fact that gun possession by criminals is already strictly illegal and largely unenforced. Increasing attacks on the Constitution and civil liberties are threatening freedoms Americans have always had. You are advised to become aware of any new laws which may be enacted. Contact your legislators to express your views on proposed legislation.

To our patient and supportive families

THE RIGHT TO BEAR ARMS 1

In the United States of America, citizens have always had the right to bear arms. The Second Amendment to the United States Constitution is the historic foundation of this right to have and use guns. The Second Amendment is entitled The Right To Keep And Bear Arms. This is what it says:

> "A well regulated Militia, being necessary to the security of a free State, the right of the people to keep and bear Arms, shall not be infringed."

The intentions of the revolutionaries who drafted the Constitution were clear at the time. It was this right to bear arms that allowed those citizens 200 years ago to break away from British rule. An armed populace was a precondition for independence and freedom from oppressive government. The founders of the United States of America were unambiguous and unequivocal in their intent:

No free man shall be debarred the use of arms.
–Thomas Jefferson

The Constitution shall never be construed to authorize Congress to prevent the people of the United States, who are peaceable citizens, from keeping their own arms.
–Samuel Adams

Little more can reasonably be aimed at with respect to the people at large than to have them properly armed.
–Alexander Hamilton

Americans have the right and advantage of being armed.
–James Madison

The great object is that every man be armed.
Everyone who is able may have a gun.
–Patrick Henry

Today the issue is controversial and emotionally charged. There are powerful and vocal groups on all sides of the topic of guns. Some people have taken to saying that the Second Amendment doesn't mean what it always used to mean, and there have been calls to repeal it. The Supreme Court has been mostly quiet on the subject, and its few pronouncements have been used to support all sides of the debate. Importantly, all 50 states recognize a citizen's right to act in self-defense, completely apart from firearms debates.

Nothing in Texas law may conflict with our fundamental creed, the U.S. Constitution, and so the right to bear arms is passed down to Texans, as it is to the citizens of all the states in the union. The states, however, have passed laws to organize and control the arms which people bear within their borders. That's what this book is about.

In addition to the Second Amendment to the U.S. Constitution, the Constitution of the State of Texas reaffirms the right of its citizens to bear arms to protect themselves:

**Texas State Constitution
Article 1, Section 23:**

RIGHT TO KEEP AND BEAR ARMS

"Every citizen shall have the right to keep and bear arms in the lawful defense of himself or the State; but the Legislature shall have power, by law, to regulate the wearing of arms, with a view to prevent crime."

The state of Texas has a *rule of preemption* about gun laws, which can be found in §1.08 of the Penal Code. This means that local authorities within the state cannot pass laws or regulations which conflict with the state's laws and regulations. Power is delegated only to the state to regulate firearms, which provides uniform rules statewide.

The majority of Texas "gun laws" can be found in the Texas Penal Code and the Code of Criminal Procedure. The complete Penal Code and Code of Criminal Procedure are both contained in an 800-page book called *Texas Criminal Laws.* It is widely available in libraries, and a copy may be obtained inexpensively from the Texas Dept. of Public Safety.

You'll find the main relevant sections of state gun law printed in this book in Appendix D. Many of the fine details concerning guns come from other sources, listed in Appendix C.

The Dreaded "§" Section Symbol:
Texas Penal Code §46.02"

The character "§" means "section." You read it aloud (or to yourself) as "section" whenever it appears. Every individually named chunk of law in America is called a section and has a section number, so you see this symbol a lot. It's an integral part of the written name for every statute on the books. A section may be just a few words or extremely long, and it may be amended by new laws. Penal Code section forty six oh two, the law shown above, is one of the main Texas gun laws.

The section "§" symbol intimidates many people and as such, is valuable for keeping the law mysterious and somehow unknowable to the general public. Don't let it scare you. Just think "section" whenever you see "§." To write a section symbol, make a capital "S" on top of another capital "S."

To make a "section" symbol
draw an "S" over another "S"

A Word About Federal Law

The TEXAS Gun Owner's Guide covers the federal laws that relate to the right of the people to keep and bear arms.

Federal law generally does not control the day-to-day details of how you can carry a firearm in any given state, or the rules for self defense and crime resistance, or where you can go for target practice. The individual states control these things. Federal law focuses on commercial aspects, interstate transportation, certain prohibited weapons, crimes against the nation and other specifically defined areas.

It's a common mistake to think that federal laws are "higher" than state laws, or that they somehow come first. They control different things, and the states and the feds each have full jurisdiction over their respective areas.

REASONS FOR THE TEXAS GUN LAWS

Texas criminal law begins with a list of reasons for its existence (see Penal Code §1.02), all of which have direct impact on gun ownership and use:

1–To safeguard conduct that isn't criminal;

2–To define what the state can and can't do in criminal matters;

3–To guide and limit official discretion in law enforcement;

4–To insure public safety by prohibiting conduct which might harm people;

5–To give people fair warning of what is considered prohibited behavior and the consequences of violating the law;

6–To discourage crimes by providing penalties;

7–To provide punishment that discourages future criminal activity;

8–To rehabilitate people who are convicted.

WHAT IS A FIREARM?

In Texas, a firearm is defined in §1.07 of the Penal Code as a *deadly weapon*, a term that includes anything that is designed for lethal use (like a gun or a bayonet), or can be used lethally (like a kitchen knife or a baseball bat). Specifically, state law says that *firearm* means:

> "any device designed, made, or adapted to expel a projectile through a barrel by using the energy generated by an explosion or burning substance or any device readily convertible to that use."

Antique or curio firearms made before 1899 are excluded, including those having a folding knife blade as part of their design. Guns that have been thoroughly disabled and are only for show are not regarded as guns under federal law. Questions about how to make a specific gun unserviceable can be directed to the Firearms Technology Branch of the Bureau of Alcohol, Tobacco and Firearms.

A BB, pellet or dart gun (using compressed air or CO_2 gas to propel the projectile) does not meet the definition of a firearm under state law. BB guns may sometimes be treated almost as if they were regular firearms by some authorities, although the definition clearly excludes them. Although there are no specific state requirements for BB guns, some types designed for hunting are quite powerful and the safest course of action is to always treat them as if they are regular firearms.

A zip gun is anything that was not originally a firearm, but has been adapted to work like a firearm. These fall into the Prohibited Weapons category, described in Chapter 3.

For the letter of the law and the strict legal wording of the various weapons definitions, see §46.01 of the Penal Code.

In this book, the words *gun*, *firearm* and *arms* are used interchangeably to refer to all handguns and long guns. When you see the terms *handgun*, *rifle*, *shotgun*, *long gun*, *semiautomatic pistol* or *semiauto*, or *revolver*, the reference is to that specific type of firearm only.

WHO CAN BEAR ARMS IN TEXAS?

If you are a resident of Texas you may have a gun unless:

1–You have been convicted of a felony. A felon may not possess a gun until five years after release from prison (or from parole, community supervision, etc., whichever is later) and then, only at the premises where the person lives (see Penal Code §46.04). A violation is a third degree felony;

2–You are serving a term of imprisonment in any correctional or detention facility.

Having a firearm if you are in one of these categories is a third degree felony (see Penal Code §46.04 and §46.10).

Under Penal Code §46.06, it is a class A misdemeanor to transfer a handgun to a person you know will use it unlawfully, or to a person you know is subject to an active protective order (sometimes referred to as a court restraining order). The same penalty applies to knowingly selling a firearm or ammunition to anyone who is intoxicated, or to a person who has been convicted of a felony, in less than five years from their release date.

Transferring a firearm to a child under 18 is a class A misdemeanor (Penal Code §46.06), unless the transfer is with the permission of the child's parent or legal guardian. If the transfer is a sale, the permission must be in writing.

3–In addition, you may also be prohibited from firearm possession under federal laws designed to keep weapons out of the hands of criminals. These overriding restrictions are listed in Section 8 of the Firearms Transaction Record, Form #4473, which must be completed when you buy a gun from a federally licensed dealer. Federal law prohibits gun purchase by, or transfer to, anyone who:

• Is charged with or has been convicted of a crime which carries more than a one-year sentence (except two-year state misdemeanors);

• Is a fugitive from justice;

• Unlawfully uses or is addicted to marijuana, a depressant, a stimulant or a narcotic drug;

- Is mentally defective;
- Is mentally incompetent;
- Is committed to a mental institution;
- Has been dishonorably discharged from the armed forces;
- Has renounced U.S. citizenship;
- Is an illegal alien;
- Is under a court order restraining harassment, stalking or threatening of an intimate partner or partner's child.

When filling out a Firearm Transaction Record form you're required to state that you are not in any of these categories. It's a felony to make false statements on a Firearms Transaction Record form.

Juveniles

Texas law sets no legal minimum age at which a child can have or use a firearm. This is a choice made by parents or legal guardians of the minor, who have a legal obligation to act in a responsible manner. However, selling a gun to a minor without *written* consent from the minor's parent or legal guardian, or transferring one in any other way without the responsible adult's approval, is a class A misdemeanor. (See Penal Code §46.06 for the letter of the law.)

Child Safety Law

If a child under 17 years old gains access to an unsecured and loaded firearm (whether a round is in the chamber or not) because it was left where an adult knew or should have known the child could get it, the adult can be charged with a class C misdemeanor. If the child fires the gun and hurts or kills anyone the adult can be charged with a class A misdemeanor. See Penal Code §46.13 for the letter of the law.

A firearm is secured, for the purposes of this law, when you've taken the steps a reasonable person would take to prevent child access, including (but not limited to) putting it in a locked container, using a trigger lock, or by other means.

There is a defense to prosecution under this law if: 1–someone older than 18 is supervising the child in hunting, sporting or other lawful purpose; 2–if the child uses the weapon for lawful defense of people or property; 3–if the child was involved in an agricultural enterprise at the time; or 4–if the child got the weapon through illegal entry.

Law enforcement officials must wait seven days before arresting the adult who made the gun available if the child is a member of that same family and the child self-inflicted death or serious injury.

Firearms dealers must post a sign in block letters at least one inch high stating: "It is unlawful to store, transport, or abandon an unsecured firearm in a place where children are likely to be and can obtain access to the firearm."

If a court allows community supervision for an adult who has violated this law, it may require the person to give public service at the court's discretion, or to pay for and attend a firearms safety course, for as long as 17 hours, that meets or exceeds National Rifle Association requirements (see Code of Criminal Procedure Article 42.12 §13B).

Federal Regulation of Juveniles

New federal rules generally prohibit people under 18 from having handguns or matching ammunition, or providing these to juveniles, unless they meet some additional requirements. While carrying written consent from a parent or guardian (who must not be prohibited from possessing a firearm themselves), a minor may have a handgun:

1–in the course of employment;

2–in legitimate ranching or farming;

3–for target practice;

4–for hunting;

5–for a class in the safe and lawful use of a handgun;

6–for transport, unloaded in a locked case, directly to and from such activities.

Also excluded is a minor who uses a handgun against an intruder, at home or in another home where the minor is an invited guest. If a handgun or ammunition is legally transferred to a minor, who then commits an offense with the firearm, the firearm must be returned to its lawful owner after due process. Minors may inherit title (but not possession) of a handgun. Violation of this law carries fines and a one-year jail term.

Texas Gun-Free School Zone Laws

It is a felony, punishable by up to five years in the state penitentiary for a first offense, to interfere in any way with the normal operation of any type of school (public, private, vocational, technical, at any grade or degree level), or any portion of its campus, or a school bus transporting children, by exhibiting, using, or threatening to exhibit or use a firearm. See Education Code §4.31 for the letter of the law.

Penal Code §46.03 makes it a third degree felony for a person, even with a concealed-handgun license, to intentionally, knowingly or recklessly bring a firearm on the premises of a public or private school or educational institution, or a passenger vehicle of such an establishment, without written permission from them or under their written regulations.

CHL holders are prohibited, under Penal Code §46.035 from carrying a handgun on the premises where a high school, collegiate or professional sporting event, or an interscholastic event, is taking place (unless they're using the handgun in the event).

Under Penal Code §46.11 an offense under any of the state weapons laws (except for §46.03-a-1) carries the next higher penalty if it's proven that you knew you were:

1–Within 300 feet of a school;

2–On the premises where a school function was taking place;

3–At events sponsored by the University Interscholastic League.

HOW DO YOU OBTAIN FIREARMS?

Guns and ammunition may be bought or sold between private residents of this state under the same conditions as any other private sale of merchandise, provided you comply with all other laws (you can't sell to prohibited possessors or to minors, etc.). Sale *and delivery* of firearms by a private resident to any non-resident is prohibited by federal law. Such sales are allowed, but delivery must take place through licensed dealers in the two people's states—it's a violation to transport the firearm interstate yourself. Details are in this chapter under *Transport and Shipping*. As long as all other laws are complied with, a non-resident may temporarily borrow or rent a firearm for any lawful sporting purposes from a dealer or a resident. You may own any number of firearms and any amount of ammunition.

If you are going to deal in guns (or for that matter, import, manufacture or ship firearms in interstate or foreign commerce), you need a license from the Bureau of Alcohol, Tobacco and Firearms. Federally licensed dealers of firearms and ammunition are spread across the state. Residents need no special license or permit to walk in and buy a regular firearm from a regular dealer. Firearms may be paid for in the same ways as any other retail merchandise. You may sell a gun you own to any dealer in the state.

To buy a handgun and matching ammunition you must be at least 21 years old. Your request to buy a handgun from a dealer is made on a written form and reported to local authorities, who must conduct a criminal-history background check, required by the Brady Law. A waiting period of zero to eight days applies while the check is conducted (see Chapter 7 for more on the federal Brady Law). The Brady Law waives the waiting period altogether in many cases (18 USC § 922-s), including for a person with a proper concealed-weapon license. The Texas concealed-handgun license seems to meet the Brady requirements (as do the licenses in many states), but while the license program is new, it would be wise to anticipate some confusion, conflicting rules and unsettled conditions.

To buy a rifle or shotgun and matching ammunition you must be at least 18 years old, and there is no Brady waiting period or background check (see Chapter 7 for changes that will occur if the Brady national instant background check is established). Some ammunition may be used in either a handgun or a rifle. This type of ammo can be sold to a person between the ages of 18 and 21 only if the dealer is satisfied it will be used in a rifle and not a handgun.

In-State Purchase

Government-issued identification that establishes your name, address, date of birth and signature (it must also have your photo if you want to buy a handgun) must be shown to the dealer. A driver's license (or state ID card issued in place of a driver's license) is the usual form of ID expected by most dealers.

When you buy firearms from a licensed dealer you must fill out a federal Firearms Transaction Record, form 4473. There are no duplicate copies made of this form and the original is permanently filed by the dealer. The form requires personal identification information, identification of the gun and its serial number, and your signature. By signing the form you are stating that you are not ineligible to obtain firearms under federal law. Licensed dealers keep copies of this form available. Forms required by the Brady Law are also kept by dealers, and are described in Chapter 7.

The purchase of more than one handgun from the same dealer in a five-day period is reported to the Bureau of Alcohol, Tobacco and Firearms and, under the Brady Law, to local authorities as well, before the close of business on the day of the sale.

Out-of-State Purchases

Residents of this state, including businesses and corporations, are specifically granted permission in the state statutes (see Penal Code §46.07) to buy guns anywhere in the United States. Such purchases must conform to the local laws at the place of purchase. However, the overlapping local, state and federal gun laws in the U.S. are frequently incompatible, and can sometimes make this difficult.

When you buy a long gun out of state from a licensed dealer you may take delivery immediately if the laws of that state allow it. Federal law requires, however, that handguns bought out of state must be shipped to you through a licensed dealer in your home state—you cannot legally take possession of a handgun directly from a dealer outside your home state.

Gun Shows

Gun shows are periodically sponsored by national, state and local organizations devoted to the collection, competitive use or other sporting use of firearms. You may buy firearms from an in-state dealer at a gun show the same as you could on their regular retail premises. Out-of-state dealers can display their wares and take orders, but cannot make deliveries to non-licensees at the show. Purchases made from an out-of-state dealer must be transferred to a licensee within this state, from the out-of-state dealer's licensed premises.

CARRYING FIREARMS

It's basically against the law to carry a handgun intentionally, knowingly or recklessly on yourself in Texas, unless you have a concealed-handgun license, or meet other limited exceptions discussed in this chapter. The unlawful carrying of weapons on or near yourself is mainly covered in §46.02 of the Penal Code.

This apparent contradiction with the U.S. Constitution has been on the books for more than a century. It bewilders many Texas residents, though they have come to live with it. Texas is not the wild west many outsiders believe it to be.

The law is written in such a way that having a handgun on or around you is an offense. It then provides you with a number of defenses to prosecution, which you may use in court.

Even if you are legally carrying or transporting a handgun, local authorities may have little choice but to treat simple possession as sufficient cause to make an arrest, confiscate the firearm, and require you to prove your innocence later, in court. The narrow exemptions in the law (such as being a "traveler") may not be something a peace officer at the scene can verify, and may lead to arrest of an otherwise innocent citizen.

This puts law-abiding gun owners at serious risk, and every effort should be made to avoid even the slightest impression that a handgun is possessed in violation of state law. Frequently, the discretion of the authorities is all that stands between you and arrest. Because possession can be an offense but concealment is not, it is prudent to keep handguns discreetly out of sight.

Long guns are completely unaffected by the handgun restriction, and it's not uncommon to see pickup trucks with rifle racks throughout the state. Texas carrying laws make no distinction between loaded and unloaded firearms.

The old handgun-carrying restriction dates back to 1871, in the days after the War Between the States, when it was an attempt to prevent newly freed slaves and former confederates from bearing arms. A violation is a class A misdemeanor, but if the offense occurs in a place licensed or permitted to sell or serve alcohol it is a third degree felony. (See Penal Code §46.02 for the letter of the law.)

The following section of *The Texas Gun Owner's Guide* describes the requirements **if you do not have a concealed-handgun license**. To learn how a concealed-handgun license operates, read Chapter 2.

Limits of the Handgun-Carrying Restrictions

As noted above, it's an offense to carry a handgun in Texas. If you are charged, your possible defenses are described in Penal Code §46.02. There is a valid defense to prosecution under the basic handgun-carrying restriction for anyone acting officially as:

1–A member of the armed forces;

2–A member of the national guard;

3–A guard employed by a penal institution; or

4–A peace officer (covered in Penal Code §46.15).

In addition, there is a valid defense to prosecution if you are:

1–On your own premises or premises under your control (except for security guards, who must meet certain special requirements listed below under *Security Guards*);

2–Engaged in legal hunting or other sporting activity and the weapon is a type commonly used in the activity, or directly enroute to such activities;

3–Traveling (see details on following page);

4–The holder of a valid concealed-handgun license;

5–A liquor-license holder (or employee of the holder) while supervising the licensed premises.

In addition to the statutory exceptions listed above, having a handgun in your possession is permissible in an instance of self defense or other justifiable use such as crime prevention (see Chapter 5). This defense against a weapons charge is known as the defense of *necessity* (see Penal Code §9.22).

Security Guards

If you are an employee or agent of the owner of a premises, and your primary responsibility is to act as a security guard to protect people or property, you may carry a handgun if you meet these conditions:

1–You are engaged in the performance of your duties as a security officer or traveling to and from your work place;

2–You are officially commissioned by the Texas Board of Private Investigators and Private Security Agencies;

3–The handgun must be in plain view;

4–You must be wearing a distinctive uniform.

In addition, a person (sometimes referred to as a bodyguard) with a security officer commission and a personal protection authorization from the Texas Board of Private Investigators and Private Security Agencies, may carry while on duty.

See §46.02 for the letter of the law.

Traveling

The single word *traveling* is listed in state law as an exception to the handgun-carrying restriction—traveling is a "defense to prosecution." When is a person legally traveling? This is a hotly debated topic. Few areas in Texas gun law cause as much confusion. The legal basis for a definition of traveling comes from previous court decisions on the subject, called *precedents*.

A review of *case law* (court decisions that are officially published to interpret the laws on the books), along with many officials' perspectives on the subject, clearly show that you face a definite risk whenever transporting handguns in the state. Circumstances which may satisfy one peace officer that you are in fact traveling may not satisfy another. Since mere possession of the firearm may be sufficient for an arrest, the risk is substantial.

If you are found traveling with a handgun on yourself or in your car in Texas, the authorities may presume that you possess it illegally, and it's up to you to prove that you are *traveling* in the complex legal sense, or else exempt under another provision of the law. Some experts have observed that this can be interpreted as "guilty until proven innocent," contrary to the fundamental American concept of "innocent until proven guilty." You are in fact required to prove that you meet one of the exceptions provided in the law to have a weapons charge dropped, creating a substantial degree of risk. Despite this, the criminal code stipulates that nothing shall diminish the assumption of innocence:

> "All persons are presumed to be innocent and no person may be convicted of an offense unless each element of the offense is proved beyond a reasonable doubt. The fact that he has been arrested, confined, or indicted for, or otherwise charged with, the offense gives rise to no inference of guilt at his trial." (See Penal Code §2.01.)

However, many gun owners can tell chilling stories that make you wonder. The authorities don't have to prove that you're not traveling. It is prudent to avoid even the slightest inference of impropriety when transporting a handgun; do nothing to unduly draw the attention of a peace officer at such times.

Here is a review of some of the hundreds of cases decided over the years, to help provide perspective on this confusing subject. These short summaries do not provide full details and in that sense may be misleading. *For the whole story you must study the entire court decision—often many pages of involved legal text. Do not rely on these brief gists for any legal purposes whatsoever.* You'll also note that the decisions do not always agree with each other, adding another element of risk and uncertainty. Each case represents a person going to court for having been found with a handgun by the authorities.

General:
▶ Driving a herd of cattle across a county to Kansas is traveling. (Rice vs. State 1881)
▶ Fugitives are not travelers. (Shelton vs. State 1889)
▶ Borrowing a handgun to see your brothers in another county does not make you a traveler several days later in your own county. (Brownlee vs. State, 1895)

- An auditor collecting tickets and fares from railroad passengers is a traveler. (Barker vs. Satterfield, 1908)
- Taking the most direct route to a permanent boarding house from a hotel is traveling. (Ward vs. State 1911)
- A merchant going to see customers who owe money is not a traveler. (Hickman vs. State, 1913)
- Riding around a neighborhood, working and looking for work, is not traveling, even if you intend to go out of the county if you can't find work. (Younger vs. State, 1915)
- Coming to a city as a traveler does not allow you to carry a handgun around for several days after you've arrived. Also, the right to carry a handgun as a traveler is lost if you suspend your travel to burglarize a house. (Smith vs. State, 1915)
- Carrying a pistol in your car is not, by itself, traveling. (Welch vs. State, 1924)
- Carrying a gun in a car while traveling is not a violation of carrying on your person. (Christian vs. State, 1927)
- Using a gun illegally doesn't necessarily make you guilty of unlawful carry. (Grant vs. State 1929)
- Moving from one home to another is traveling. (Senters vs. State, 1983)

Purpose:
- If you are exempt as a traveler, the reason you are traveling is not relevant. (Evers vs. State, 1978)

Time and Distance:
- Going to the county seat of your own county and returning the next day is not traveling. (Darby vs. State, 1887)
- Taking a trip by wagon for two or three days is traveling. (Smith vs. State, 1875)
- Taking a handgun 60 miles away for repairs and then boarding a train with it bound for home is traveling. (Impson vs. State, 1892)
- Traveling 25 miles and then preparing to camp out is traveling (Price vs. State, 1895)

- Going 15 miles from home is not traveling. (Stanfield vs. State, 1896)
- Going 18 miles from home is not traveling. (Creswell vs. State, 1897)
- Going 35 miles from home to another county, and then returning home immediately is traveling. (Bain vs. State, 1898)
- Returning 150 miles to get home is traveling. (Thomas vs. State, 1897)
- A railroad porter going 150 miles on a daily run is traveling. (Williams vs. State, 1903)
- Going from one county to another, or planning to, and boarding a train, is traveling. (Campbell vs. State, 1910)
- Driving a car 40 miles and back on the same day in daylight is not traveling. (George vs. State, 1921)
- Going 35 miles to a place in another county is not traveling. (Wortham vs. State, 1923)
- Taking paying passengers 37 miles in a car is not traveling, even if you claim you were told you might have to go much further. (Paulk vs. State, 1924)
- The mode of travel must be considered when determining traveling, not just distance alone. (Kemp vs. State, 1930)
- Leaving at 5 p.m. and returning before midnight is not traveling. (Vogt vs. State, 1953)
- Leaving your air force base to go 120 miles to spend a weekend with your family is traveling. (Allen vs. State, 1968)

Interruption of Traveling:
- Stopping your travel for business or pleasure removes your protection as a traveler. (Stilly vs. State, 1889)
- Going out of your way to bring a doctor home while traveling, is still traveling. A mere delay does not remove the travel protection. (Irvin vs. State, 1907)
- Stopping momentarily on a business trip to discuss a debt with a creditor at the creditor's request, does not remove the travel protection. (Hunt vs. State, 1908)

▶ Stopping a journey for business relevant to the journey is traveling. (Campbell vs. State, 1910) (Kemp vs. State, 1930)

▶ Going directly from a hotel to a boarding house and stopping along the way to eat with a friend is traveling. (Ward vs. State, 1911)

▶ Turning aside from a journey that was traveling, for business not related to the original journey, is not traveling. (Pecht vs. State, 1918) (Tadlock vs. State, 1934)

Termination of Travel

▶ Traveler status ends when you arrive at your destination (U.S. vs. Pozos, 1983)

▶ Going from one county to another is traveling, but after arriving and staying overnight, you are not a traveler while going around town the next morning. (Ballard vs. State, 1914)

▶ Returning to your home from an out-of-state trip, changing your clothes, and taking your wife for a ride in the country is not traveling. (Kiles vs. State, 1966)

Temporary Residence

▶ Going from your temporary home to your permanent home in another county is traveling. (Campbell vs. State, 1889)

▶ For the purpose of determining travel, a person may have both permanent and temporary legal residences. A girl friend's home is not necessarily legal temporary residence, and so carrying a gun from your place of work to her house, after a fishing trip, is not traveling. (Smith vs. State, 1982)

Hunting

▶ You cannot carry a pistol while hunting hogs on the range, or hunting anything off your own premises. (Baird vs. State, 1873) (Titus vs. State, 1875)

▶ You cannot take a pistol out on the range to kill a beef, even if you have no other means available. (Reynolds vs. State, 1877)

▶ Government employees may carry handguns while hunting predators and rodents, if the guns are a type typically used for this. (Atty. Gen. Opinion, 1980)

Security Officers

▶ Night watchmen cannot carry while not on duty. (Robison vs. State, 1926)

Peace Officers

▶ Peace officers and people legally acting as peace officers may carry handguns while actually on duty (Atty. Gen. Opinions, 1941, 1946, 1973, 1975, 1980). Whether a person is truly a peace officer, except for those specifically spelled out in the law, and whether the person is actually acting in an official capacity is subject to question and has numerous court precedents. A peace officer in one location does not automatically have rights in another location. Being deputized, being appointed or acting under another person's authority does not automatically make you a peace officer, as the following examples show, and as is frequently the case, not all the precedents agree with each other.

▶ Being appointed a deputy constable in good faith by a constable who has no authority to make such an appointment is not a defense. (Johnson vs. State 1914)

▶ A sheriff who can appoint one deputy in a precinct but actually appoints two does not protect both appointees. (Ranson vs. State, 1914)

▶ An appointment by an adjutant general but without taking an oath, etc., is insufficient as a defense for carrying a handgun. (Ringer vs. State, 1894)

▶ Being commissioned as a deputy sheriff and allowed to carry is not a defense while you are not acting in an official capacity and are carrying for personal protection. (Gandara vs. State, 1924)

▶ Although you can be criminally prosecuted for failing to assist a peace officer if requested, a private security officer who requests such assistance and arms you is not a peace officer under the law, cannot appoint you a peace officer and provides no defense. (Bohn vs. State, 1983)

▶ A person properly deputized by a magistrate to make an arrest may carry. (Jenkins vs. State, 1904)

▶ A magistrate can name a suitable person who is not a peace officer to make an arrest in an arrest warrant, and that person may carry a gun. (Stephenson vs. State 1923) (Hawkins vs. State 1988)

Reasonable Belief

▶ If a person honestly believes to be an appointed officer and therefore carries, the person is not guilty. (Carroll vs. State 1900) (Barnett vs. State 1921) (Franklin vs. State 1944)

These are just a fraction of the cases that have come to the courts on the issue of carrying a handgun in Texas. The law is quite complex, and subject to unusual interpretation and inconsistent results. In addition, numerous cases have shown a tendency for the court to presume you have no exception or defense against having been found carrying a handgun on or about your person. It is then up to you as a defendant to prove conclusively that an exception existed at the time of the arrest and that you are innocent. You must exonerate yourself from guilt. Do be careful.

Guns In Cars

The same rules that prohibit carrying a handgun on yourself apply to carrying a gun in a car. If the gun is within your reach it is considered "on or about" you (see Penal Code §46.02) and is illegal without a specific valid exemption. Long guns are not included in this restriction.

If you meet the exemption of *traveling* then you may carry a handgun in a private vehicle. The prudent traveler, given the weight of case law as previously discussed, would do well to carry the weapon out of view in another part of the vehicle (since concealment isn't an issue—it is the carrying that is restricted). The trunk is often cited as the location of choice, unloaded, with the ammunition apart from the firearm. There is some disagreement among police, however, who may consider the trunk as "on or about" you, especially if you open the trunk.

In an ironic quirk of law that confounds many Texans, the more readily available a firearm is to you for use in an emergency, the greater the legal risk of an illegal-carrying charge.

Considering the complications, many people find it easier to keep a long gun available and not worry about it. If you have a valid Texas concealed-handgun license, you may carry a loaded handgun concealed in your car under many circumstances.

Transport and Shipping

You may ship and transport firearms around the country, but not by the U.S. Postal Service, under one of the oldest federal firearms statutes on the books, dating from Feb. 8, 1927. (The oldest federal law still in effect—except for Constitutional provisions—appears to be a firearm forfeiture law for illegal hunting in Yellowstone National Park, passed on May 7, 1894.)

You may have a weapon shipped to a licensed dealer, manufacturer or repair shop and back. However, depending upon the reason for the shipment and the shipper being used, the weapon may have to be shipped from and back to someone with a federal firearms license. You should check with the intended recipient and you must inform the shipping agent in writing before shipping firearms or ammunition.

Any firearm purchased outside Texas and shipped to you in Texas must go from a licensed dealer where you bought it to a licensed dealer here. Many dealers in the state will act as a "receiving station" for a weapon you buy elsewhere, sometimes for a fee.

If you buy a gun from a private party out of state, the gun may only be shipped to a licensed dealer within Texas. If you sell a gun to a private party out of state, the gun must be shipped to a licensed dealer in the purchaser's state. "Taking the gun with you" from a private sale, if it's going out of state, is prohibited by federal law.

The only time when you may directly receive an interstate shipment of a gun is the return of a gun that you sent for repairs, modification or replacement to a licensee in another state.

Personal possession of firearms in other states is subject to the laws of each state you are in. Federal law guarantees the right to transport (not the same as carry) a gun in a private vehicle, if you are entitled to have the gun in your home state and at your destination, if the gun is unloaded and locked in the trunk, or in a locked compartment other than the glove compartment or the console if the vehicle has no trunk. Not all states have fully honored this federal guarantee, creating a degree of risk for anyone transporting a firearm interstate.

The bottom line is that the civil right and historical record of law-abiding citizens traveling with firearms for their own safety has evaporated due to laws at the state level. People typically have no idea what the gun laws are in any state but their own (and rarely enough that), a complete set of the relevant laws is hard to get, understanding the statutes goes from difficult to nearly impossible, and you can be arrested for making a simple mistake.

The legal risk created by our own government for a family traveling interstate with a personal firearm may be greater than the actual risk of a criminal confrontation. Because of this, the days of traveling armed and being responsible for your own safety and protection have all but ended for people who leave their home state. The proper authorities are generally exempt from these restrictions.

Those readers who purchased this book hoping it would somehow enable or empower them to travel interstate with a loaded personal firearm must contact their representatives and begin to ask about the lost National Right to Carry. That right has a name, the Second Amendment, and it has quietly disappeared for interstate travelers.

Common or Contract Carriers

You may transport firearms and ammunition interstate by "common carriers" (scheduled and chartered airlines, buses, trains, ships, etc.), but you must notify them in writing and comply with their requirements. Call in advance and get precise details and the names of the people you speak with—you wouldn't be the first traveler to miss a departure because of unforeseen technicalities and bureaucratic runarounds.

For air travel, firearms must be unloaded, cased in a way deemed appropriate by the airline, and may not be possessed by or accessible to you in the "sterile" area anywhere on the gate side of the passenger security checkpoint, including on the aircraft. You may ship your firearms as baggage or you may give custody of them to the pilot, captain, conductor or operator for the duration of the trip. Airlines must comply with firearms rules found primarily in the Code of Federal Regulations, Title 14, Sections 107 and 108, and other laws. A little-known provision of the Brady Law prohibits carriers from identifying the outside of your baggage to indicate that it contains a firearm, a prime cause for theft in the past.

Local Ordinances

Texas Penal Code prohibits local authorities from passing firearms laws which conflict with state statutes. This is called *preemption*, and is found in Penal Code §1.08. Despite this rule, you may find some localities that have enacted laws that appear to conflict with state law.

An amendment to Local Government Code §215.001, made by the Right to Carry law, says that cities do not have authority to regulate the carrying of concealed handguns by concealed-handgun licensees at public parks, public meetings of a city, county or other governmental body, political rallies, parades or meeting, or nonfirearms-related school, college, or professional athletic events.

Cities *can* substantially regulate certain other aspects of firearms, from requiring people to arm themselves, to prohibiting shooting in city limits and more. These are described in Chapter 4 under *The Land of Texas.*

Most local firearm ordinances merely reiterate state statutes, giving city courts jurisdiction in some areas. This typically has no direct effect on law-abiding gun owners, but conflicting laws might. *It is important to note that* The Texas Gun Owner's Guide *does not cover local ordinances, whether they agree or conflict with state law.* The liability to citizens who obey state laws that conflict with local laws is uncertain and creates a degree of legal risk.

Prohibited Places

Always keep in mind that some places are strictly off limits to citizens with firearms, even if you are otherwise legally in possession of arms. The list of places where guns are not allowed at all, including restrictions for CHL holders, appears at the end of Chapter 2.

Product Liability Limit

Texas has a law which discourages nuisance lawsuits against manufacturers and sellers of firearms and ammunition (Civil Practices and Remedies Code § 82.006). Under this law, a suit cannot be brought because a gun is inherently dangerous and causes damage. Rather, a suit has to prove a bona fide design defect which results directly in the alleged damage. If a gun functions in the way it is normally expected to function, there is no grounds for legal action.

LOSS OF RIGHTS

The right to bear arms is not absolute. Gun control—in the true sense—means disarming criminals and is a good idea, a point on which everyone but the criminals agree. The list of people who may not bear arms at all appears earlier in this chapter. A person whose rights are whole may lose those rights, mainly for conviction of a felony.

Forfeiture of Rights

Your right to bear arms can be lost. Conviction of any felony removes your civil right to bear firearms under state and federal law. The right to bear arms is forbidden to anyone who is or becomes a prohibited possessor under federal law, as described earlier, or as defined under Penal Code §46.04. State law, under narrow conditions, allows a felon to possess a firearm at home only.

Forfeiture of Weapons

The authorities can take your weapons if they have just cause. Firearms may be seized by a peace officer during an arrest or search, and if convicted of an offense involving the use of the weapon, or if the weapon is prohibited according to Chapter 46 (the weapons section) of the Penal Code, or if it is alleged to be stolen property (in Chapter 47 of the Penal Code), the court can either order that the weapon be destroyed or that it be turned over to the state for use by the law enforcement agency that seized it. See Code of Criminal Procedure Article 18.19.

If you *are not* convicted of the charge, you have 60 days after being notified by the magistrate that the weapon was seized to make a written request to the court that it be returned. Otherwise, it will be destroyed or turned over for use by law enforcement. See Code of Criminal Procedure Article 18.19.

If you *are* convicted you may request and get the weapon back provided: 1–You ask within 60 days; 2–you have no prior convictions under state weapons laws; 3–it is not a prohibited weapon; 4–the offense wasn't committed at a playground, video arcade, youth center or school; and 5–in the court's opinion, based on your record, returning the weapon poses no threat to the community. Otherwise, the weapon is destroyed or given to the authorities that seized it.

Certain weapons are contraband if unregistered and are subject to seizure by the authorities. Included are weapons identified under the National Firearms Act (see Chapter 3), or identified as prohibited weapons under state law.

Personal property, including firearms and ammunition, may be seized by the Bureau of Alcohol, Tobacco and Firearms when used or intended to be used or involved in violation of any U.S. laws which ATF agents are empowered to enforce. Acquittal or dismissal of charges allows you to regain any confiscated property, but this may be more difficult than it sounds.

The Lost National Right to Carry

Traveling out-of-state with personal firearms presents certain legal risks. The authorities have been known to hassle, detain or arrest people who are legally traveling with weapons, due to confusion, ignorance, personal bias and for other reasons, even when those reasons are strictly illegal.

Some states have openly challenged or defied existing legal safeguards (see the federal transportation guarantee in Chapter 7) for law-abiding firearms owners. As a practical matter, because each state's laws differ, the right to bear arms as you travel interstate has basically evaporated. The 14th amendment guarantee that no state shall deny the rights of an American citizen has not been applied to this situation.

Transporting a firearm (unloaded and locked away) is somewhat risky even with the federal guarantee. *Carrying* one (armed and ready) is practically impossible unless you're willing to face felony criminal charges. The legal risk from our own government may be greater than the threat of a criminal attack.

Countless people have asked Bloomfield Press for a book that would cover all 50 states, to resolve the problem. This is an appealing idea, but it's not the answer for many reasons: there's no way for the readers to be assured of accuracy; the amount of labor needed to do such a work is prohibitive; keeping the information current in such a book is impossible; and using a book fifty times the size of this one is, well, a joke. Having such a book won't save you from arrest either, as you leave one state where, say, a loaded gun in the glovebox is perfectly all right (Arizona for example), to another state where such a gun counts for two crimes (loaded gun, accessible gun) as in California.

The main fault with the "just write a book" fix is that it's the wrong approach. You don't fix a major national problem like this by writing a book. You fix it by restoring the lost National Right to Carry, also known as the Second Amendment, to the position it always held in America until the last few decades, during which its erosion has been nearly total for interstate travelers.

Restoration of Rights

Federal law (18 USC § 925) provides a method for restoring a lost right to bear arms and this has been useful to some citizens who are responsible community members and whose restrictions were based on decades old convictions of youth, or other circumstances that pose little threat. The Treasury Dept., responsible for this law, has claimed for several years that they have no budget with which to accomplish this work, and the restoration of rights process has effectively ground to a halt.

WHAT DOES IT ALL MEAN?

Law books don't use the word *crime*; they use the terms *felony* and *misdemeanor*. Crimes are divided into these categories to help match the punishment to the crime. Felonies are extremely serious; misdemeanors are less serious.

Felonies are divided into three categories (see Penal Code §12.31 through §12.35), starting with the most serious: Capital felony, then 1st degree, 2nd degree and 3rd degree felonies, and a third category called state felonies.

Misdemeanors are grouped into three *classes* (see Penal Code §12.21 through 12.23). Class A is the most serious charge, followed by class B and class C.

The punishments are matched to the seriousness of the crime. This ranges from a capital felony, which can be punishable by death or life imprisonment, to a class C misdemeanor, which carries a fine of under $500 and no jail sentence. See the Crime and Punishment Chart in Appendix B for the basic penalties for each type of crime.

WHAT DO YOU NEED TO GET A FIREARM?

WHAT DO YOU NEED TO GET A FIREARM FROM A FEDERALLY LICENSED DEALER?

- You must be at least 18 years old for a long gun, or 21 years old for a handgun (and not be a prohibited possessor);

- You need a government-issued ID which establishes your name, address, date of birth and signature, and has a photo for a handgun purchase;

- You must fill out a federal form 4473, identifying yourself, the firearm you are buying, and certifying that you are not a prohibited possessor;

- You must file a form with the dealer and wait from zero to nine days to meet the Brady Law requirements before taking delivery of a handgun. It is unclear at this point whether the concealed-handgun license will exempt licensees, as it does in many other states, from Brady paperwork and delays. The wait and paperwork do not apply for long guns (see Chapter 7 for more Brady details);

- If you are not a Texas resident, it must be legal for you to have the weapon in your home state. You may take possession of a long gun over the counter if you could in your home state, but if you purchase a handgun, it must be shipped to a dealer in your home state—you cannot legally take possession of it here yourself; and

- You must be able to pay for your purchase.

THE RIGHT TO CARRY LAW 2

In the closing days of the 1995 Texas legislative session, Senate Bill 60, The Right to Carry law, made it through conference committee and was passed by both houses. A tense few days later the governor signed it, and a new era had dawned. More than a century of severe handgun restrictions were relaxed for residents of the state.

Gov. George W. Bush signed the bill on May 26, 1995. Its effective date is Sep. 1, 1995, and no license to carry becomes effective before Jan. 1, 1996.

In Texas, without a license under the Right to Carry law, it's generally against the law to carry a handgun (or illegal knife or club) on yourself, either openly or concealed. Carrying a handgun if you have no legal affirmative defense, no license and aren't otherwise exempt is a class A misdemeanor or higher.

The ability to legally carry a handgun in Texas is so heavily restricted that the only practical way to carry one legally for personal safety is with a valid license, issued by the Dept. of Public Safety (DPS). The requirements are rigorous, but the license grants broad immunity from the restrictions that limit unlicensed citizens.

Under certain conditions, local, state and federal employees may be authorized to carry weapons. Peace officers may carry statewide, on or off duty. As of Jan. 1, 1996, Texas residents may also exercise a license for carrying a concealed handgun, under the 1995 Right to Carry law.

The Concealed-Handgun License (CHL)

A license to Carry a Concealed Weapon is called a CCW license in various parts of the country. In Texas this is actually a Concealed Handgun License or CHL, since no other weapon may be carried. It is available to any resident who is qualified as described below. Qualified license holders are exempt from most but not all the restrictions which normally prohibit handgun carry in Texas, and a few new limitations have been created. For the first time in 124 years, Texans may legally carry personal handguns for self defense.

Unlike some states, the Texas concealed-carry law is a "must issue" law. The statute prohibits DPS, which administers the CHL program, from denying a license "on the basis of a capricious or arbitrary decision," and says that DPS "shall issue" a license to anyone who qualifies. Basically, it means that if you meet the qualifications, you get the license.

This is an awesome responsibility. The legislative battles to establish this new law were long and hard-fought, and the law is not perfect. It is now up to the citizens to demonstrate intelligent use of this law, to exhibit restraint in all but the most life-threatening situations, and to work hard to make Texas a better place to live.

For the word of the law (which license applicants must certify they have read *and* understand), see the actual law as passed, *Senate Bill 60* in Appendix D. The CHL portion of the new law will go on the books as *Article 4413 (29ee) Revised Statutes.*

General Conditions

- You must carry the license with you whenever you carry a concealed handgun and must show the license, along with your driver's license (or DPS ID card), to any peace officer or magistrate on request, when you are armed. Failure to cooperate or not having your license with you is a class B misdemeanor.

- You must keep a concealed handgun concealed. Deliberately letting it show is a class A misdemeanor, unless you are using it in a situation that legally justifies the use of deadly force (sometimes called "the defense of *necessity*").

- It's a class A misdemeanor for a person with a CHL to be armed while intoxicated.

- If you are arrested or indicted for an offense that would disqualify you for a CHL after you have obtained one, the license is suspended. Upon conviction, the license is revoked.

- DPS maintains a database to confirm the validity of all CHLs. If you are found without your license while carrying a concealed handgun a peace officer can check to see if you are in fact licensed. If you're not, an arrest is possible or even likely. If you are licensed, you face the officer's discretion similar to driving without your driver's license—a deep sweat you won't soon forget and definite potential for arrest.

- The law requires DPS to keep statistics on incidents involving CHL holders, including arrests for carrying in prohibited places, and records about handgun discharges. Discharges would include accidental ones, unjustified or criminal firings, and justifiable uses of deadly force (crime prevention). A reasonable person would take care not to be a statistic in any of those categories if at all possible. DPS must adopt procedures to gather reports from local authorities.

- On or before Jan. 31, 1997, DPS will report on the feasibility of substituting a written exam for the classroom instruction that is otherwise required of license applicants.

QUALIFICATIONS FOR A CONCEALED-HANDGUN LICENSE

The Dept. of Public Safety is required by law to issue your concealed-handgun license (CHL) if you:

1–Are a legal Texas resident for six months before your date of application;

2–Are at least 21 years of age;

3–Have not been convicted of a felony;

4–Have not been convicted of disorderly conduct or a class A or class B misdemeanor in the last five years;

5–Are not *charged* with a class A or B misdemeanor, disorderly conduct or a felony (this restriction does not require a judgment of guilt, just that a charge is filed);

6–Are not a fugitive from justice;

7–For ten years prior to applying have not had any delinquent conduct violations of a felony grade;

8–Have not had two class B misdemeanors or worse in the preceding ten years for alcohol or illegal drug violations;

9–Are not of unsound mind, which means you:

A–Have not been adjudicated mentally incompetent, mentally ill, or not guilty of a criminal offense by reason of insanity; or

B–Have not been diagnosed by a doctor as having a mental disorder that makes you incapable of handling your affairs, or that you are suffering from depression, manic depression, or post-traumatic stress syndrome. If you have been diagnosed with any of these conditions, you must provide a certificate from a doctor stating you are no longer disabled or under any medication for treatment of these conditions;

12–Are not a chemically dependent person;

13–Have not been judged delinquent on any back taxes or child support payments in the state of Texas, or payments for a student loan made under the Texas Guaranteed Student Loan Corporation;

14–Are not under a restraining order from your spouse, except for one regarding property only;

15–Are qualified under federal and state law to purchase a handgun;

16–Pass a DPS-approved handgun safety training program and obtain a *Handgun Proficiency Certificate*;

17–Are cleared through a local, state and federal criminal history background check, and a non-criminal history check if DPS decides it's needed;

18–Pay the fee.

Preliminary CHL Application

To obtain a CHL, you must first make an application to receive the application materials. This "application for the application" is available free of charge from licensed handgun dealers, DPS, or any other person or entity approved by DPS. It may seem like an unneeded extra step, but it could save you the $140 non-refundable fee if it turns out you're ineligible for any reason from overdue back taxes to a prior criminal record.

The law requires your name, address, race, sex, height, date of birth and driver's license number, and DPS is authorized to require other information on the form. The completed form is sent to DPS at its Austin address (listed in Appendix C).

If you are disqualified at this stage you are notified and have an opportunity to have the decision reversed. DPS offers disqualified applicants an opportunity for informal review, in person or by telephone, to help reverse erroneous findings. This courtesy is provided in addition to all your other legal remedies (described later under *Application Denials*). It must be said that DPS has worked diligently to implement this complex new law.

If you are not disqualified at the preliminary review, you will get the complete CHL application packet.

Actual CHL Application

The actual CHL application requires your name, place and date of birth, race, sex, hair and eye color, height, weight, driver's license number or DPS identification certificate number, criminal history information, drug, alcohol and psychiatric treatment history for the past five years, and your residence and business addresses for the preceding five years. Filling out the form untruthfully is grounds to revoke the license. A completed CHL application packet includes:

1–Concealed-handgun license Application form;

2–Two recent color passport photos that meet the strict DPS standards for composition, size and likeness;

3–Birth certificate or other certified proof of age;

4–Two sets of fingerprints taken by a properly trained person who works for a law enforcement agency (the finger printer has certain responsibilities to verify that you are who you claim to be);

5–Proof of residency (detailed below);

6–An official Handgun Proficiency Certificate from an approved CHL course;

7–Affidavits, signed by you, stating that you have: 1–read and understand the concealed-handgun license law and all statutes of Texas state law regarding the use of deadly force; 2–that you meet the eligibility requirements listed above; and 3–authorizing DPS to investigate your non-criminal background history as far as they deem necessary;

8–A fee set by the DPS Director, currently $140 for four years, which may be paid by cashier's check or a money order payable to the Texas Dept. of Public Safety. The fee is non-refundable, and DPS may decide to allow other forms of payment. The fee for senior citizens (60 or over) and people whose income is at or below the federal poverty level, is 50% of the full rate, presently $70 for four years.

You should also note that:

• If an application is incomplete, not legible or all the elements are not submitted, the application will not be processed. You have 90 days from the time DPS gets your application to correct any problems, and you can request an additional 90 days. The application is not considered received until it is complete.

• Only original DPS forms are accepted—do not send photocopies, but you should keep photocopies for your own records.

Application Background Checks

When DPS receives your completed application, they conduct a background check through their computerized criminal history system. Within 30 days, DPS must forward your application to officials in your geographic area for a local check to verify the accuracy of your application. There is no time frame provided for the local officials to act. DPS is also required to send your fingerprints to the FBI for a national criminal history check.

The scope of the DPS investigation is at the "sole discretion of the department." The unlimited nature of this investigation may cause some residents to think twice about applying for the license. Juvenile records which might otherwise be sealed may be opened and inspected.

When done, the local authorities return your application to Austin, with either approval or disapproval recommended. Disapproval must include an affidavit stating personal knowledge or naming people with personal knowledge of information that would make you ineligible for a license.

DPS must by law issue or deny a license within 90 days of the date the local authorities receive your packet—which comes to a maximum of 120 days. Instead of notifying you, DPS may simply wait 30 days from when they should act (the 120 day point), and their lack of notice constitutes denial. In the worst case, then, you could apply, wait 150 days, hear nothing, and thus be denied. Typically, however, DPS makes a good faith effort to process applications as quickly as practical. After

January 1, 1997, the first 90-day period is shortened to 60 days, moving the whole time frame up by 30 days.

Your county sheriff is notified that you have been issued a license, and local law enforcement agencies may request notification from DPS as well.

A license is valid from the date of issue (but no license is effective before Jan. 1, 1996). The license includes an ID number, an expiration date, your color photo, name, date of birth, residence address, hair and eye color, height, weight, signature and driver's license (or DPS ID card) number. There are two categories of license, *SA* which covers all handguns, and *NSA* which covers non-semi-automatic handguns.

Residency

Applicants must prove that they have been legal residents of Texas for at least six months prior to applying for a CHL. Residency may be shown by:

1–A Texas driver's license issued at least six months ago (note that a person with a driver's license in another state is considered a resident of that state);

2–Proof that you've been registered to vote in Texas for at least six months;

3–Proof that you've owned or leased a residence in Texas for at least the past six months (Deed records, rental contracts, rental receipts or canceled checks may be used as evidence);

4–Records of utility payments; or

5–Other proof DPS finds acceptable.

Application Denials

If DPS denies your license after the background check and notifies you in writing, there are three reasons they can give: 1-You don't meet all of the qualifications; 2-the local authorities disapproved; or 3-your certified instructor disapproved. When you receive the denial, you may request a hearing, in writing, if you wish to have it reversed. The request is made to DPS at its

Austin address and must reach them within 29 days of your receipt of the denial. DPS must *schedule* a hearing within 30 days of receiving your request, in your local county justice court. The hearing must be *held* within 60 days of your request. A justice of the peace acts as an administrative hearing officer for the proceeding. DPS may be represented by a district attorney, county attorney, the attorney general or a designated member of the department.

The court will decide if there is a "preponderance of the evidence" or overwhelming evidence to support the denial. You have an opportunity to present evidence as well. If the court decides that there is not enough evidence to support the denial of a CHL, DPS is ordered to immediately issue or return the license. If the judgment goes against you, you are entitled to appeal the ruling within 30 days.

Similar procedures apply for the return or reinstatement of a license that is suspended or revoked.

Modifying or Replacing a License

If you have a CHL and change your name or address, or if your license is lost, stolen, or destroyed, you must notify DPS, on a form they provide, within 30 days. The department will issue a modified or duplicate license for a fee of $25. If your license is lost, stolen, or destroyed and was due to be renewed within 60 days, you may renew the license instead and pay only the nonrefundable renewal fee. Expiration dates remain unchanged for modified or replaced licenses. Failure to notify the department as described can result in suspension of your license. Your local sheriff (and other agencies if they ask) are notified of license changes.

You may also modify a license to allow you to carry a handgun of a different category than your license indicates. You must pass a proficiency exam for the new category within six months of applying to modify your license. Along with the application, you must submit a copy of a Handgun Proficiency Certificate from a certified instructor, a fee of $25, two recent color passport photos and a form provided by DPS. If you're qualified, the department must issue your modified license within 45 days after they receive your application materials. When you get the modified license, you must return your old one to DPS or your new one can be suspended.

Duration and Renewal

A license is valid for up to 4 years from the day it is issued, plus the time to your next birthday. This could amount to four years and one day to five full years, and makes everyone's birthdate their renewal date. Many states have chosen time frames of five years or less, to comply with Brady law exemptions for license holders (permits must be less than five years old to exempt holders from the Brady delay and paperwork, other conditions apply, see Chapter 7). The CHL renewal process will actually be phased in in two years, to help stagger the workload.

To get a renewal you must complete a DPS-approved continuing education course in handgun proficiency no more than six months before you apply for renewal. If you pass the course you get a new Handgun Proficiency Certificate. Send a copy of it, along with a renewal application form provided by DPS, a non-refundable fee (which DPS will set when the first renewal dates approach), and two recent color passport photos to the address DPS announces when renewals come due.

DPS is required to send license holders a renewal form within 60 days of their expiration date. Applicants must be renewed or denied within 45 days of their application. The renewal fee for senior citizens and the indigent will be half of the regular fee. A renewed license is good for four years.

The renewal procedure can be done by mail. If you choose to renew by mail, you must include a signed form that says you understand state law regarding the use of deadly force and places where carrying a concealed handgun is prohibited.

Revoked License

Your license may be revoked if :

1–You were not legally entitled to have it in the first place;

2–You lied on the application;

3–You become ineligible after getting it (for example, if you were convicted of a felony);

4–You're convicted of carrying a firearm in a place prohibited under Penal Code §46.035.

Administrative details are provided in the law to guide law enforcement in the revocation process, and to allow licensees to respond. Details to reapply for a license, two years after one is revoked, are also provided.

Suspended License

Your license may be suspended if:

1–You are convicted of class C misdemeanor disorderly conduct;

2–You fail to show your license to authorities when required to do so;

3–You fail to notify DPS in 30 days of a change of name or address, or of a lost, stolen or destroyed license;

4–You carry a firearm that doesn't match your license category (the revolver and semi-auto distinction, described later);

5–You are *charged* with an offense which would disqualify you if you are convicted;

6–You don't return an old license after a modified one is issued.

Administrative details are provided in the law to guide law enforcement in the suspension process, and to allow licensees to respond. A license may not be suspended for less than one year or more than three years.

License Seizure

If you are arrested and taken into custody while carrying a CHL and handgun, the peace officer must confiscate the license and weapon. You may have the handgun returned (as described in Article 18.19 of the Code of Criminal Procedure) if you're not guilty.

Peace Officer May Disarm License Holder

If a peace officer believes it's necessary for your protection, or for the protection of the peace officer or other individuals, the officer is authorized to disarm you, and to return your firearm at the scene when the danger has subsided (provided you have broken no rules yourself).

Immunity for State Government and Instructors

Courts are prohibited from finding any part of the government, or a qualified handgun instructor, liable for damages for any actions or omissions as a result of the Right to Carry law, or any actions an applicant or licensee takes after getting or being denied a license. DPS is not responsible for any injury or damage done by a license holder. A case for damages may not even be brought to court with one exception. The only exception to these immunities are actions or omissions by the state that are "capricious or arbitrary."

Records and Privacy

DPS can disclose that you hold a CHL to any criminal justice agency, and is required to notify your sheriff. It's a chilling thought, however, to realize that when they receive a request in writing plus a fee to cover copying costs, the law requires them to provide this information to any individual who asks about you. The information they may disclose is your name, date of birth, gender, race, and zip code. DPS must notify you if a request is made and provide the name of the agency or person who made the request.

Reciprocity

Texas will honor a concealed-carry license from another state if:

- The license is current and valid.
- The eligibility requirement is at least as rigorous as in Texas.
- The state that issued the license has reciprocity with Texas.

MANDATORY CONCEALED-HANDGUN TRAINING

The Dept. of Public Safety (DPS) is required by law to establish training standards for concealed-handgun instructors and the programs they teach. Any resident who seeks a license (or a renewal or category-modified license) to carry a concealed handgun must earn a Handgun Proficiency Certificate by taking and passing an approved course with a qualified instructor.

DPS develops and distributes the directions and materials for the course, testing and recordkeeping. You go to the qualified instructor, not to DPS, to take a course for a license. (The course to become a certified instructor is given only by DPS, and is described later.) DPS maintains files of all test results, and the individual instructors keep records of their own. The course includes both classroom instruction and firing range instruction, and DPS officials may sit in and observe a class.

Minimum Course Requirements

The law and subsequent regulations set out certain minimum training requirements for a license. By law, each course must be between 10 and 15 hours in length (DPS recommends 14 hours) and is based on the curriculum developed by DPS. It must be conducted within Texas at facilities acceptable to DPS ("you can't just teach under an oak tree somewhere"). The range where you take the shooting test must have an official DPS ID number, which the range operator obtains after an on-site visit from DPS. The training program must include at least:

1–The laws related to weapons (federal and state laws affect weapons);

2–The laws related to the use of deadly force (state laws regulate the use or threatened use of deadly force);

3–Handgun use, proficiency and safety;

4–Actual demonstration that you can safely and proficiently handle firearms of your choice (of at least 9mm or .38 caliber);

5–Non-violent dispute resolution;

6–Proper storage practices for handguns, with an emphasis on eliminating accidental injuries to children.

By regulation, all applicants must pass a 50-question written exam based on this material with a minimum 70% score to qualify. More than one attempt to pass may be allowed. You must pass within six months of your application.

A continuing education course will also be developed by DPS to meet the license renewal requirement. That course must include at least four hours of instruction on one or more of the same topics covered above, plus whatever else DPS decides is appropriate.

Handgun Categories

The Right to Carry law introduces a new legal concept in Texas—distinctions between handgun types and calibers. The smallest caliber allowed for qualifying is .38 with a revolver, and 9mm for semiautomatics (the .380 is considered acceptable) and larger calibers are permitted as well. Semiautomatics are category "SA," and all other handguns are designated category "NSA." Instructors must qualify with both, license applicants may choose. A person who qualifies as SA may carry any type of legal handgun. An NSA licensee may only carry non-semiautomatics. Licensees may carry any caliber within their category. Applicants provide their own firearms for the test.

Marksmanship Requirements

The minimum requirements set by law to qualify for a Handgun Proficiency Certificate are:

1–Passing a written exam on the topics covered in the class;

2–Firing your handgun or handguns for qualifying scores.

DPS is charged with setting minimum standards for the ability to safely and proficiently handle and fire a handgun. The course of fire appears in a chart on the inside back cover of this book, and is subject to change by DPS. The basic requirements include:

- An unmodified DPS TX-PT blue silhouette target (life-sized with 5, 4 and 3 point scoring zones)

- A 50-round course of fire, using your own handgun, with timed shots fired at 3, 7 and 15 yards.

- 90% of maximum possible score to pass (225 out of 250) for instructors; 70% of maximum score to pass for licensees (175). Instructors and license applicants are given up to three attempts to pass.

- Firearms are to be held at the ready before and between firing strings, finger outside the trigger guard, muzzle pointed 45° ahead of you. No drawing is included in the test. Firing double action or from safety-on or decocked is recommended from a tactical and safety standpoint.

- Turning targets or whistles can be used to time strings. The time between strings is regulated at the range officer's discretion.

- A shot fired late deducts one highest-scoring shot. A shot lost to a malfunction cannot be made up (just as in a real emergency). An accidental discharge, firing out of sequence or unsafe handling of a firearm is grounds for removal from the course of fire or disqualification. Makeups depend on available time and the instructor's discretion.

INSTRUCTOR QUALIFICATIONS

To be eligible to take the DPS instructor's course you must meet the qualifications of a regular license applicant (residency, no criminal record, etc., described above) and have at least one of the following certifications:

- Commission on Law Enforcement Officer Standards and Education;
- Texas Board of Private Investigators and Private Security Agencies;
- National Rifle Association of America handgun instructor;
- You regularly instruct others in the use of handguns and have graduated from a school that uses a nationally accepted course designed to train handgun instructors.
- In addition, by rule, DPS has provided extended training for instructor applicants with less intensive training backgrounds.

An eligible instructor applicant must successfully complete a 25 - hour or 40-hour DPS-provided course of instruction to become certified as a CHL instructor. To qualify for the shorter 25-hour course, an applicant must pass a written pre-test with a 70% score, and a marksmanship pre-test with a 90% score for both revolver and semiauto. Applicants have one chance only to pass the pre-test. If you don't pass the pre-test, you're given some preference in reapplying for the regular training program.

The non-refundable fee for the course is $100. If you pass, the requirement for your own Handgun Proficiency Certificate is automatically waived if you apply for a CHL (though the $140 fee still applies). Instructors are not required to be licensed to carry concealed—and certification to instruct is *not* a license to carry. If an instructor becomes ineligible for a carry license, DPS will take action against the person's instructor status as well.

Training is currently provided only at DPS Austin headquarters and applicants must make their own arrangements for room and board while attending. Handgun instructor certification is good for two years. Retraining is required every two years and includes another $100 fee.

Any disruptive or unsafe behavior is grounds for immediate dismissal from training, at the instructor's sole discretion. Use of alcohol or illegal drugs during training is also grounds for immediate removal. Applicants must comply with all Texas laws and Training Academy operational procedures.

By law, an instructor must be able to teach, and the DPS training includes:

- The laws concerning weapons and the use of deadly force (state laws regulate the use of deadly force; state and federal laws regulate firearms);
- Handgun use, proficiency, and safety;
- Non-violent dispute resolution;
- Proper storage practices for handguns, especially to prevent accidents involving children.

DPS also provides training in techniques of group instruction and other subjects as deemed necessary. Instructor applicants must bring their own equipment, including:

- A revolver of at least .38 caliber;
- A semi-automatic handgun of at least 9mm (including .380);
- At least 200 rounds of factory-made ammunition per firearm (check with DPS for approved brands, reloads not allowed);
- Eye and ear protection, and protective clothing;
- Any other gear DPS determines is needed.

Handguns may have no modifications that compromise the safety of the weapon. Handguns are subject to inspection before and during training and may be rejected if the course instructor finds one to be unsafe.

Instructor applications are similar to carry-license applications, except that no photograph is required. An instructor applicant who is denied certification to instruct has similar options to have the decision reversed that a CHL applicant has (described under *Application Denials*). An instructor applicant who fails to qualify is given some preference in reapplying.

Prior notice must be given to DPS for each training session an instructor holds, including date, time, classroom location, range location and ID number, and the instructor(s) giving the course. Records and reports of all classes held must be securely stored by instructors for three years, are subject to inspection, and include license applicant records, test scores, critiques, course materials, and copies of all reports sent to DPS. Reports on students who've taken a class must be submitted on official forms within five business days.

Instructors must use official, sequentially numbered Handgun Proficiency Certificates, available from DPS at $5 each in lots of ten or more. Certificates may only be transferred to students as stipulated by law, must be kept in secure locked storage, and loss, theft or destruction must be reported to DPS in 5 business days.

Video tapes or guests instructors who are not themselves certified may be allowed by prior written approval from DPS. Such approval is obtained from the Austin DPS office, c/o the Pistol Range.

Miscellaneous

- DPS distributes a list of certified handgun instructors on request, at no cost, and keeps track of scheduled classes (which instructors must report to DPS prior to beginning). For a reasonable fee you may request a statistical report on CHLs issued, denied, revoked or suspended during the previous month, with breakouts by age, gender, race and zip code.

- The fees collected under the CHL program are used exclusively to run the program. Any excess at the end of the fiscal year is transferred to the Crime Victims Compensation Fund.

- Written notices required by the Right to Carry law must be sent by certified mail. Your official address is the last address you provided to DPS. If a certified letter to you is returned as undeliverable, DPS can give you legal notice by publishing one announcement in a local newspaper.

- Although *The Texas Gun Owner's Guide* doesn't specifically cover gun laws designed for peace officers and other officials, note that the Right to Carry law has full provisions for issuing CHLs to honorably retired peace officers who meet basic requirements. The license has the same duration as a civilian license, though the conditions and other factors are somewhat different (such as a proficiency requirement based on Local Government Code §415.035). A set of requirements is also established for active and retired judicial officers. Both of these appear in their entirety in Appendix D.

• DPS must provide a copy of the standards, course requirements and examinations to any qualified handgun instructor on request.

A WORD TO THE WISE

You should **expect changes** to the recently issued policies surrounding the new concealed-carry license. Anticipate a shakedown period while everything comes up to speed, with new regs possible, and old ones adjusted, eliminated or interpreted differently. Everyone may not agree on everything, and **elements of this book will undoubtedly change**. Remember that you face serious repercussions for what may be seemingly minor infractions. _The TEXAS Gun Owner's Guide is just one tool for helping you on a long road to knowledge._ That road has many turns and pitfalls— you should not rely on a single tool for such a complicated route, and be extremely cautious as you travel its course. Take steps to stay current.

Bloomfield Press will be preparing **updates** periodically. To receive a copy send us a stamped, self-addressed envelope. The address is on page two.

PROHIBITED PLACES

Many of the restrictions on possession of firearms are found in the Texas Penal Code. Other prohibitions are found in federal statutes and regulations, and land office and agency regulations, codes and laws. The prohibited places listed generally do not apply to the proper authorities (peace officers, commissioned security guards and bodyguards, members of the military and prison guards, special exempt agents of the government).

See Chapter 4 for information on where *shooting* firearms is prohibited. This section deals with places where *bearing* arms is prohibited. CHL holders are required to certify that they know where firearms are prohibited to obtain a renewal license by mail, and the subject is included in training classes.

Under §46.03 of the Penal Code it's a third degree felony for a person, even with a valid concealed-handgun license, to intentionally, knowingly or recklessly bring a firearm:

1–On the premises of a public or private school or educational institution, or a passenger vehicle of such an establishment, without written permission from them or under their written regulations;

2–On the premises of a public polling place on the day of an election or while early voting is in progress;

3–In any government court or offices used by the court, unless by written regulations or with written authorization from the court;

4–To a racetrack;

5–To the secured area of an airport (with an exception for properly checked baggage).

Under Penal Code §46.035, established by the Right to Carry law, CHL holders are prohibited from carrying:

1–On the premises where a high school, collegiate or professional sporting event, or an interscholastic event, is taking place (unless you're using the handgun in the event);

2–In an amusement park;

3–On the premises of a church, synagogue or other established place of worship;

4–At any meeting of a government entity;

5–On the premises of a correctional facility;

6–On the premises of hospitals or nursing homes (without written authorization);

7–On the premises of establishments that get 51% or more of their income from selling alcoholic beverages for on-premises consumption (typically known as *bars* though other places might qualify).

Note that hospitals, nursing homes and watering holes must prominently display a sign at each entrance, with block letters at least one inch in height, in contrasting colors, stating in both English and Spanish that it's unlawful to carry a handgun on the premises. DPS recommends this language: "State law prohibits carrying a handgun on these premises."

The word *premises* means a building or part of a building. It does not include a public or private driveway, street, sidewalk or walkway, parking lot or garage, or other parking area. This allows you to disarm before entering a prohibited place, and allows travel in the vicinity of those places.

Carrying a firearm at the places listed in §46.035 is a class A misdemeanor, except for bars and correctional facilities, where it is a third degree felony. An overall exception is made for the justified use of deadly force (self defense, etc.) under chapter 9 of the Penal Code.

Under Penal Code §46.11 an offense under any of the weapons laws (Penal Code chapter 46) carries the next higher penalty if it's proven that you knew you were:

1–within 300 feet of a school;

2–On the premises where an official school function was taking place;

3–at an event sponsored by the University Interscholastic League.

The places listed under item 1 for §46.03 (above) are excluded from the increase in penalties.

Also note that:

- Individual municipalities have some regulatory control over firearms within municipal limits (see Chapter 4) but may not make regulations that affect concealed-handgun licensees.

- Licensed security officers are subject to the same CHL requirements as regular residents, in addition to their own requirements as licensed guards.

- A separate law (Education Code §4.31) makes it a five-year felony to interfere with the normal activities of any type of school, or a school bus carrying children, by showing or using a firearm, or by threatening to show or use one.

- The Texas Parks and Wildlife Dept. is authorized to close areas to firearm possession, use, or to possession or use of specific types of firearms, under a number of different laws and regulations in the Parks and Wildlife Code.

- Under Parks and Wildlife Code §62.081, it's illegal to possess firearms on Lower Colorado River Authority land, except at official non-profit target ranges, by members of the boy scouts, girl scouts, or other non-profit public service groups, under the supervision of an authorized instructor.

- Possession of firearms on Lavaca-Navidad River Authority property is prohibited.

Private Property and No-Guns-Allowed Signs

Property owners have explicit rights and control the terms by which others may enter their property. Access to a private residence is legally under near-total control of the resident. A place open to the public, however, has limitations on the right to discriminate or refuse access to a member of the public.

The actual words of the Right to Carry law don't prevent or empower public and private employers from restricting CHL holders from their business premises. This creates two gray areas of control—limiting public access and setting conditions of employment—to be resolved by the courts.

There is little preventing a public place from posting signs of any reasonable nature. Whether a public place may discriminate against a person for exercising a Constitutional right, or for earning a government-issued license, remains to be seen. Does a place that restricts your ability to respond in an emergency take on a liability to protect you? Are you more safe or less safe at a place that has a no-guns-allowed policy? Will insurance companies refuse to pay for damages if a store has a no-guns sign, or if it doesn't have one? Are you really easier pickins when you're in a "gun-free" zone? Will foot traffic go up or down at a store with no-guns-allowed signs?

One thing to keep in mind is that boisterous arguments with store managers in public will serve little productive purpose, and creating too much commotion, especially if armed, can have decidedly negative repercussions.

A property owner may post a sign to forbid access (for example, "keep out" "no unauthorized personnel") or to set conditions for access ("open from 9–5" "no shirt, no shoes, no service") but it's illegal to discriminate on the basis of age, sex, race, religion, disability, national origin, or, creed. Banning legally armed citizens defeats the whole purpose of the Right-to-Carry law—to allow a person to respond in a dire criminal emergency. It's not perfectly clear what law is broken by walking past a private no-guns-allowed sign, or how a resident who is licensed to carry concealed could be charged for such an act. A person who is asked to leave private property and refuses faces a trespassing charge (see Penal Code §30.05).

The Texas Attorney General's Office issued two opinions on Aug. 30, 1995, concerning these gray areas. In one they suggest that a CHL-licensee commits criminal trespass by disregarding a no-guns-allowed sign, and in the other they propose that a rapid transit system can regulate firearms on its conveyances. Key legislators involved in passing the Right-to-Carry law disagree. Which "endangers the public safety" more—allowing CHLs to travel freely, or prohibiting their presence? It will take a court decision (or several) to help resolve the matter. It would be prudent to follow this unsettled issue carefully to see where it leads, and not to take any unnecessary risks.

Criminal trespass is a class B misdemeanor, unless it's committed in a home, a shelter center or with a deadly weapon, in which case it's a class A misdemeanor.

Bars

Intentionally, knowingly or recklessly carrying a handgun into a liquor store or place that serves alcoholic drinks is a third degree felony (see Penal Code §46.02). A concealed-handgun license does not exempt you from this requirement. A bar or liquor store that knowingly allows a person to have a firearm on the premises can have its liquor license revoked. These restrictions do not apply to the liquor-license holder (or the holder's employee) while supervising the licensed premises.

The liquor commission can adopt certain rules related to firearms. They may allow a gun show on the premises of a liquor license holder, if the premises is a government entity or a non-profit civic, religious, charitable, fraternal or veterans' organization. They may allow an off-premises-consumption license holder to hold a gun show if the license holder also has a federal firearms license. Finally, they may allow the ceremonial display of firearms at a licensed establishment.

Federal Facilities

- Guns are generally prohibited in federal facilities. Knowingly having a gun or other dangerous weapon (except a pocket knife with a blade under 2-1/2 inches) in a federal facility is punishable by a fine and up to one year imprisonment. Exceptions include authorities performing their duties, possession while hunting, or possession for other lawful purpose. You cannot be convicted of this offense unless notice of the law is posted at each public entrance or if you had actual notice of the law. A federal facility is a building (or part), federally leased or owned, where federal employees regularly work.

- Except for limited hunting privileges, there is a fine of up to $500 for carrying a gun in the National Parks.

- Possession of firearms on any military base is subject to control by the commanding officer.

- Firearm possession is prohibited by federal law on the gate side of airport-passenger security checkpoints. You are allowed to check firearms as baggage if you do it in accordance with federal rules (see *Common and Contract Carriers* in Chapter 1).

WHEN CAN YOU CONCEAL A FIREARM?

In Texas, the question isn't really about concealment, it's whether you can carry a handgun at all. Unless you have a valid Texas concealed-handgun license, the five *instances* where you may conceal a gun on yourself are:

1–In your residence;

2–On your business premises;

3–On land owned or leased by you;

4–While "traveling," according to the legal definition discussed in Chapter 1;

5–While engaging in lawful hunting, fishing, or other sporting activity, or directly enroute to such activity.

For private citizens without a license, there are no other "times" allowed under the law.

With a valid concealed-handgun license, you can legally carry a handgun anywhere in the state (though it must be concealed), except for the prohibited places listed in this chapter.

TYPES OF WEAPONS 3

There are weapons and there are weapons. A gun may be perfectly legal, but if you take it from your home or place of business, under many circumstances, it becomes an offense under current Texas law. If a gun has been modified in certain ways, it becomes a *prohibited weapon* and it may be a crime to have it at all. Certain weapons, defined by name or by operating characteristics and appearance, may only be owned if they were made before Sep. 13, 1994.

Weapons include *dangerous instruments,* things that can be deadly depending on their use, like fireplace tools or a baseball bat. The term *deadly weapons* specifically refers to things designed for lethal use. Guns are only one kind of deadly weapon.

A responsible gun owner needs an understanding of the different types of firearms, their methods of operation, selections for personal defense, holstering options, ammunition types, loading and unloading, cleaning and maintenance, accessories, safe storage and more. Many fine books cover these areas. This chapter of *The Texas Gun Owner's Guide* only covers weapons from the standpoint of those which are illegal, restricted or otherwise specially regulated.

PROHIBITED WEAPONS

In 1934, responding to mob violence spawned by Prohibition, Congress passed the National Firearms Act (NFA), the first major federal law concerning guns since the Constitution. This was an attempt to control what Congress called "gangster-type weapons." Items like machine guns, silencers, short rifles and sawed-off shotguns were put under strict government control and registration. These became known as "NFA weapons."

This gave authorities an edge in the fight against crime. Criminals never registered their weapons, and now simple possession of an unregistered "gangster gun" was a federal offense. Failure to pay the required transfer tax on the weapon compounded the charge. Regular types of personal firearms were completely unaffected.

Political assassinations in the 1960s led to a public outcry for greater gun controls. In 1968, the federal Gun Control Act was passed, which absorbed the provisions of earlier statutes and added bombs and other destructive devices to the list of strictly controlled weapons. Texas calls these *prohibited weapons* (see Penal Code §46.05 for the letter of the law), though a more accurate title might be *controlled weapons,* as you'll see under Machine Guns. It is generally illegal to make, have, transport, sell or transfer any prohibited weapon without prior approval and registration. Violation of this is generally a third degree felony under state law (see Penal Code §46.05), and carries federal penalties of up to 10 years in jail and up to a $10,000 fine.

Defaced Deadly Weapons

Removing, altering or destroying the manufacturer's serial number on a gun is a federal felony. Knowingly having a defaced gun is a federal felony.

State Prohibited Weapons

Penal Code §46.05 makes it illegal to intentionally or knowingly have, make, transport, repair or sell:

1–An explosive weapon;

2–A machine gun;

3–A short-barrel firearm;

4–A firearm silencer;

5–Armor-piercing ammunition;

6–A switchblade knife;

7–A chemical dispensing device (not including small personal self-defense sprays available commercially);

8–Knuckles;

9–A zip gun.

A violation is a third degree felony, except for items 7 or 8, which are class A misdemeanors. The first six items are also regulated under federal law.

Prohibited Weapon Exceptions

It is legal to intentionally or knowingly have, make, transport, repair or sell a prohibited weapon if:

1–You are performing official duties as a member of the armed forces, national guard, a governmental law enforcement agency or a penal institution;

2–You are acting within the boundaries of federal NFA weapons laws;

3–In the case of a switchblade or springblade knife or short-barrel firearm, you are dealing with it solely as an antique or curio;

4–In the case of armor-piercing ammunition, you are only acting to make it available to the armed forces, the national guard, a governmental law enforcement agency, or a penal institution.

ILLEGAL GUNS

(Also called NFA weapons or prohibited weapons)

These weapons and destructive devices are among those that are legal only if they are pre-registered with the Bureau of Alcohol, Tobacco and Firearms.

1–A rifle with a barrel less than 16 inches long;

2–A shotgun with a barrel less than 18 inches long;

3–A modified rifle or shotgun less than 26 inches overall;

4–Machine guns;

5–Silencers of any kind;

6–Firearms over .50 caliber;

7–Street Sweeper, Striker-12 and USAS-12 shotguns.

Guns with a bore of greater than one-half inch are technically known as destructive devices. Some antique and black powder firearms have such large bores but are not prohibited, as determined on a case-by-case basis by the Bureau of Alcohol, Tobacco and Firearms.

AFFECTED WEAPONS

The federal Public Safety and Recreational Firearms Use Protection Act (also called the Crime Bill, set to expire on Sep. 13, 2004), allows citizens to possess certain firearms and accessories only if they were made before Sep. 13, 1994. New products must have a date stamp and are off-limits for the public. If you have an affected weapon or accessory that has no date stamp, there is a legal presumption that the item is *not* affected (that is, it is a pre-crime-bill version) and is OK. Affected weapons (there are about 200) include all firearms, copies or duplicates, in any caliber, known as:

Norinco, Mitchell, and Poly Technologies (Avtomat Kalashnikovs, all models); Action Arms Israeli Military Industries Uzi and Galil;

Beretta AR-70 (SC-70); Colt AR-15; Fabrique National FN/FAL, FN/LAR, and FNC; SWD M-10, -11, -11/9, and -12; Steyr AUG; Intratec TEC-9, -DC9, and -22; and revolving cylinder shotguns, such as (or similar to) the Street Sweeper and Striker 12, and, any rifle that can accept a detachable magazine and has at least 2 of these features: a folding or telescoping stock; a pistol grip that protrudes conspicuously beneath the action; a bayonet mount; a flash suppressor or threaded barrel for one; and a grenade launcher, and, any semiautomatic pistol that can accept a detachable magazine and has at least 2 of these features: a magazine that attaches outside of the pistol grip; a threaded barrel that can accept a barrel extender, flash suppressor, forward handgrip, or silencer; a shroud that is attached to, or partially or completely encircles, the barrel and permits the shooter to hold the firearm with the nontrigger hand without being burned; a manufactured weight of 50 ounces (3-1/8 lbs.) or more when unloaded; and a semiautomatic version of an automatic firearm, and, any semiautomatic shotgun that has at least 2 of these features: a folding or telescoping stock; a pistol grip that protrudes conspicuously beneath the action; a fixed magazine capacity in excess of 5 rounds; and an ability to accept a detachable magazine, and, any magazines, belts, drums, feed strips and similar devices if they can accept more than 10 rounds of ammunition (fixed tubular devices for .22 caliber rimfire ammo are not included).

OTHER ILLEGAL DEADLY WEAPONS

(Also called destructive devices)

A number of other deadly weapons that are not guns are also prohibited under state and federal law. Possession of these devices is a third degree felony, unless it is a switchblade knife or knuckles, in which case it is a class A misdemeanor. (See Penal Code §46.05 for the letter of the law, §46.01 for definitions.)

1–Explosive, incendiary or poison gas bombs;

2–Explosive, incendiary or poison gas grenades;

3–Explosive, incendiary or poison gas rockets with more than 4 ounces of propellant (includes bazooka);

4–Explosive, incendiary or poison gas mines;

5–Mortars;

6–Molotov cocktails;

7–Nunchaku (a martial arts weapon made of two sticks, clubs, bars or rods, connected by a rope, cord, wire or chain, Nunchaku are not prohibited in lawful martial arts pursuits);

8–Armor piercing ammunition (a handgun bullet with at least a core of steel, iron, brass, bronze, beryllium, copper, depleted uranium, or one or a combination of tungsten alloys. Excluded are nontoxic shotgun shot, frangible projectiles designed for target shooting, projectiles intended for industrial purposes, oil- and gas-well perforating devices, and ammunition that is intended for sporting purposes);

9–Missiles with an explosive or incendiary charge greater than 1/4 ounce;

10–An unregistered machine gun;

11–A short-barrel firearm (rifle with a barrel length of less than 16 inches or a shotgun with a barrel length of less than 18 inches, or any weapon made from a shotgun or rifle if, as altered, it has an overall length of less than 26 inches);

12–A firearm silencer;

13–A switchblade knife;

14–Knuckles;

15–A chemical dispensing device ("a small chemical dispenser sold commercially for personal protection" is *not* prohibited);

16–A zip gun.

NOTE: Effective Mar. 1, 1994, Street Sweeper, Striker-12 and USAS-12 shotguns are classified as destructive devices, subject to NFA regulations (similar to machine guns), and *must now be registered even if you acquired it before that date*. The tax is waived for all such weapons owned before the effective date. If you own and do not wish to register such a weapon, or wish to transfer ownership without filing federal transfer papers, you may transfer the weapon to a properly qualified dealer, manufacturer or importer (with their ~~ssion~~), or to a law enforcement agency.

MACHINE GUNS

Under ~~conditions, private citizens~~ weapons ~~the machine~~

Unlike normal ~~possession~~, the cloak of privacy afforded gun ownership is removed in the case of so-called "NFA weapons"—those which were originally restricted by the National Firearms Act of 1934. The list has grown since that time, through subsequent legislation. As a law-abiding private citizen, if you want to have an NFA weapon you must meet five conditions. These requirements are designed to keep the weapons out of criminal hands or to prosecute criminals for possession.

1–You must register the weapon itself in the National Firearms Registry and Transfer Records of the Treasury Dept. This list of arms includes about 193,000 machine guns.

2–You must obtain permission in advance to transfer the weapon by filing "ATF Form 4 (5320.4)" available from the Bureau of Alcohol, Tobacco and Firearms.

3–An FBI check of your background is performed to locate any criminal record that would disqualify you from possessing the weapon. This is done with the help of a recent 2" x 2" photograph of yourself and your fingerprints on an FBI form FD-258 Fingerprint Card, which must be submitted with the application.

4–The transfer of the weapon from its lawful owner to you must be federally registered. In other words, a central record is kept of every NFA weapon and its current owner.

5–You must pay a $200 transfer tax. For some NFA weapons, the transfer tax is $5.

A properly licensed dealer can sell a registered machine gun to a qualified private buyer.

You may apply for approval to make NFA weapons, such as short rifles or sawed-off shotguns. The application process is similar to the process for buying such weapons. Unregistered NFA weapons are contraband and are subject to seizure. Having the unassembled parts needed to make an NFA weapon counts as having one.

The authorities are generally exempt from these provisions. Texas allows open trade in automatic weapons between manufacturers and dealers, and includes state and city police, prisons, the state and federal military, museums, educational institutions, and people with special licenses and permits.

The official trade in machine guns is specifically prohibited from becoming a source of commercial supply. Only those machine guns (and other NFA weapons) which were in the National Firearms Registry and Transfer Records as of May 19, 1986, may be privately held. This includes about 15,500 machine guns in Texas. The number available nationally will likely drop, since no new full-autos are being added to the registry, and the existing supply will decrease through attrition. Texans own about 30,000 NFA weapons in total.

CURIOS, RELICS AND ANTIQUES

Curios and relics are guns that have special value as antiquities, for historical purposes, or other reasons that make it unlikely they will be used currently as weapons. The Curio and Relic List is a 60-page document available from the Bureau of Alcohol, Tobacco and Firearms. They can also tell you how to apply to obtain curio or relic status for a particular weapon.

Antique firearms, defined as firearms with matchlock, flintlock, percussion cap or similar ignition systems, manufactured in or before 1898, and replicas meeting specific guidelines, are exempt from certain federal laws. For complete details contact the Bureau of Alcohol, Tobacco and Firearms. Remember, though, if it can fire or readily be made to fire it is a f... under state law.

Congress has been considering a variety of selective and categorical firearms bans. Citizens are advised to follow developments and remain keenly aware of any firearms or accessories that were formerly legal and then declared illegal. One such example is the Striker-12 shotgun, described earlier.

WHAT'S WRONG WITH THIS PICTURE?

These weapons and destructive devices are illegal unless they are pre-registered with the Bureau of Alcohol, Tobacco and Firearms.

- A rifle with a barrel less than 16 inches long
- A shotgun with a barrel less than 18 inches long
- A modified rifle or shotgun less than 26 inches overall
- Street Sweeper, Striker-12 or USAS-12 shotguns
- Machine guns or machine pistols
- Silencers of any kind
- Firearms using fixed ammunition over .50 caliber
- Armor-piercing ammunition
- Explosive, incendiary or poison gas bombs
- Explosive, incendiary or poison gas grenades
- Explosive, incendiary or poison gas mines
- Explosive, incendiary or poison gas rockets with more than 4 ounces of propellant (includes bazooka)
- Missiles with an explosive or incendiary charge greater than 1/4 ounce
- Mortars

Keep in mind that additional weapons may be added to this list in the future.

WHERE CAN YOU SHOOT? 4

Once you own a gun, it's natural to want to go out and fire it. In fact, it makes good sense. If you've decided to keep a gun, you should learn how it works and be able to handle it with confidence. Most hunting and shooting in Texas takes place on private land, although there is some limited access to national and state land for these purposes. Public ranges, both indoor and outdoor, provide an excellent and safe opportunity.

Ninety-six percent of the 267,338 square miles of Texas is in private hands. The remainder is regulated by many different authorities, and it's important to know the laws if you're contemplating hunting or shooting outdoors.

In order to understand where you can shoot outdoors in this state, you must first know where you cannot shoot. The restrictions come first when determining if shooting in an area is permissible.

Certain legal justifications may allow shooting, even if it would otherwise be illegal. An example is self-defense. A list of justifications is in Chapter 5.

GENERAL RESTRICTIONS

These are restrictions that apply whether you are on private land or land owned by the federal, state or local government.

Illegal Trajectory

It's illegal to shoot in such a manner that bullets will travel anywhere they may create a hazard to life or property. In National Forests, you may not shoot from or across a body of water adjacent to a road.

Aside from being a violation of several laws, there is a general rule of gun safety here: Be sure of your backstop. Take this a step further: Be sure of your line of fire. Never fire if you are unaware of (or not in full control of) the complete possible trajectory of the bullet, and are sure that the shot poses no threat to life or property.

Discharge in City Limits

It is a class A misdemeanor to recklessly fire a gun in a municipality with a population of 100,000 or more. This is sometimes called the accidental discharge law.

From Vehicles or Boats

It is illegal to shoot from a vehicle on or across a public road or from a boat on public water while hunting. The only exception is that migratory waterfowl (ducks, geese, brant and coot) may be hunted from a boat or any floating craft (except a sink box) that is beached, anchored or tied (see Parks & Wildlife Code §62.003). Chapter 6 discusses the laws and regulations governing hunting in Texas in more detail.

It's also illegal to knowingly shoot upon, from, across or into a public road or railway while hunting, including roads in the National Forests. Authorities frown on "road shooting" of any kind, and it's extremely unsafe. Shooting from vehicles or on public roads carries a heavy penalty and is just not a good idea.

Posted Areas

Under certain circumstances signs can be posted that restrict firearms use, possession or access to land or premises.

- *Private Land* may be posted by authority of the landowner or lessee.
- *State Land* controlled by the Texas Parks and Wildlife Dept. may be posted to restrict hunting and/or shooting.
- *National Forests* may have areas posted by the authorities for a number of reasons.

Most private, local, tribal, state and federal authorities may legally post an area under their control. The penalty for a violation varies widely, depending upon who posted what area. A different condition exists in posting private property open to the public, such as a store, as described in Chapter 2.

Public Nuisance

Maintaining a public place that is not a sanctioned shooting range, where people habitually go shooting, is a common nuisance. Going to such a place is a public nuisance.

THE LAND OF TEXAS

The land of Texas is divided up several different ways. The General Land Office divides the state into 34 Land Districts, and there are 254 counties in Texas.

Texas General Land Office

The Texas General Land Office has preserved and maintained records about Texas lands since 1836. Their collection, dating from the middle 1700s, includes land grants issued by the Spanish Crown, the Mexican Government and the Republic and State of Texas, and documents land distribution through original surveys, titles, registers, patents, reports, clerk returns, contracts, legislative acts, deeds of acquittance and other records. The GLO does not have any authority to make regulations concerning firearms, but they can tell you about the background for any ground in Texas.

Cities, Towns and Villages

In general, a municipality can't adopt regulations concerning the private ownership, keeping, transportation, transfer, licensing, or registration of firearms, ammunition, or firearm supplies (see §215.001 of the Local Government Code for the letter of the law). There are exceptions, however, and a municipality may require or regulate:

- Citizens or public employees to be armed for personal or national defense, law enforcement, or other lawful purpose;

- The discharge of firearms within city or town limits;

- The use of property or the locations of businesses under the city's fire code, zoning ordinances, or land use regulations;

- The use of firearms in the event of an insurrection, riot, or natural disaster where the city finds such measures necessary to protect public health and safety;

- The storage or transportation of explosives to protect public safety (Up to 25 lbs. of black powder for each private resident and up to 50 lbs. of black powder for each retail dealer are not subject to regulation);

- Carrying of firearms at public parks or public governmental meetings, political rallies, parades or official political meetings, or at non-firearms related school, college or professional athletic event. Exempt from this are any areas designated for hunting, fishing or firearms sporting event and the weapon is the type commonly used in that activity.

Under an amendment to the Local Government Code §215.001 provided by the Right to Carry law, municipalities do not have authority to regulate the carrying of concealed handguns by license holders at the locations mentioned in the paragraph above (public parks, etc.).

Special Cases

- *BB Guns*—Individual cities may have their own rules concerning BB guns (which are not firearms under state law). It may be permissible to set up a BB gun range indoors or outdoors within municipal boundaries if proper safety measures are taken. Check with local authorities for exact details at your location. BB guns are prohibited for hunting game.

- *Control of Nuisance Wildlife*—A required permit is available for this purpose from the Texas Parks & Wildlife Dept. (in Parks and Wildlife Code §43.154 through §43.157) or from the United States Fish and Wildlife Service. Problems with nuisance wildlife can often be handled best by contacting an exterminator who has the proper permits.

- *Special Permits*—The chief of police of a municipality may issue a special permit for firing guns within city limits (typically related to celebrations, parades, etc.).

- *Legally Justified Cases*—The law allows shooting within city limits under certain narrow circumstances called *justification*. An example is self-defense. For details, see Chapter 5.

County Land

The state of Texas is divided into 254 counties. County land may contain authorized shooting ranges, and information about these can be best obtained from the county sheriff's department where you want to shoot. You may notice that each county sheriff has a "style" to how they run their counties.

To promote public safety, the commissioners court of a county may regulate or prohibit the shooting (but no other aspects) of firearms on lots that are ten acres or smaller, in certain unincorporated areas of a county (see Local Government Code §240.021).

In counties with a population of 2,000,000 or more, you must have written consent of the landowner (or the landowner's legal representative) in order to hunt or target shoot (see Parks and Wildlife Code §62.012). You must have the consent with you and to be valid it must contain your name, identify the land involved, be signed by the owner or the owner's representative, and have the address and phone number of the person signing.

Indian Country

There are three Indian reservations in Texas, belonging to the Alabama-Coushatta, the Tigua (Ysleta del Sur Pueblo) and the Kickapoo Traditional Tribe of Texas. The tribes do not allow public hunting or shooting on tribal lands at this time.

Generally, those who live on Indian lands in Texas are under the same regulations that apply to other residents of the state. However, overlapping federal, state, tribal and local authority creates confusion when laws are violated in Indian country. Enforcement of laws on Indian reservations can cause a fundamental conflict over jurisdiction. Actual penalties for violations may be the subject of dispute.

National Forests

Approximately 673,000 acres in Texas is made up of National Forests and National Grasslands operated by the Forest Service of the U.S. Dept. of Agriculture. You may carry firearms at anytime and anywhere in the National Forests, as long as you and your gun are in compliance with the law. Call the local National Forest office (listed in Appendix C) for details before venturing out. Don't confuse the National Forests with the National Parks, where you normally may not even carry a loaded gun.

Hunting is allowed in the National Forests, but requires proper licenses. Contact the Texas Parks and Wildlife Dept. for details, and see Chapter 6 on Hunting Regulations. You cannot shoot inside a designated recreation area, at a crossroads, near a trail or in a posted area. Special conditions may apply in Wildlife Management Areas. It's best to call first if you're not sure about a particular location.

Target shooters are required to use removable targets in designated areas only. Clay pigeons, bottles, trash and other targets which leave debris are prohibited. Your choice of a target site should be against an embankment which will prevent bullets from causing a hazard. Your location should be *remote* from populated sites.

The laws controlling the National Forests are in a book called *Code of Federal Regulations, Title 36*, available at larger libraries. These federal rules prohibit shooting:

- Within 150 yards of a residence, building, campsite, developed recreation site or occupied area;
- Across or on a Forest Development road;
- Across or on a body of water adjacent to a Forest Development road;
- In any way which puts people at risk of injury or puts property at risk of damage;
- Which kills or injures any timber, tree or forest product;
- Which makes unreasonable noise;
- Which damages any natural feature or property of the United States.

Violation of these restrictions carries a possible $500 fine and a maximum prison sentence of 6 months under federal law.

The Forest Supervisor or other proper authority may issue special restrictions on firearm possession or use, or close a section to access if it seems necessary to protect public safety, or for other good reason.

It's always recommended to check with a representative of the Forest Service about any piece of National Forest land you're planning on using. National Forests and their offices within the state of Texas are listed in Appendix C.

National Parks Service Land

The National Parks Service of the U.S. Dept. of the Interior manages six national sites in Texas including National Parks, National Monuments, National Historic Sites, National Seashore and National Recreation Areas.

Limited hunting privileges exist in National Recreation Areas by special agreement of the Dept. of the Interior and the Texas Parks and Wildlife Dept. Except for this, it's illegal to even carry a loaded firearm into National Parks Service lands. Firearms must be unloaded, cased and out of sight, and broken down (bolt or magazine removed or otherwise temporarily inoperable). A list of Texas's National Parks Service sites is in Appendix C.

Private Land

Most hunting and shooting in Texas occurs on the 96% of the state that is in private hands. Land owners may grant permission for others to shoot on their land. To shoot on someone else's private land, you must first obtain permission from the owner. This can be an informal arrangement between you and the landowner, or you may pay for entry to the property as part of a leasing arrangement. In counties with more than 2,000,000 people, you need *written* consent to shoot on private land (see the entry under County Land).

If you have a simple agreement with a landowner and are granted permission, it's important to remember that this is not "for life." Just because you were allowed to hunt or shoot one time, doesn't mean you're automatically allowed the next time. You would do well to ask each time. If you enter someone else's property, for shooting or any other purpose, without permission, you can be charged with trespassing.

Owners of private land may allow access to the public for hunting, fishing, wildlife watching, photography, and other outdoor activities, through a lease arrangement. A list of the many Texas landowners who participate in this program can be found in a brochure called the *Hunter's Clearinghouse Directory.* Updated annually, it's published by the Texas Parks & Wildlife Dept. It's divided into seven areas or geographic regions–the Panhandle, Rolling Plains, West, Central, East, Gulf Coast and South–and then is arranged alphabetically by county within those regions. All arrangements relating to private land leased to the public should be made with the landowner, *not* the Parks & Wildlife Dept.

The private lands that are leased to the Texas Parks and Wildlife Dept. become part of Texas' Public Hunting Lands, totaling about 1,400,000 acres, including land owned by the Parks & Wildlife Dept. and land leased to them by the U.S. Forest Service, the Army Corps of Engineers, Texas Utilities, the Sabine River Authority, timber companies and private citizens. For more information on leasing your land for public hunting, contact Parks and Wildlife.

River Authorities

At least 14 agencies govern Texas waterways: 12 River
Authorities, the International Boundary and Water Commission,
and the U.S. Army Corps of Engineers. Five River Authorities
allow at least some kind of recreation on the land and waters
under their jurisdiction:

The Brazos River Authority

The waters under the authority of the BRA are Lake Granbury,
Lake Limestone and Possum Kingdom Lake. There are
designated target ranges where firearms are permitted. Hunting
of waterfowl is permitted in season, and special hunting
privileges may be authorized by the Board of Directors of the
Authority.

The Lavaca-Navidad River Authority

The possession or use of firearms on L-NRA property is
prohibited, because "all project lands and water are a wildlife
preserve." This includes BB or pellet guns, rifles, sidearms, and
shotguns. An exception to this, however, is in some limited
areas designated by the Authority for hunting small game and
water fowl, and then only by written permission issued by the
Authority.

The Lower Colorado River Authority

Possession of firearms, hunting or shooting on or across the land
of the Lower Colorado River Authority is prohibited, unless the
LCRA decides to lease land for a nonprofit target rifle range.
Violation is a P&W Code class C misdemeanor (see §62.081 of
the Parks & Wildlife Code). Nonprofit public service groups like
the boy scouts or girl scouts may bring in a qualified instructor
that has been registered with and approved by the LCRA on
designated ranges. This is for target shooting only. No hunting is
allowed. A map showing designated ranges and a list of
approved and registered instructors is maintained at the LCRA's
Austin office, listed in Appendix C.

The Sabine River Authority

The waters of the SRA are actually controlled by the Texas Parks
& Wildlife Dept. when it comes to hunting and shooting. Areas
may be posted by the SRA in places close to facilities or on

lands or waters where the SRA has deemed it hazardous to allow hunting or shooting.

The Trinity River Authority
Other than at Lake Livingston, where hunting is allowed, the discharge of a firearm on TRA land is prohibited. Law enforcement officials in the course of their duties are the only exception.

Shooting Ranges

Officially-approved and commercially operating shooting ranges may be the best place to learn and practice the shooting sports. Ranges may be legally set up within city limits as long as they conform to local requirements and ordinances. State regulations for operating outdoor shooting ranges are found beginning at Health and Safety Code §756.041. A special statute, Local Government Code §250.001, helps protect sport shooting ranges from nuisance lawsuits and government, civil or criminal charges due to noise.

The list of fine shooting ranges in Texas is a long list, and there's no way to fairly represent a portion of them in *The Texas Gun Owner's Guide*. Each county sheriff's office is usually familiar with the ranges in their county, and the yellow pages include lists of indoor and outdoor ranges. The Texas State Rifle Association, listed in Appendix C, can help you locate ranges in your area, and it organizes shooting events and competitions statewide. With passage of the concealed-handgun law, DPS has issued ID numbers to ranges that meet their standards and are authorized to conduct handgun proficiency tests for license applicants. The list is available on request.

Anyone who keeps a gun for personal safety would be wise to visit a range regularly and practice.

State and Federal Military Land

Land reserved for military use, whether under the jurisdiction of the National Guard or a branch of the federal armed forces such as the Army or the Air Force, is controlled by a military commander. What a commander says, goes. Possession or use of firearms on a military base is subject to control by the commanding officer.

You can't do much of anything on military land without prior approval. Anyone on military land is subject to a search. For details concerning a specific military installation, contact the base provost Marshall or the base commander's office.

Military ranges are frequently made available to the public or to organized groups on a controlled basis. Federal law actually says that a range built with any federal funds may be used by the military "and by persons capable of bearing arms." The rules for use are set by whoever controls the range, and the military has first call on use of the range.

Under the federal Civilian Marksmanship Program, the Army is required to provide range time, .22 and .30 caliber ammunition free of charge, and practice and instruction in firearms for citizens and for youths in the Boy Scouts, 4-H and similar clubs. For details see Title 10 of the United States Code, starting at section 4307. This program is part of the historical record of cooperation between the government and the citizens in keeping the population trained in the use of small arms.

Carrying firearms while traveling on a public road which passes through military land is subject to standard state regulations.

Certain State Lands

The Texas Parks and Wildlife Dept. can restrict shooting on land under its jurisdiction. By the general authority granted to the Dept. under the Parks & Wildlife Code §13.101 and §13.102, it can make regulations governing the health, safety, and protection of people and property in:

- State parks;
- State property adjacent to state parks and within 200 yards of their boundaries (see Parks & Wildlife Code §13.201);
- Historic sites;
- Scientific areas;
- Forts under its control;
- Public water within the above areas.

For example, discharging a firearm in, on, along, or across Lake Lavon in Collin County is a misdemeanor and is punishable by a fine of not less than $10 and not more than $200 plus costs, or confinement in the county jail for not more than one year, or both. This does not apply if you are hunting with a shotgun during a lawful hunting season (see Parks & Wildlife Code §143.023).

At the very least, you can be ejected from an area. In addition, a court order can be issued to prevent you from returning for any period the court determines (see Parks & Wildlife Code §13.108).

As you can see, shooting outdoors in this day and age is not just a matter of leaning off your back porch (well, not for most of us). You may ask, "how am I supposed to know all that?" The answer is, it's always best to call ahead and be sure before going hunting or setting up target practice on any land not your own. Even on your own land, depending on where your property is located, there may be subtle or total restrictions (especially true in cities). Call your local authorities to be sure, and recognize that nothing in life is completely free from risk.

Transporting Firearms for Shooting

Texas law allows you to have a handgun on or near yourself while you are directly enroute to a sporting activity where it can be lawfully used (see Penal Code §46.02). Because of the high legal risk for presence of a handgun (discussed in Chapter 1) no transportation method is foolproof. Rifles and shotguns have no such restrictions.

Some experts feel that a handgun brought to a range should be unloaded, in the trunk and separate from ammunition. A securely locked container is a possible option for vehicles without a trunk. Neither of these methods offer guarantees, since if you are stopped by a peace officer for any reason, the mere presence of a handgun can lead to criminal charges. Technically, while you are directly on the way to a range, a handgun, loaded and at your side or even holstered, is as legal as it is at the range. It's just that there's no way to demonstrate that legality convincingly and you're subject to arrest. If you have a concealed-handgun license, it's much less complicated to transport a handgun for recreational shooting or any other legal purpose. See Chapters 1 and 2 for more detail on "traveling" and the laws that affect CHL holders.

WHAT'S WRONG WITH THIS PICTURE?

1–Shooting within city limits is normally prohibited.

2–It's illegal to deface signs.

3–Trespassing is illegal.

4–You can't use targets which leave debris.

5–Shooting at wildlife requires a permit or license.

6–The target has no backstop. The shooter is not controlling the entire trajectory of the bullet.

7–The shooter isn't wearing eye or ear protection.

THERE'S NOTHING WRONG WITH THIS PICTURE!

THERE'S NOTHING WRONG WITH THIS PICTURE!

Practicing the shooting sports outdoors is all right as long as you comply with the laws.

- The shooters are at a remote location, on land which isn't restricted.
- The target leaves no debris.
- The target has a backstop which prevents bullets from causing a potential hazard.
- No wildlife or protected plants are in the line of fire.
- The shooters are using eye and ear protection.

DEADLY FORCE and SELF-DEFENSE 5

"I got my questionnaire baby,
You know I'm headed off for war,
Well now I'm gonna kill somebody
Don't have to break no kind of law."

- from a traditional blues song

There are times when you may shoot and kill another person and be guilty of no crime under Texas law. The law calls this *justification*, and says justification is a complete defense against any criminal charges (see Penal Code Chapter 9 for the letter of the law). The specific circumstances of a shooting determine whether the shooting is justified, and if not, which crime has been committed.

Whenever a shooting occurs, a crime has been committed. Either the shooting is legal as a defense against a crime or attempted crime, or else the shooting is not justified, in which case the shooting itself is the crime.

Your civil liability in a shooting can be a greater risk than criminal charges. You can be charged with both, and your legal protections are less vigorous in civil cases than in criminal ones. With very narrow exceptions, overcoming criminal charges does not protect you from a civil lawsuit—you can be tried twice.

Justification in killing someone does not provide criminal or civil protection for recklessly killing an innocent third person in the process. A stray shot you make can be as dangerous to you legally as committing a homicide. Using lethal force is so risky legally it is yet another reason to avoid it if at all possible—for your own safety.

USE OF DEADLY PHYSICAL FORCE

A reasonable person hopes it will never be necessary to raise a weapon in self-defense. It's smart to always avoid such confrontations. In the unlikely event that you must resort to force to defend yourself, **you are generally required to use as little force as necessary to control a situation. Deadly force can only be used in the most narrowly defined circumstances, and it is highly unlikely that you will ever encounter such circumstances in your life.** You have probably never been near such an event in your life so far. Your own life is permanently changed if you ever kill a person, intentionally or otherwise.

When can you "shoot to kill" and not be convicted of a crime? When the authorities or a jury, after the fact, determine that your actions were justifiable. *You never know beforehand.* And as a strategic matter, the Dept. of Public Safety teaches students to "shoot to stop."

No matter how well you understand the law, or how justified you may feel you are in a shooting incident, your fate will probably be determined much later, in a court of law. Establishing all the facts precisely is basically an impossible task and adds to your legal risks.

What were the exact circumstances during the moments of greatest stress, as best you remember them? Were there witnesses, who are they, what will they remember and what will they say to the authorities—each time they're asked—and in a courtroom? What was your relationship to the deceased person? How did you feel at the moment you fired? Did you have any options besides pulling the trigger? Can you look at it differently after the fact? Has there been even one case recently affecting how the law is now interpreted? Was a new law put into place yesterday? How good is your lawyer? How tough is the prosecutor? How convincing are you? Are the police on your side? Does the judge like your face? What will the jury think?

Be smart and never shoot at anyone if there is any way at all to avoid it. Avoiding the use of deadly force is usually a much safer course of action, at least from a legal point of view. You could be on much safer ground if you use a gun to protect yourself *without* actually firing a shot. Even though it's highly unlikely you'll ever need to draw a gun in self-defense, the number of crimes prevented by the presence of a citizen's gun— *that isn't fired*—are estimated to be in the millions. And yet, just pulling a gun can subject you to serious penalties. Think of it in reverse—if someone pulled a gun on you, would you want to press charges because they put your life in danger? You must be careful about opening yourself up to such charges.

Still, the law recognizes your right to protect yourself, your loved ones and other people from certain severe criminal acts. In the most extreme incident you may decide it is immediately necessary to use lethal force to survive and deal with the repercussions later. **You are urged to read the actual language of the law about this critical subject,** and even then, to avoid using deadly force if at all possible. Get the annotated criminal statutes in a library and read some case law to get a deeper understanding of the ramifications of using deadly force—and dealing with the legal system after the fact.

***The Texas Gun Owner's Guide* is intended to help you on a long journey to competence. Do not rely solely on the information in this book or on any other single source, and recognize that by deciding to prepare to use deadly physical force if it ever becomes necessary you are accepting substantial degrees of risk.**

Even with a good understanding of the rules, there may be more to it than meets the eye. As an example, shooting a criminal who is fleeing a crime is very different than shooting a criminal who's committing a crime. You may be justified in shooting to kill in a circumstance, and you might miss and only wound, but if you ever shoot to intentionally wound you'll have an uphill battle in court. The law is strict, complex and not something to take chances with in the heat of the moment if you don't have to.

It's natural to want to know, beforehand, just when it's OK to shoot to kill and be able to claim self-defense later. Unfortunately, you will never know for sure until *after* a situation arises. You make your moves whatever they are, and the authorities or a jury decides. The law doesn't physically control what you can or can't do—it gives the authorities guidelines on how to evaluate what you did after it occurs. **There are extreme legal risks when you choose to use force of any kind.**

Because cases of murder outnumber cases of justifiable homicide, the authorities have a distinct tendency to think of the person holding a smoking gun as the perpetrator, later as the suspect, and finally as the defendant, while the person who gets shot, or was merely threatened with a gun, is the victim and in need of protection. If you ever come close to pulling the trigger, remember there is a likelihood you will face charges when it's all over. The effects of the shot last long after the ringing in your ears stops.

"The quotations which follow are plain, conversational expressions of the gist of the law." This is followed by a more precise description of the law. Finally, each subject is cross-referenced to the actual section ("§") of the law.

Public Duty
"The use of deadly force is justified if it is required by law."

This includes circumstances such as combat during a war, executions, actions of peace officers, required assistance to a public servant, and other situations required by statute. You must reasonably believe your actions are justified by law in such circumstances. This instance of legal justification has little direct effect on the average citizen. See Penal Code §9.21 for the letter of the law.

Necessity
"This justification, called *the defense of necessity*, applies to an immediate need to act to prevent harm, regardless of laws which might otherwise prohibit your actions."

When you believe that action is immediately necessary to avoid imminent harm, and the harm you seek to avoid is urgent and clearly greater than the harm your actions would cause (and that is otherwise usually prohibited by law, such as carrying a handgun), and no specific exclusion for your actions have been established by law, your actions may be justified, if the authorities or a jury agree, after the fact, that you were justified.

The "defense of necessity" is frequently what allows a proper case of self defense to exclude charges of illegal possession of a handgun. See Penal Code §9.22 for the letter of the law.

Self-Defense

<u>"Only when someone is about to kill you unlawfully, can you kill them first."</u>

Except for the special cases below, you are justified in threatening or using deadly physical force against another person to protect your life, only if you reasonably believe that your life is immediately and illegally threatened by the other person, and a reasonable person in your situation would stand their ground, if the authorities or a jury agree, after the fact, that you were justified.

You cannot use deadly force:

- In response to insults or "verbal provocation" alone;

- To resist arrest or search by a peace officer (or someone acting for the officer), even if it's an unlawful arrest or search, unless the officer (or the person acting for the officer) is using undue force, you haven't offered any resistance up to that point, and only when and only to the degree you reasonably believe it's immediately necessary to use force to protect yourself from the undue force being used or threatened against you;

- If you've agreed to the force of another person against you— the "let's step outside and settle this" scenario, sometimes referred to as *dueling* (or in old West terms, a *showdown*);

- If you've provoked the force of another person against you. However, if you then back down and the other person refuses to back down, you may be justified;

- If you go to discuss your differences with someone and bring along a prohibited weapon (under Penal Code §46.05) or a handgun in violation of the carrying restriction (Penal Code §46.02).

See Penal Code §9.31 and §9.32 for the letter of the law. Under Civil Practice and Remedies Code §83.001 you have an affirmative defense to a civil lawsuit if you act in self defense, under Penal Code §9.32, and the person you act against has unlawfully entered your home.

Defense of a Third Person
"You can protect someone else the same as you can protect yourself."

You are justified in threatening or using deadly physical force to protect a third person under the same circumstances as you would to protect yourself: if you reasonably believe your actions are immediately necessary to protect the third person against the use of unlawful deadly force, if the authorities or a jury agree, after the fact, that you were justified.

See Penal Code §9.33 for the letter of the law.

Crime Prevention
"Deadly force is justified to prevent certain crimes."

Texas law says you are justified in using deadly physical force when and to the degree you reasonably believe it is immediately necessary to prevent someone's use or attempted use of force on you, and a reasonable person in your situation wouldn't retreat, and to prevent someone from committing:

1–Aggravated kidnapping,

2–Murder,

3–Sexual assault,

4–Aggravated sexual assault,

5–Robbery, or

6–Aggravated robbery,

if the authorities or a jury agree, after the fact, that you were justified.

See Penal Code §9.32 for the letter of the law.

Law Enforcement

"Deadly force is justified to control certain criminal activities related to arrest and escape."

If you are a peace officer or acting in an officer's presence and at the officer's direction, you may use or threaten deadly force to assist in making an arrest or search, or to prevent an escape after arrest, if the authorities or a jury agree, after the fact, that you were justified. See Penal Code §9.51 thru 9.53 for the letter of the law. There are certain things you must be sure of in this tense situation, including:

• Whether the arrest or search is lawful;

• If there's a warrant, that the warrant is valid;

• That the person directing you is indeed a peace officer, and has the legal authority to empower your actions.

If you believe you're being directed by a peace officer, who later turns out not to be one, you may have a difficult defense. The same is true if it turns out after the fact that the officer acted improperly. In some cases, a person believing they were duly authorized was enough, in other cases that belief was not valid as a defense against prosecution.

Protection of Life or Health

"You are justified in using deadly force against a person when and only to the degree you reasonably believe it is immediately necessary to protect that person's life in an emergency, if the authorities or a jury agree, after the fact, that you were justified."

See Penal Code §9.34 for the letter of the law.

Protecting Property

<See important note at end of section>

"Deadly force is justified to prevent another person from committing certain property crimes or to keep them from fleeing after committing these crimes."

Texas law says that you can use deadly force to protect land or tangible movable property if you reasonably think it is immediately necessary to prevent another person from committing:

- Arson;
- Burglary;
- Robbery;
- Aggravated robbery;
- Theft during the nighttime; and
- Criminal mischief during the nighttime;

if the authorities or a jury agree, after the fact, that you were justified.

The law adds that you can shoot to prevent a person from fleeing after committing burglary, robbery, aggravated robbery or theft during the nighttime, and from escaping with the property, if you reasonably believe you can't protect or recover the property any other way. It also says you are justified if using less than deadly force would expose you or another to serious risk of death or bodily injury. (See Penal Code §9.42)

Included is protecting property for a third person if the other person would do the same (under the law) themselves, and you have been asked by the third person to protect the property or have a legal duty to do so. You may also protect a third person's property if the third person is your spouse, parent, child, lives with you or is in your care. (See Penal Code §9.43)

Important Note: Some experts feel that use of deadly force in a property crime, which doesn't involve a threat to life or limb, would be difficult or even impossible to defend in court. Shooting an escaping thief in the back (per §9.42) creates a risky legal defense. Many of the precedent-setting cases are old and may not reflect the current state of jurisprudence. Some Supreme Court decisions suggest that the use of deadly force in property-only crimes, or to stop a criminal who is fleeing once the crime has ended, may not be justifiable. Civil liability is not necessarily removed by being cleared of criminal charges (you run the risk of a lawsuit by the perpetrator's kin). Also note that theft/criminal mischief in the nighttime are not defined by statute.

These and other factors make reliance on this law quite risky and not recommended. Yes, it is the law, but remember that justice is not always served. Remember that you are only justified if the authorities or a jury agree, after the fact, that you were justified. Remember that a prosecutor's role is to work hard to convict, regardless of your guilt or innocence. The pursuit of high conviction rates may lead to what some would consider dirty lawyer tricks, with your future on the line. There's an old saying that has some merit here, "Better a criminal goes free than a lien on your home." It is admittedly a very tough and risky choice.

RELATED LAWS

Aggravated Assault
"You can't shoot or threaten to shoot someone without a legal reason."

Intentionally, knowingly or recklessly shooting a person (or causing serious bodily injury in any other way, for that matter), without legal justification, is aggravated assault, a second degree felony. Threatening to shoot someone or just exhibiting a weapon during an assault is considered aggravated assault. See Penal Code §22.02 and §22.021 for the letter of the law.

Disorderly Conduct
"You must act seriously with guns."

It's illegal to discharge a firearm in a public place other than a sport shooting range, to display a gun in a public place with the purpose of creating alarm, or to shoot a gun on or across a public road. See Penal Code §42.01 for the letter of the law.

Deadly Conduct
"It's illegal to endanger the life of another person through the use of firearms."

You must not discharge or even point a firearm near people, in the direction of a house, building or vehicle where people might be inside. This is a third degree felony. See Penal Code §22.05 for the letter of the law.

Reporting Gunshot Wounds
"It's a crime to treat a gunshot wound and not report it."

A physician, administrator, superintendent, or other person in charge of a medical facility who is called on to treat a gunshot wound, regardless of the activity that may have caused it, must immediately notify the authorities and report the circumstances. Failure to make a report is a misdemeanor and carries a six month jail sentence or a fine of up to $100. See Health and Safety Code §161.041 for the letter of the law.

Responsibility

"Everyone is not equally criminally responsible for their acts."

A person under the age of 15 when an offense occurs can't be charged criminally for a shooting. No one can be given the death penalty for a crime committed when under the age of 17. (See Penal Code §8.07 for the letter of the law.) Certain mental states may have an affect on your legal responsibility for your actions.

Common or Public Nuisance

Maintaining a public place where people habitually go shooting (except for approved shooting ranges) is a common nuisance. A person who habitually goes shooting at such a place is a public nuisance. See the Civil Practices and Remedies Code beginning at §125.001 for the letter of the law.

Booby Traps

It's illegal to rig a gun as a booby trap (see Penal Code §9.44).

IF YOU SHOOT A CROOK OUTSIDE YOUR HOUSE
DO YOU HAVE TO DRAG HIM INSIDE?

IF YOU SHOOT A CROOK OUTSIDE YOUR HOUSE DO YOU HAVE TO DRAG HIM INSIDE?

No! Acting on this wide-spread myth is a completely terrible idea. You're talking about tampering with evidence, obstructing justice, interfering with public duties, false reporting and more. If you're involved in a shooting, leave everything at the scene just as it is and call for the police and an ambulance.

Don't think for a minute that modern forensics won't detect an altered scene of a crime. At any shooting a crime has been committed. Either the shooting is justified, which means you were in your rights and the victim was acting illegally, or you exceeded your rights in the shooting, regardless of the victim's circumstance. The situation will be investigated to determine the facts, and believe it, the facts will come out. Police tell time-worn jokes about finding "black heel marks on the linoleum." And once you're caught in a lie, your credibility is shot.

If you tamper with the evidence, you have to lie to all the authorities to back it up. Then you have to commit perjury to follow through. Can you pull it off?

If the guy with the mask was shot from the front, armed as he is, the homeowner has a good case for self-defense. If the masked man was shot from behind, the homeowner has a case for acting to prevent aggravated burglary. Either way, he's better off leaving the body where it falls.

Suppose you shoot an armed intruder coming through your window, and the body falls outside the house. You'll have a better time convincing a jury that you were scared to death, than trying to explain how the dead crook in your living room got blood stains on your lawn.

The reason this fable gets so much play is because there is a big difference between a homeowner shooting a crook in the kitchen, and one person shooting another outdoors. Shooting at a stranger outside your house can be murder.

CAN YOU POINT A GUN AT SOMEONE?

No matter how many aces a person is holding, you can't settle the matter with a gun. This also shows how the law can be interpreted in more than one way.

Using a gun to put a person in reasonable fear of imminent physical injury is *aggravated assault*—a second degree felony. A more lenient view would be to say that this is reckless display of a gun, which is *disorderly conduct,* a class B misdemeanor.

When you go to court, it could be argued that this is actually *attempted murder,* a felony. And if the guy with the gun is angry enough to take back his money, it becomes *aggravated robbery,* also a first degree felony.

By drawing your gun, the other guy may be able to shoot you dead and legally claim self-defense. You may never pull a gun to leverage an argument. Merely having the gun with you may violate the handgun-carrying prohibition of Texas law and if the scene is taking place in a bar, the crime goes from a misdemeanor to a felony.

If someone pointed a gun at you, would you get angry and want to see them arrested? Consider how someone would feel if roles were reversed and it was you who pulled the gun when it wasn't absolutely necessary to prevent a life-threatening situation.

Despite all this, the law recognizes your right to defend yourself, your loved ones, and other people. The law also recognizes a citizen's right to act to prevent certain crimes. These cases, when you *can* point a gun at another person, are described in Chapter 5.

HUNTING REGULATIONS 6

Texas hunting regulations are complex, highly-detailed and mandatory requirements issued for the most part by the Texas Parks and Wildlife Dept. This chapter is intended to point you in the right direction. Hunters need more information than just the firearms details provided here. For more detailed information and complete hunting regulations and procedures, contact the Texas Parks and Wildlife Dept.

A hunting license is required for any person, of any age, who hunts in the state of Texas. The Texas Parks and Wildlife Dept. requires every hunter whose date of birth is on or after September 2, 1971 to take and pass a Hunter Education Course through a program administered by Parks & Wildlife. Those who wish to hunt and are aged 12 through 16 can either successfully complete the course or they must be accompanied by a licensed hunter 17 years of age or older. Children under 12 must be accompanied by a licensed hunter 17 or older. You must carry proof of certification of completing the course on your person (called Hunter Safety Certification) while you are hunting. Failure to carry this certification is a class C misdemeanor under the Parks & Wildlife Code and carries a fine of $25 to $500.

The Hunter Education Training Course costs five dollars. To get information on a course near you, contact your local Texas Parks and Wildlife Dept. Law Enforcement office (see Appendix C for contact information). You may be exempted from the course if you have been certified in the voluntary Texas Hunter Safety Education Program, or if you have been certified through another state. To find out if you qualify call the Texas Parks and Wildlife Hunter Education Section to see if your prior training is acceptable.

The Hunter Education Program is governed by §62.014 of the Parks & Wildlife Code. The course must cover at least:

- the safe handling and use of firearms and archery equipment;
- wildlife conservation and management;
- hunting laws and applicable rules and regulations;
- hunting safety and ethics, including landowners' rights;

A certificate is issued by the department upon completion of the course.

A Texas hunting license is valid only from Sep. 1 or the date it's issued, whichever comes later, to Aug. 31 of the following year. It must be renewed each year. To be considered a resident, you must have lived in the state continuously for six months immediately before applying for your license, or be an active duty member of the U.S. armed forces. Dependents of active members of the armed forces are included. This does not, however, apply to the National Guard.

Hunting on Leased Land

The annual *Hunter's Clearinghouse Directory* gives detailed information from the nearly 300 private landowners who lease their land for hunting and other outdoor activities. It divides these lands into seven geographic areas. Information for each area is then arranged alphabetically by county and is presented in chart form. Charts include such information as types of game available, acreage, lodging and amenities.

Anyone who leases hunting rights and charges a fee for hunting on their property or property they control must have a Hunting Lease License and must keep detailed records in a Hunting Lease Record Book provided by the Texas Parks and Wildlife Dept.

Hunting on U.S. Army Corps of Engineers Land

The U.S. Army Corps of Engineers manages certain lands around the state, and allows hunting at many of these locations in accordance with local, state and federal laws. Prohibited areas include lands around dams, outlet facilities, project offices and areas leased for recreational purposes. Since each area has its own unique environment that might affect hunting and firearms safety, you must contact the local authorities to be sure. You can also get a guide published by the Southwestern Division of the U.S. Army Corps of Engineers. Their address is in Appendix C.

Public Lands Regulated by Texas Parks and Wildlife Dept.

A booklet describing certain public hunting lands in Texas is issued to purchasers of an annual hunting permit. It's called the *Public Hunting Lands Map Booklet*, and contains detailed maps and instructions for hunting on land owned or controlled by the Texas Parks & Wildlife Dept. or leased from the U.S. Forest Service, Army Corps of Engineers, Texas Utilities, Sabine River Authority, timber companies or private landowners. The tracts range from 500 acres to 400 square miles.

Loaded firearms are not allowed in or on a motor vehicle or in a designated campsite on these lands and buckshot is prohibited altogether. Muzzleloading firearms are legal for taking deer, provided they are .45 caliber or larger. It is illegal to discharge a firearm (or bow and arrow) from, onto, along or across a road or campsite. Using or displaying a firearm in an unsafe or threatening manner is also illegal.

Only certain areas are designated for target practice, so be sure to check the map booklet for the appropriate information. Also be aware that certain areas have their own specific regulations and you're responsible for following these. As an example, on Unit #747, the Alazan Bayou WMA in Nacogdoches County it's illegal to have a rifle or handgun greater than .22 caliber rimfire during squirrel hunting season, and taking feral hogs during the general season is prohibited with anything other than a muzzleloader.

Some Key Hunting Regulations

Below you'll find the main general rules about the use of firearms while hunting. Remember, hunting regulations are not limited to guns and include archery and falconry. A free general booklet called the *Texas Hunting Guide* is available from the Texas Parks & Wildlife Dept. and is updated annually.

- A valid hunting license is required to hunt any animal (terrestrial vertebrates) or bird.

- It's illegal to use another person's license, stamp or game tags to hunt or fish.

- Generally, you can't hunt from a motor vehicle, aircraft or any airborne device, powerboat, sailboat or other floating device. However, you may hunt non-migratory animals and birds from a motor vehicle or boat if you are within the boundaries of private property or on private water and you stay clear of the state road system (see Parks & Wildlife Code §62.003).

- You must carry your driver's license or personal ID certificate (issued by the Texas Dept. of Public Safety) on yourself while hunting, if you're 17 years old or older. Non-residents must carry similar documents issued by their state or country of residence.

- It's Illegal to hunt at night or to use artificial light to "blind" prey, and you can't use artificial light to help you take game animals and game birds, but battery-powered scoping devices that project a light or dot only inside the scope are OK.

- It's illegal to let any edible portion of an animal you take go to waste.

- Many hunting regulations concern the types of firearms allowed depending on the game and the season. Some examples are listed below:

  Only muzzleloading weapons (includes handguns) of .45 caliber or larger are legal for hunting deer during a muzzleloader-only deer season

There's no restriction on the number of shells a shotgun or rifle may hold when hunting birds or animals, with the exception of migratory game birds where the limit is two in the magazine, one in the chamber.

It's illegal to take game animals or game birds with fully automatic weapons or using silencers.

It's illegal to use rimfire ammunition for taking deer, pronghorn or elk anywhere in the state, or for taking aoudad sheep in certain Panhandle counties.

It's illegal to shoot migratory game birds with any gun other than a shotgun that's not larger than 10 gauge.

- It's illegal to shoot any mammal, reptile, amphibian or bird listed by the state or federal authorities as an endangered species or threatened species.

- Residents are requested to report sightings of mountain lions dead or alive, and to report the shooting of a mountain lion (which may be legally hunted). The state is trying to gather information on the number and distribution of these animals.

- Poaching (hunting in violation of any of the regulations) is a serious crime. Hunters (and others) are encouraged to report poaching incidents, by calling Operation Game Thief (see Appendix C).

- It's illegal to take otter with firearms.

- It's illegal to shoot at, take or attempt to take any fur-bearing animal, from a boat on public waters in Texas.

- It's illegal to discharge a firearm on, along or across a public road.

- It's illegal to possess a firearm or be accompanied by a person possessing a firearm while taking game animals, game birds and fur-bearing animals by falconry.

- It's illegal to use smoke, explosives or chemicals of any kind to kill or flush fur-bearing animals in the wild.

- A firearm (and other things) may be confiscated if you are charged with using it in a Parks and Wildlife violation. Upon conviction, anything confiscated may be auctioned off or kept by the department. Upon acquittal the goods are returned to the owner.

A Hunter's Pledge

Responsible hunting provides unique challenges and rewards. However, the future of the sport depends on each hunter's behavior and ethics. Therefore, as a hunter, I pledge to:

- Respect the environment and wildlife;
- Respect property and landowners;
- Show consideration for nonhunters;
- Hunt safely;
- Know and obey the law;
- Support wildlife and habitat conservation;
- Pass on an ethical hunting tradition;
- Strive to improve my outdoor skills and understanding of wildlife;
- Hunt only with ethical hunters.

By following these principles of conduct each time I go afield, I will give my best to the sport, the public, the environment and myself. The responsibility to hunt ethically is mine; the future of hunting depends on me.

The Hunter's Pledge was created cooperatively by:

International Association of Fish and Wildlife Agencies
Izaak Walton League of America
National Rifle Association
Rocky Mountain Elk Foundation
Tread Lightly! Inc.
Sport Fishing Institute
Times Mirror Magazines Conservation Council
U.S. Dept. of Agriculture Extension Service
Wildlife Management Institute

NOTES ON
FEDERAL LAW 7

Although federal laws regulate firearms to a great degree, the same laws prohibit the federal and local government from encroaching on the right to bear arms. This is seen in the 2nd, 9th and 14th Amendments to the Constitution, and in federal statutory laws, which number about 230.

Dealers of firearms must be licensed by the Bureau of Alcohol, Tobacco and Firearms (ATF). Federal law requires licensed dealers to keep records of each sale, but prohibits using this information in any sort of national registration plan. The information is permanently saved by the dealer and is not centrally recorded by the federal authorities. If a dealer goes out of business the records are sent to a central federal depository for storage (or a state site if approved by the Treasury Dept.). Federal law prohibits using these records to establish a national firearms registration system.

Paperwork required by the Brady Law is collected by local authorities, but must be destroyed shortly after it is used to conduct background checks, and by law, no records of the checks may be kept. Local authorities are required to certify their compliance with record destruction to the U.S. Attorney General every six months.

This means there's no central place for anyone to go and see if a given individual owns a firearm. For someone to find out if you have a gun they would have to check all the records of all the dealers in the country, a daunting task. Only ATF is authorized to check the records of manufacture, importation and sale of firearms.

The dealer's records allow guns to be *traced,* a very different and important matter. When a gun is involved in a crime, ATF can find out, from the manufacturer's serial number, which licensed dealer originally received the gun. The dealer can then look through the records and see who purchased the weapon. It's a one-way street—a gun can be linked to a purchaser but owners can't be traced to their guns. One study of successful traces showed that four out of five were of some value to law enforcement authorities.

When President Reagan was shot by John Hinckley Jr., the weapon was traced and in fourteen minutes time, a retail sale to Hinckley was confirmed.

Buying, selling, having, making, transferring and transporting guns is in many cases regulated by federal laws. These regulations are covered in *The Texas Gun Owner's Guide,* but for the most part, only state penalties are noted. There may be federal penalties as well. (A book describing all the federal gun laws in plain English, *Gun Laws of America*, is available from Bloomfield Press. See the listing in the back of this book.)

Under the Assimilative Crimes Act, state law controls if there is no federal law covering a situation. It is important to recognize that there can be a question of jurisdiction in some cases. Additional federal requirements may be found in the Code of Federal Regulations and the United States Code.

A long history of federal regulation exists with regard to firearms and other weapons. The main laws include:

- Second Amendment to the Constitution (1791)
- Ninth Amendment to the Constitution (1791)
- Fourteenth Amendment to the Constitution (1868)
- National Firearms Act (1934)
- Federal Firearms Act (1938)
- Omnibus Crime Control and Safe Streets Act (1968)
- Gun Control Act (1968)
- Organized Crime Control Act (1970)
- Omnibus Crime Control Act (1986)
- Firearm Owner's Protection Act (1986)
- Brady Handgun Violence Prevention Act (1993)
- Public Safety and Recreational Firearms Use Protection Act (The Crime Bill) (1994)

Federal Firearms Transportation Guarantee

Passed on July 8, 1986 as part of the Firearm Owner's Protection Act, federal law guarantees that a person may legally transport a firearm from one place where its possession is legal to another place where possession is legal, provided it is unloaded and the firearm and ammunition is not readily accessible from the passenger compartment of the vehicle. The law doesn't say it in so many words, but the only non-accessible spot in the average passenger car is the trunk. If a vehicle has no separate compartment for storage, the firearm and ammunition may be in a locked container other than the glove compartment or console.

There have been cases, especially in Eastern states, where local authorities have not complied with this law, creating a degree of risk for people otherwise legally transporting firearms. To avoid any confusion, the text of the federal guarantee is printed here word for word:

Federal Law Number 18 USC § 926A
Interstate transportation of firearms

Notwithstanding any other provision of any law or any rule or regulation of a State or any political subdivision thereof, any person who is not otherwise prohibited by this chapter from transporting, shipping, or receiving a firearm shall be entitled to transport a firearm for any lawful purpose from any place where he may lawfully possess and carry such firearm to any other place where he may lawfully possess and carry such firearm if, during such transportation the firearm is unloaded, and neither the firearm nor any ammunition being transported is readily accessible or is directly accessible from the passenger compartment of such transporting vehicle: Provided, That in the case of a vehicle without a compartment separate from the driver's compartment the firearm or ammunition shall be contained in a locked container other than the glove compartment or console.

Anyone interested in a complete copy of the federal gun laws, with plain English summaries of every law, can get a copy of *Gun Laws of America*, published by Bloomfield Press. See the back section of this book for details.

The Brady Law

The Brady Handgun Violence Prevention Act was signed into law on Nov. 30, 1993. Its provisions for common carriers, reporting multiple handgun sales and license fee increases are among the rules affecting private citizens which took effect immediately. The waiting-period provisions took effect on Feb. 28, 1994, and were set to expire on Feb. 27, 1999.

In addition to the regulation of private citizens described below, the Brady Law: places special requirements on dealers, sets timetables and budgets for the U.S. Attorney General to implement the law, provides funding, sets basic computer system requirements, mandates criminal-history record sharing among authorities, enhances penalties for gun thieves and more. Your federal legislators can send you the full 12-page Brady Law.

The Brady Law refers to a "chief law enforcement officer," defined as the chief of police, the sheriff, an equivalent officer or their designee. The description below refers to such persons as "the authorities." Where the law refers to an individual who is unlicensed under §923 of USC Title 18, this description says "private citizen" or "you." Federally licensed dealers, manufacturers and importers are referred to as "dealers." The act of selling, delivering or transferring is called "transferring." The law defines *handgun* as, "a firearm which has a short stock and is designed to be held and fired by the use of a single hand." A combination of parts which can be assembled into a handgun counts as a handgun.

Under the Brady Law, to legally obtain a handgun from a dealer you must provide:

• A valid picture ID for the dealer to examine;

• A written statement with only the date the statement was made, notice of your intent to obtain a handgun from the dealer, your name, address, date of birth, the type of ID you used and a statement that you are not: 1–under indictment and haven't been convicted of a crime which carries a prison term of more than one year, 2–a fugitive from justice, 3–an unlawful user of or addicted to any controlled substance, 4–an adjudicated mental defective, 5–a person who has been committed to a mental institution, 6–an illegal alien, 7–dishonorably discharged from the armed forces, 8–a person who has renounced U.S. citizenship.

Then, before transferring the handgun to you, the dealer must:

• Within one day, provide notice of the content and send a copy of the statement to the authorities where you live;

• Keep a copy of your statement and evidence that it was sent to the authorities;

• Wait five days during which state offices are open, from the day the dealer gave the authorities notice, and during that time,

• Receive no information from the authorities that your possession of the handgun would violate federal, state or local laws.

The waiting period ends early if the authorities notify the dealer early that you're eligible. The authorities "shall make a reasonable effort" to check your background in local, state and federal records. Long guns are unaffected by the Brady Law until the National Instant Check described below comes on line.

You are excluded from the Brady waiting-period process:

1–If you have a written statement from the authorities, valid for 10 days, that you need a handgun because of a threat to your life or a member of your household's life; or

2–With a handgun permit, in the state which issued it, if the permit is less than five years old and required a background check (if the Texas concealed-handgun license qualifies, it will eliminate the need for license holders to wait for handgun purchases or to do additional paperwork or background checks, see details later); or

3–In states which have their own handgun background check (Texas does not have one); or

4–If the transfer is already regulated by the National Firearms Act of 1934, as with Class III weapons; or

5–If the dealer has been certified as being in an extremely remote location of a sparsely populated state and there are no telecommunications near the dealer's business premises (written for Alaska, but other localities may qualify).

If a dealer is notified after a transfer that your possession of the handgun is illegal, the dealer must, within one business day, provide any information they have about you to the authorities at the dealer's place of business and at your residence. The information a dealer receives may only be communicated to you, the authorities or by court order. If you are denied a handgun, you may ask the authorities why, and they are required to provide the reason in writing within 20 business days of your request.

Unless the authorities determine that the handgun transfer to you would be illegal, they must, within 20 days of the date of your statement, destroy all records of the process. The authorities are expressly forbidden to convey or use the information in your statement for anything other than what's needed to carry out the Brady process.

The authorities may not be held liable for damages for either allowing an illegal handgun transfer or preventing a legal one. If you are denied a firearm unjustly, you may sue the political entity responsible and get the information corrected or have the transfer approved, and you may collect reasonable attorney's fees.

National Instant Check: The Brady Law requires the U.S. Attorney General (AG) to establish a National Instant Criminal Background Check system (NICBC) before Nov. 30, 1998. Once this in effect, the previous waiting process is eliminated. In order to transfer any firearm, not just handguns, when the NICBC system is in place, a dealer must:

* verify your identity from a valid photo-ID card, contact the system, identify you and receive a unique transfer number, or

* wait three days during which state offices are open and the system provides no notice that the transfer would violate relevant laws.

The NICBC system is required to issue the transfer number if the transfer would violate no relevant laws, and it destroys all records of approved inquiries except for the identifying number and the date it was issued. If the transfer is legal, the dealer includes the transfer number in the record of the transaction. The NICBC system is bypassed under conditions similar to 2, 4 and 5 listed above as exceptions to the waiting period (with number 2 broadened to include "firearms" permit).

Whoever violates these requirements is subject to a fine of up to $1,000 and a jail term of up to 1 year.

If you are denied a firearm under the NICBC, you may request the reason and the system must present you with a written answer within five business days. You may also request the reason from the AG, who must respond immediately. You may provide information to fix any errors in the system, and the AG must immediately consider the information, investigate further, correct any erroneous federal records and notify any federal or state agency that was the source of the errors.

Multiple sales of handguns (two or more from the same dealer in a five day period) have long been reported to the Bureau of Alcohol, Tobacco and Firearms, and must now be reported to local authorities as well. Local authorities may not disclose the information, must destroy the records within 20 days from receipt if the transfer is not illegal and must certify every six months to the AG that they are complying with these provisions.

Common or contract carriers (airlines, buses, trains, etc.) may not label your luggage or packages to indicate that they contain firearms. (Federal law requires you to notify the carrier in writing if you are transporting firearms or ammunition. The long-time labeling practice had been responsible for the frequent theft of luggage containing firearms.)

Licensing fees for obtaining a new federal firearms license are increased to $200 for three years. The fee for renewing a currently valid license is $90 for three years.

Brady Law CHL Note

While the Brady Law is new it would be prudent to anticipate a degree of confusion, inconsistent policies and enforcement, conflicting regulations and jurisdictions, regulations which do not match the letter of the law, denials of responsibility, and court cases to clarify the intent, practicalities and legality of the law. With the law being challenged in federal courts, changes to it, repeal or partial repeal are possible.

For example, under normal conditions, a proper handgun-carry permit exempts the holder from the Brady delay and paperwork. If the permit is less than five years old, required a background check, and the sale is in the same state as the permit is from, the sale is exempt from further red tape. The Bureau of Alcohol, Tobacco and Firearms however has taken an initial stand that the Texas CHL is faulty and doesn't meet the Brady requirements, for reasons that are under scrutiny.

By law, DPS maintains constant watch for felony charges and other disqualifying indications against CHL holders, which causes automatic suspension or revocation of a CHL. Because of this, years from now, license renewals won't require separate background checks (at least as currently written). This means the license fails to meet federal standards, says BATF. You may not think this makes sense, but it is BATF's position as we go to press.

BATF goes on to say that the Texas CHL law is further flawed, because active and retired judges, and honorably retired peace officers may obtain CHLs if they meet stringent state law requirements, but they aren't subjected to separate background checks either.

Now of course, if DPS is allowing judges or honorably retired peace officers who are felons or illegal aliens (or in any other prohibited category) to get CHLs, then this must be corrected immediately. What is more likely perhaps is that the BATF policy must adjust to conform with the law and not deprive honest citizens of their rights under the law. Which side do you believe is right? What will the authorities decide? Only time will tell.

Public Safety and Recreational Firearms Use Protection Act

This law, popularized as the 1994 Crime Bill, affected three areas of existing firearms law: 1-Possession and use of firearms by juveniles; 2-Purchase of firearms by people under domestic violence restraining orders, and 3-it created a new class of regulated firearms and accessories. The information on juveniles is found in Chapter 1 since it relates to who can bear arms. The new class of prohibited purchasers (for domestic violence cases) is also in Chapter 1, as part of the list for federal form 4473—the form dealers use with all sales.

The portion of the law that affected certain weapons and accessories, the so-called assault-weapons ban, has been poorly reported and many people have an inaccurate notion of what this law accomplished. Nothing is actually banned— Americans may still buy, own, sell, trade, have and use any of the millions of affected firearms and accessories.

What the law actually did was to prohibit *manufacturers and importers* from selling newly made goods of that type to the public (and it's a crime for the public to get them). Maybe that is a ban, but not in the sense that's been popularized. Contrary to news reports, the law did nothing about the very real problem of getting armed criminals off the street. The list of affected weapons is in Chapter 2.

The net effect of the law was to motivate manufacturers to create stockpiles before the law took affect, then to introduce new products that are not affected and to step up marketing efforts overseas for affected products. In addition, demand and prices skyrocketed for the now fixed supply of goods domestically, and then adjusted downward when it became obvious that supplies were still available. None of this applies after the law expires in 2004. If this is all news to you, it's time to question your source of news.

Court challenges are actively underway with regard to the Brady law and the 1991 Gun-Free School Zones act was overturned by the U.S. Supreme Court in April, 1995. **New laws may be passed at any time, and it is your responsibility to be fully up-to-date when handling firearms under all circumstances. The information contained in this book is guaranteed to age.**

Failure to comply with new laws and regulations can have serious consequences to you personally, even if you believe your Constitutional rights have been compromised. In fact, many experts have noted that increasing latitudes are being taken by some governmental authorities with respect to Constitutional guarantees. Legislative and regulatory changes present serious risks to currently law-abiding citizens, since what is legal today may not be tomorrow. The entire body of U.S. law is growing at a significant rate and it represents some potential for threats to freedoms Americans have always enjoyed. It is prudent to take whatever steps you feel are reasonable to minimize any risks.

GUN SAFETY and Concealed-Handgun Training 8

Many fine books and classes exist which teach the current wisdom on gun safety and use. In Texas, some of the best public classes are given by the Texas Parks and Wildlife Dept. and the Texas State Rifle Association, both listed in Appendix C. There are also firearms proficiency and safety trainers spread across the state, including 2,800 hunting instructors for Parks and Wildlife. The list of CHL trainers is available on request from the Dept. of Public Safety.

When studying firearm safety (and every gun owner should), you will likely come across the Ten Commandments of Gun Safety. These well-intentioned lists have serious drawbacks— no two lists are ever the same and there are many more than ten rules to follow for safe gun use. In addition, hunters must learn many rules which don't apply to other shooters. For instance, a hunter should never openly carry game—it makes you an unwitting target of other hunters.

The Commandments of Safety are actually a way of saying, "Here's how people have accidents with guns." Each rule implies a kind of mishap. It's good exercise to look at each rule and read between the lines to find its counterpart—the potential disaster the rule will help you avoid. For example, Rule 1 translates into, "People have accidents with guns which they think are empty." Always keep in mind the prime directive: Take time to be safe instead of forever being sorry.

THE GUN OWNER'S COMMANDMENTS OF SAFETY

1–Treat every gun as if it is loaded until you have personally proven otherwise.

2–Always keep a gun pointed in a safe direction.

3–Don't touch the trigger until you're ready to fire.

4–Be certain of your target and what is beyond it before pulling the trigger.

5–Keep a gun you carry discretely holstered or otherwise concealed unless you're ready to use it.

6–Use but never rely on the safety.

7–Never load a gun until ready to use. Unload a gun immediately after use.

8–Only use ammunition which exactly matches the markings on your gun.

9–Always read and follow manufacturers' instructions carefully.

10–At a shooting range, always keep a gun pointed downrange.

11–Always obey a range officer's commands immediately.

12–Always wear adequate eye and ear protection when shooting.

13–If a gun fails to fire: a) keep it pointed in a safe direction; b) wait thirty seconds in case of a delayed firing; c) unload the gun carefully, avoiding exposure to the breech.

14–Don't climb fences or trees, or jump logs or ditches with a chambered round.

15–Be able to control the direction of the muzzle even if you stumble.

16–Keep the barrel and action clear of obstructions.

17–Avoid carrying ammunition which doesn't match the gun you are carrying.

18–Be aware that customized guns may require ammunition which doesn't match the gun's original markings.

19–Store guns with the action open.

20–Store ammunition and guns separately, and out of reach of children and careless adults.

21–Never pull a gun toward you by the muzzle.

22–Never horseplay with a firearm.

23–Never shoot at a hard flat surface, or at water, to prevent ricochets.

24–Be sure you have an adequate backstop for target shooting.

25–On open terrain with other people present, keep guns pointed upwards, or downwards and away from the people.

26–Never handle a gun you are not familiar with.

27–Learn to operate a gun empty before attempting to load and shoot it.

28–Be cautious transporting a loaded firearm in a vehicle.

29–Never lean a firearm where it may slip and fall.

30–Do not use alcohol or mood-altering drugs when you are handling firearms.

31–When loading or unloading a firearm, always keep the muzzle pointed in a safe direction.

32–Never use a rifle scope instead of a pair of binoculars.

33–Always remember that removing the magazine (sometimes called the clip) from semi-automatic and automatic weapons may still leave a live round, ready to fire, in the chamber.

34–Never rely on one empty cylinder next to the barrel of a revolver as a guarantee of safety, since different revolvers rotate in opposite directions.

35–Never step into a boat holding a loaded firearm.

36–It's difficult to use a gun safely until you become a marksman.

37–It's difficult to handle a gun safely if you need corrective lenses and are not wearing them.

38–Know the effective range and the maximum range of a firearm and the ammunition you are using.

39–Be sure that anyone with access to a firearm kept in a home understands its safe use.

40–Don't fire a large caliber weapon if you cannot control the recoil.

41–Never put your finger in the trigger guard when drawing a gun from a holster.

42–Never put your hand in front of the cylinder of a revolver when firing.

43–Never put your hand in back of the slide of a semi-automatic pistol when firing.

44–Always leave the hammer of a revolver resting over an empty chamber.

45–Never leave ammunition around when cleaning a gun.

46–Clean firearms after they have been used. A dirty gun is not as safe as a clean one.

47–Never fire a blank round directly at a person. Blanks can blind, maim, and at close range, they can kill.

48–Only use modern firearms in good working condition, and ammunition which is fresh.

49–Accidents don't happen, they are caused, and it's up to you and you alone to prevent them in all cases. Every "accident" which ever happened could have been avoided. Where there are firearms there is a need for caution.

50–Always think first and shoot second.

It is the responsibility of every American to prevent firearms from being instruments of tragedy.

TEACH YOUR CHILDREN WELL

School Firearms Safety Program

Texas school districts are authorized and "strongly encouraged," under Education Code §21.118, to provide firearms safety programs for students in grades Kindergarten through 12. The districts must consult with a certified firearms instructor before implementing a program, and the program must meet the standards set by the National Rifle Association Eddie Eagle Children's Gun Safety Course.

Parents may give written notice to deny firearm safety training for their children, and the school district must comply. At no time may a student on school property be allowed to handle a readily dischargeable firearm.

Keeping Children Safe

Choosing to own a firearm—or choosing not to—has serious implications for the safety of your children and family. Your ability to respond in an emergency or not, and a child's dangerous access to a loaded firearm without your approval, should motivate you to take serious precautions for safety where firearms are concerned.

Firearms are dangerous; they're supposed to be dangerous; they wouldn't be very valuable if they weren't dangerous. The same as with power tools, automobiles, medicines, kitchen knives, balconies, swimming pools, electricity and everything else, it is up to responsible adults and their actions to help ensure the safety of those they love and the rest of the community.

In Texas these are not just good ideas, it's the law. A firearm owner has a direct responsibility to control a child's access to a loaded firearm (see Penal Code §46.13). Knowing about child safety and guns is required by DPS as part of the instruction needed to qualify for a CHL.

It is your responsibility to see that your own children, children who might visit you and careless adults are prevented from unauthorized access to any firearms you possess.

A delicate balance exists between keeping a gun immediately ready for response in an emergency, and protecting it from careless adults and children. This is the paradox of home-defense firearms. The more out-of-reach a gun is for safety's sake, the less accessible it is for self-defense (also for safety's sake).

Secured Storage

Leaving a loaded gun out in the open where careless adults or children could get at it is not being responsible and subjects you to criminal charges if an accident occurs.

Putting a loaded gun in a hard-to-find spot may fool some kids (and it's better than doing nothing), but remember how easily you found your folks' stuff when you were a kid.

Putting a gun in a hard-to-get-to spot (like the top of a closet) has advantages over hard-to-find spots when small children (like toddlers) are involved. Remember that kids reach an age where they like to climb. And you really have no idea what goes on when the babysitter is around.

Hinged false picture frames, when done well, provide a readily available firearm that most people will simply never notice. The frame must be in a spot that can't be bumped, and if ever the frame is detected its value is completely and immediately compromised.

Trigger guards warn that a gun is loaded, but they provide a low level of child-proofing since they are typically designed to be removed easily.

Gun locks can be effective in preventing accidents but are completely compromised if a child can get at the key. The location of the key then becomes the paradox factor in keeping the gun at-the-ready yet safe. The closer together you keep the gun and its key the less safety the lock provides.

Gun safes used properly can prevent accidents and provide reasonable access to personal firearms, but it is an expensive option. Many people with gun collections keep their firearms in a floor-standing safe, for theft and fire protection, simultaneously providing a high degree of accident proofing. Single-gun handgun safes are made for floor or wall mounting and use finger touch buttons that can be operated quickly in the dark. This is an excellent option for keeping a gun available yet highly protected from unauthorized use.

A home that doesn't have many visitors and never has kids around has a different challenge than a home with four kids growing up, when it comes to staying safe. Be sure that your home is safe for your kids—safe from those who would do you harm, and safe from the potential for harm your own home holds.

Disabling

Disabling a gun provides a safety margin. The more disabled a gun is the greater the safety, but the more difficult it becomes to bring the gun to bear if it should be needed.

The least disabled condition, and hence the least safe (though better than nothing), is a safety lever engaged on a semi-automatic or an appropriate empty cylinder on a revolver.

An unloaded firearm is disabled in a sense, and incapable of firing, though that reverses completely upon the presence of ammunition. The margin of safety here, for both preventing accidents and providing defense, is as wide as the distance between the gun and its ammunition.

Removing a firing pin or otherwise disassembling a firearm represents a high degree of disabling, essentially lowering chances of accidents to zero, and removing the possibility of putting the weapon to use in an emergency.

Keeping no firearm at home eliminates the ability to respond for safety if necessary, and still leaves a child at risk when visiting friends (especially if the child is not firearms aware).

The bottom line is that there are no perfect solutions, and that life has risks. You trade some for others, and make personal choices that affect everything you do. Be sure you make the hard choices necessary to keep your family safe in your own home.

One Man's Approach

Internationally recognized firearms instructor and author Massad Ayoob believes it's wiser to educate your children than attempting to childproof your gun. For a detailed discussion of his approach to guns and child safety, read his booklet, *Gun-Proof Your Children,* available from Bloomfield Press.

The Eddie Eagle Program

If you look behind all the hot political rhetoric, you'll notice that the main provider of firearms safety training in America is the National Rifle Association, fulfilling a century-old historic tradition that is actually embodied in federal law. Handgun Control, Inc. and the NRA agree that child accidents are tragic and that responsible citizens must take steps to protect youngsters. In response to this well perceived need, the NRA developed its highly acclaimed and widely used Eddie Eagle Safety Program. For teacher lesson plans, class materials, parent kits, video tapes, coloring books, posters and more, contact the NRA, listed in the Appendix.

THE EDDIE EAGLE SAFETY RULES FOR KIDS —
If you find a gun:
STOP! Don't touch. Leave the area. Tell an adult.

HOW WELL DO YOU KNOW YOUR GUN?

Safe and effective use of firearms demands that you understand your weapon thoroughly. This knowledge is best gained through a combination of reading, classes and practice with a qualified instructor. The simple test below will help tell you if you are properly trained in the use of firearms. If you're not sure what all the terms mean, can you be absolutely sure that you're qualified to handle firearms safely?

- ☐ Action
- ☐ Ammunition
- ☐ Automatic
- ☐ Ballistics
- ☐ Barrel
- ☐ Black powder
- ☐ Bolt
- ☐ Bore
- ☐ Break action
- ☐ Breech
- ☐ Buckshot
- ☐ Bullet
- ☐ Butt
- ☐ Caliber
- ☐ Cartridge
- ☐ Case
- ☐ Casing
- ☐ Centerfire
- ☐ Chamber
- ☐ Checkering
- ☐ Choke
- ☐ Clip
- ☐ Cock
- ☐ Comb
- ☐ Cylinder
- ☐ Discharge
- ☐ Dominant eye
- ☐ Effective range
- ☐ Firearm
- ☐ Firing Pin
- ☐ Firing Line

- ☐ Forearm
- ☐ Fouling
- ☐ Frame
- ☐ Gauge
- ☐ Grip
- ☐ Grip panels
- ☐ Grooves
- ☐ Gunpowder
- ☐ Half cock
- ☐ Hammer
- ☐ Handgun
- ☐ Hangfire
- ☐ Hunter orange
- ☐ Ignition
- ☐ Kneeling
- ☐ Lands
- ☐ Lever action
- ☐ Magazine
- ☐ Mainspring
- ☐ Maximum range
- ☐ Misfire
- ☐ Muzzle
- ☐ Muzzleloader
- ☐ Pattern
- ☐ Pistol
- ☐ Powder
- ☐ Primer
- ☐ Projectile
- ☐ Prone
- ☐ Pump action
- ☐ Pyrodex

- ☐ Receiver
- ☐ Repeater
- ☐ Revolver rifle
- ☐ Rifling
- ☐ Rimfire
- ☐ Safety
- ☐ Sear
- ☐ Semi-automatic
- ☐ Shell
- ☐ Shooting positions
- ☐ Shot
- ☐ Shotgun
- ☐ Sights
- ☐ Sighting-in
- ☐ Sitting
- ☐ Smokeless powder
- ☐ Smoothbore
- ☐ Standing
- ☐ Stock
- ☐ Trigger
- ☐ Trigger guard
- ☐ Unplugged shotgun

CONCEALED-HANDGUN TRAINING

Texas requires its Concealed-Handgun-License (CHL) holders to study legal issues related to firearms, use of deadly force and more (see Chapter 2 for details), and to pass written and handgun proficiency tests in order to qualify for the license. The law requires the course to be 10 to 15 hours in length.

The written test is based on a set of questions created by DPS and provided to instructors. Individual tests are made up of questions drawn from the master set.

Handgun proficiency standards are developed by DPS and appear in Chapter 2 and on the inside back cover. The details may change—so send us a self-addressed stamped envelope and we'll return a free update when one is available.

The subjects you must study in the CHL course are based on the statutory requirements and regulations issued by DPS. Here are some sample test questions that CHL applicants—and all responsible gun owners—probably should know:

Areas of Study

1–Where are firearms prohibited in Texas?
   (At least 10 places, study chapter 2)

2–What are the penalties for improper display of a handgun?
   (It depends on the charges that are filed, study chapter 5)

3–What risks exist in drawing a firearm in public?
   (Could be used to justify a self-defense claim by another party, accidental discharge, discharge in prohibited area, more, study chapter 5)

4–When does state law justify the use of deadly force?
   (The circumstances are described, study chapter 5)

5–What factors mitigate the strict legal definitions for justifiable use of deadly force?
   (This is a complex issue frequently subject to debate and interpretation, fact-intensive and specific to the

circumstances, study chapters 5, 8, and other books, such as In The Gravest Extreme, *by Massad Ayoob)*

6–What responsibility does a shooter have for shots fired that miss the intended target?
(Severe liabilities and penalties can result from the effect of stray bullets, study chapters 4 and 5)

7–Can you bring a firearm into a bar?
(Usually prohibited, but certain exceptions apply, study chapter 2)

8–What types of weapons are illegal?
(For federal- and state-law restrictions, study chapter 3)

9–Who can legally bear arms in Texas?
(Age, background, mental condition and more are taken into account, study chapter 1)

10–Under what circumstances can minors bear arms?
(Study chapters 1 and 6)

11–How can firearms be carried throughout the state?
(Different rules apply depending on what you're doing, for minors and for a person with a concealed handgun license, study chapters 1, 2 and 5)

12–What are the requirements for getting a carry license?
(Personal background, training, testing and a fee are involved, study chapters 2 and 8)

13–What do you have to do to ship firearms or carry them with you on a train, plane, or as you travel by car?
(Federal regulations control transit, study chapter 1)

14–Under what circumstances can you practice target shooting outdoors?
(Official shooting ranges are OK, regulations apply to most other land, study chapter 4)

15–How much judgment is involved in deciding whether you can use deadly force in a situation?
(No easy answers to this, read everything you can find on the subject, study chapters 5 and 8, and recognize that in using deadly force you accept very definite and substantial legal risks that cannot be fully assessed before the fact.)

16–What are the main rules of firearm safety?
(We've come up with 50, more exist, study chapter 8.)

17–What types of weapons are suitable for self-defense, and what are the best choices for you?
(A very important topic not covered in this book. You should discuss this at length with your instructor and other professionals.)

18–How do the various types of firearms operate?
(This topic should be covered by your instructor.)

19–What are the options for carrying a concealed handgun?
(This topic should be covered by your instructor.)

20–Have any new laws passed that you should know about?
(This requires ongoing information and vigilance. Send Bloomfield Press a self-addressed stamped envelope for an update when one becomes available.)

21–Are you mentally prepared to use deadly force?
(Mental conditioning for the use of deadly force is a critical component in preparing for armed defense if it should ever be needed, and one that is not easily addressed. Until a moment arrives you may never truly know the answer to this question.)

As you can see, the responsibilities of gun ownership are substantial and numerous. Make the smart choice and obtain professional training, read extensively, practice regularly, keep up on the important issues, and refresh your training periodically.

Practice Test Questions

Approved CHL-training programs use test questions that are developed and approved by the Dept. of Public Safety.

The questions presented here are designed for study—to challenge your understanding, provoke thought and encourage discussion. Some of these have obvious yes-no or true-false (T or F) answers, while others require a deeper understanding of the issues and must be answered with "maybe" or "it depends." *Some questions defy clear answers.* If you have trouble with any of these, ask your firearms safety instructor (not the publisher!) for assistance.

1–Is it legal to point an empty gun at a person?

2–Is it legal to point an empty gun at anything?

3–Is it legal to put a gun in your pocket?

4–Is home defense with a machine gun legal?

5–Never tell family members that you keep a loaded gun in the house. T or F?

6–Always tell family members that you keep a loaded gun in the house. T or F?

7–Texas requires you to lock your guns in a safe. T or F?

8–Texas requires you to put a trigger lock on your guns. T or F?

9–Does the law say you may kill if your life is in danger?

10–Does the law say you may kill if your friend is in danger?

11–If a peace officer is in danger may you shoot to kill?

12–You may conceal weapons in Texas without a license. T or F?

13–Carrying weapons openly in Texas, unlicensed, is OK. T or F?

14–A CHL prohibits concealing a bayonet. T or F?

15–A CHL prohibits bringing a gun onto a plane. T or F?

16–A CHL prohibits concealing explosives. T or F?

17–It's always illegal to bring a gun into a bar. T or F?

18–A bar owner may carry a handgun in the bar. T or F?

19–A bar owner may allow the employees to be armed. T or F?

20–A bar owner may allow patrons to be armed. T or F?

21–Drawing a gun to settle a severe argument is legal. T or F?

22–Drawing a gun wrongly may lead to criminal charges. T or F?

23–Drawing a gun wrongly is allowed if you don't shoot. T or F?

24–If someone else draws a gun, you may too. T or F?

25–If your life is immediately at risk you may draw a gun. T or F?

26–May you draw a gun to stop a serious crime in progress?

27–May you draw a gun to stop a kidnapping?

28–May you draw a gun to stop a robbery?

29–May you draw a gun to stop an armed robbery?

30–May you draw a gun to stop a sexual assault?

31–May you draw a gun to stop child molestation?

32–May you draw a gun to stop a serious traffic violation?

33–May you draw a gun to stop criminal trespass?

34–May you draw a gun to stop an arsonist?

35–May you draw a gun to stop vandals?

36–May you draw a gun to stop shoplifting?

37–May you draw a gun to stop an escape from the custody of law enforcement?

38–May you shoot in items 24 through 37 above?

39–Do you want to ever have to shoot someone?

40–All states treat self-defense shooting the same way. T or F?

41–Federal law guarantees your rights no matter what. T or F?

42–Shooting criminals is legal if they are "in the act." T or F?

43–You should declare you have a CHL to the police. True of false?

44–Never mention your CCW license unless asked. T or F?

45–It's OK to let a concealed handgun show occasionally. T or F?

46–If you shoot a criminal you don't have to report it. T or F?

47–You should report any shooting incident to authorities. T or F?

48–If you shoot a criminal leave the body where it falls. T or F?

49–If you shoot a criminal outside your home drag him inside. T or F?

50–You're normally aware of everything around you. T or F?

51–When danger lurks, your awareness always goes up. T or F?

52–Even if you're cautious, danger can surprise you. T or F?

53–When you're surprised you're not always predictable. T or F?

54–Acting under stress can lead to surprising responses. T or F?

55–Name the four modes of mental awareness.

56–Describe the four modes of mental awareness.

57–The only official way to shoot is the Weaver stance. T or F?

58–You must grip a firearm with both hands to be legal. T or F?

59–Any shooting position you like is legal for self-defense. T or F?

60–If you pass your CHL exam, you're perfectly qualified. T or F?

61–A CHL increases your personal safety. T or F?

62–A CHL increases your ability to respond. T or F?

63–A CHL will allow you to take back the streets. T or F?

64–With a CHL you may go wherever you want. T or F?

65–If a man charges you with a knife may you shoot him?

66–If a man charges you with a bat may you shoot him?

67–If a woman charges you with a bat may you shoot her?

68–If a man hits your spouse with a bat may you shoot him?

69–If a man threatens you with a bat may you shoot him?

70–If a man enrages you for no reason may you shoot him?

71–If a man won't let you get gasoline may you change his mind by drawing a gun?

72–If someone starts shooting someone else, may you shoot the first person to stop the attack?

73–Methods for controlling a violent confrontation are something that cannot be learned. T or F?

74–Will you need a gun more after you have a CHL than you did before you had a permit?

75–Have you ever witnessed a serious crime that would justify drawing a gun, such as a kidnapping, sexual assault, armed robbery or murder?

76–How much more likely are you to witness a serious crime once you have a CHL?

77–Is it a good idea to qualify in your CHL proficiency test with the same gun you plan on carrying regularly?

78–Unless you need to use it in an emergency, you should never let a concealed handgun show. T or F?

79–If you sell a gun to a person who uses it to commit a crime can you be charged with a crime?

80–What happens if you are found in Texas with an unregistered handgun in your possession?

81–What is the legal maximum distance for a self-defense shooting in Texas?

82–Texas has preemption, which means that cities and counties may pass their own gun laws. T or F?

83–Many cities in Texas have different gun laws that you must know and follow. T or F?

84–Many locations in Texas interpret the laws differently and are allowed to do so by their courts. T or F?

85–What is a "citizens arrest," how do you make one, and is it a good idea to make one if you witness a crime?

86–If you see a drug deal going down, may you draw your gun and use deadly force to stop it?

87–If you see a prostitute working in your neighborhood, may you threaten deadly force, without using it, to make the person leave?

88–If you use a gun legitimately to defend yourself there is a possibility you will be charged with a serious offense. T or F?

89–Many people who are charged with murder claim self-defense or accidental discharge. T or F?

90–Many people who use deadly force in self-defense are charged with murder. T or F?

91–The person who survives a lethal confrontation is often referred to as the defendant by the authorities. T or F?

92–If someone starts hitting you is that justification for threatening to use deadly force?

93–If someone starts hitting you is that considered justification for using deadly force?

94–If someone says they're going to start hitting you is that justification for threatening to use deadly force?

95–If someone hits you repeatedly in the face until you're bleeding and then stops, you may draw your gun and shoot the attacker. T or F?

96–If someone comes into your place of business and commits a robbery, may you respond with deadly force?

97–A man says he's going to shoot you and sticks his hand in his pocket. May you shoot him first?

98–A woman says she's going to shoot you and sticks her hand in her pocketbook. May you shoot her first?

99–If you are armed may you operate as a free-lance police officer?

100–The police may use or threaten deadly force in certain situations that you may not. T or F?

101–Tactics refers to the steps you take in an emergency. T or F?

102–Strategy refers to the plans you make in the event you are ever in an emergency. T or F?

103–A crime avoidance plan includes tactics and strategy. T or F?

104–"Shoot first and ask questions later," is bad advice for personal self-defense. T or F?

105–It's always better not to shoot at someone if you can safely avoid it. T or F?

106–If you get a CHL, does that change anything with respect to the number and seriousness of the threats you normally face in your daily routine?

107–Why does it make sense for you personally to get a concealed-handgun license?

108–If you own a gun, spending regular practice time on a shooting range is a good idea.

In addition to questions such as the ones presented here, you should study material and be able to answer questions on topics not covered in *The Texas Gun Owner's Guide*, such as:

What are the various types of firearms, what are their component parts, and how do they operate; what are the various types of ammunition; what are the criteria for selecting a self-defense weapon and ammunition; what are the options for holsters and carrying weapons; how can you reduce the chances of unintentional firing and what are the primary firearm safety rules; what affects aiming and firing accurately; how should guns and ammunition be stored; how are guns cleaned, lubricated and checked, what are the tactics and strategies for personal self-defense and having weapons accessible; what alternatives are there to confrontation; how can threatening situations be managed; how can confrontations be avoided.

JUDGMENTAL SHOOTING

All gun owners, and CHL holders in particular, should study issues related to judgmental shooting. Anyone considering armed response needs an understanding of the issues involved.

The decision to use deadly force is rarely a clear-cut choice. Regardless of your familiarity with the laws, your degree of training, the quality of your judgmental skills and your physical location and condition at the time of a deadly threat, the demands placed on you at the critical moment are as intense as anything you will normally experience in your life, and your actual performance is an unknown.

Every situation is different. The answers to many questions relating to deadly force are subject to debate. To be prepared for armed response you must recognize that such situations are not black or white, and that your actions, no matter how well intentioned, will be evaluated by others, probably long after you act.

The chances that you will come away from a lethal encounter without any scars—legal, physical or psychological—are small, and the legal risks are substantial. That's why it's usually best to practice prevention and avoidance rather than confrontation, whenever possible.

Most people can think about it this way: You've gotten along this far in life without ever having pulled a weapon on someone, much less having fired it. The odds of that changing once you have a CHL are about the same, practically zero. A concealed handgun may make you feel more secure, but it doesn't change how safe your surroundings actually are, in the places you normally travel, one bit. And it certainly isn't safe to think of a firearm as a license (or a talisman) for walking through potentially dangerous areas you would otherwise avoid like the plague.

Remember that the person holding a gun after a shooting is frequently thought of as the bad guy—the perpetrator—even if it's you and you acted in self-defense. The person who is

shot has a different, more sympathetic name—the victim—
and gets the benefit of a prosecutor even if, perhaps, you
learn later it's a hardened criminal with a long record. Maybe
your defense will improve if it is indeed a serious repeat
offender, but you won't know that until after the fact, and
don't count on it. If you ever have to raise a gun to a
criminal, you'll find out quickly how good they can be at
portraying you as the bad guy and themselves as the
helpless innocents, at the mercy of a crazed wacko—you.

Situational Analysis

Think about the deadly force encounters described below,
and consider discussing them with your firearms-safety
trainer:

1–If you are being seriously attacked by a man with a club, is
it legal for you to aim for his leg so you can stop the attack
without killing him?

2–If you enter your home and find a person looting your
possessions are you justified in shooting to kill?

3–If you enter your home and find a person looting your
possessions, who runs out the back door as he hears you
arrive, can you shoot him to stop him from escaping?

4–If you enter your home and find a person looting your
possessions, who turns and whirls toward you when you
enter, literally scaring you to death, may you shoot to kill
and expect to be justified?

5–If you enter your home and find a stranger in it who
charges you with a knife, may you shoot to kill?

6–A stranger in your home has just stabbed your spouse
and is about to stab your spouse again. May you shoot
the stranger from behind to stop the attack?

7–As you walk past a park at night, you notice a woman tied
to a tree and a man tearing off her clothing. May you use
deadly force to stop his actions?

8–A police officer is bleeding badly and chasing a man in
prison coveralls who runs right past you. May you shoot
the fleeing suspect while he is in close range to you?

9–You're in your home at night when a man with a ski mask on comes through an open window in the hallway. May you shoot to kill?

10–You're in your home at night, sleeping, when a noise at the other end of the house awakens you. Taking your revolver you quietly walk over to investigate and notice a short person going through your silverware drawer, 45 feet from where you're standing. The person doesn't notice you. May you shoot to kill?

11–As you approach your parked car in a dark and remote section of a parking lot, three youthful toughs approach you from three separate directions. You probably can't unlock your vehicle and get in before they reach you and you're carrying a gun. What should you do?

12–From outside a convenience store you observe what clearly appears to be an armed robbery—four people are being held at gunpoint while the store clerk is putting money into a paper bag. You're armed. What should you do?

13–You're waiting to cross the street in downtown and a beggar asks you for money. He's insistent and begins to insult you when you refuse to ante up. Finally, he gets loud and belligerent and says he'll kill you if you don't give him ten dollars. May you shoot him?

14–You get in your car, roll down the windows, and before you can drive off a man sticks a knife in the window and orders you to get out. Can you shoot him?

15-You get in your car and before you start it a man points a gun at you and tells you to get out. You have a gun in the pocket on the door, another under the seat, and a gun in a holster in your pants. What should you do?

16–Before you get in your car, a man with a gun comes up from behind, demands your car keys, takes them, and while holding you at gun point, starts your car and drives away. Can you shoot at him while he's escaping?

17–You're walking to your car in the mall parking lot after a movie when two armed hoods jump out of a shadow and demand your money. You've got a gun in your back pocket. What should you do?

18–A masked person with a gun stops you on the street, demands and takes your valuables, then flees down the street on foot. You're carrying a concealed handgun. What should you do?

19–A youngster runs right by you down the street and an old lady shouts, "Stop him, he killed my husband!" May you shoot to stop his getaway?

20–You're at work when two ornery-looking dudes amble in. You can smell trouble, so you walk to a good vantage point behind a showcase. Sure enough, they pull guns and announce a stick-up. You and your four employees are armed and there are several customers in the store. What's your move?

21–Your friend and you have been drinking, and now you're arguing over a football bet. You say the spread was six points, he says four. There's $500 hanging in the balance of a five-point game, and it represents your mortgage payment. He pulls a knife and says, "Pay me or I'll slice you up." You've got a gun in your pocket. What should you do?

22–At a gas station, the lines are long, it's hot, and the guy next in line starts getting surly. You're not done pumping and he hits you in the face and tells you to finish up. He shuts off your pump and says he'll kick your butt if you don't move on. Should you pull your gun to put him in his place?

Observations about the situations presented:

1–It's an unlikely case where the justification to use deadly force would be justification to intentionally wound. Firing and missing is a different story, but it could be argued that if the threat wasn't sufficient to shoot to kill then there was no justification to shoot at all.

2–Not enough information is provided to make an informed choice.

3–Although Texas statutes do justify the use of deadly force in certain property crimes and to prevent escape under certain conditions, acting in such a situation, according to many experts, presents an unacceptable legal risk to the shooter. Once the danger to you is over— and it generally is once the criminal is fleeing—it is probably best to hold your fire.

4–Probably. But do you always enter your home prepared for mortal combat? Does your story have other holes a prosecutor will notice?

5–It's hard to imagine not being justified in this situation, but stranger things have happened.

6–It's hard to imagine not being justified in this situation, but stranger things have happened. Will the bullet exit the attacker and wound your spouse?

7–Not necessarily, since you don't know if the people are consenting adults who like this sort of thing. A seasoned police officer might cautiously approach the couple, weapon drawn, and with words instead of force determine what's happening, and then make further choices depending on the outcome.

8–Not enough information is provided to make an informed choice.

9–Probably, though a well-trained expert might instead confront the intruder from a secure position and succeed in holding the person for arrest, which is no easy task. The longer you must hold the suspect the greater the risk to you. Armed and from good cover, you might just convince the intruder to leave the way he came.

10–Perhaps, but the distance and lack of immediate threat will make for a difficult explanation when the police arrive, and if the perpetrator has an accomplice that you didn't notice, the danger to you is severe. If the perpetrator turns out to be a thief with a long rap sheet, you might not even be charged. If it turns out that the intruder is 11 years old your court defense will be extremely difficult. Remember, you're obligated to not shoot if you don't absolutely have to. A shot would be in conflict with a prime safety rule—clearly identify your target before firing. Has your training prepared you for this?

11–That's a good question, and you should never have parked there in the first place.

12–Call for assistance, go to a defensible position, continue to observe, and recognize that charging into such a volatile situation is incredibly risky for all parties.

13–You are never justified in using deadly force in response to verbal provocation alone, no matter how severe.

14–The prosecutor will make it clear that if you could have stepped on the gas and escaped, the threat to you would have ended, and the need to shoot did not exist. If you were boxed into a parking space, the need to defend yourself would be hard for a prosecutor to refute. These things often come down to the exact circumstances and the quality of the attorneys.

15–Get out quietly and don't provoke someone who has the drop on you. All your guns are no match for a drawn weapon. This is where a real understanding of tactics comes into play.

16–The statutes suggest that you may fire in this case, but the legal risk to you is so severe (as described in #3 above) that it's probably best to hold your fire. Once the threat to you is over, the justification for using lethal force is less reliable.

17–Not enough information is provided to make an informed choice.

18–Anyone crazy enough to rob you at gunpoint must be considered capable of doing anything, and the smart move is to avoid further confrontation and stay alive. You could draw and fire, but the justification for using deadly force on the street is not as reliable if your life is not in immediate danger (even though Texas statutes say it is permissible). If you miss in the adrenaline-filled rush of the moment your shot could pose a threat to a bystander, and it could encourage return fire from the fleeing criminal. You could chase after him, but it's extremely unwise and risky to you. Many experts advise that once the danger to you is over don't escalate the situation by firing.

19–You don't have enough information. When in doubt, don't shoot.

20–This is where strategy and tactics are critical. If you allow your employees to carry and are prepared for armed defense of your premises you better get plenty of advanced training in gunfighting and self-defense. You'll need it to survive, and you'll need it to meet the legal challenges later. If a customer gets shot by one of your own, even if you get the villains, you're in for big time trouble and grief. If no one gets hurt but the criminals, you'll be a hero. Either outcome remains burned in memory. Tough choice.

21–Too many killings occur between people who know each other. Your chance of a successful legal defense in a case like this are remote. Would he really have killed you? Probably not. Did you have any other options besides killing him? Probably so. Have you fought like this before? Maybe. What would the witnesses say? Nothing you could count on, and probably all the wrong things. The fact that you have a firearm and can use it doesn't mean you should, the likelihood of absolutely having to use it is small, and using it to settle a bet with a friend over a point spread may not be the worst thing you can do, but it's close.

22–Cap your tank and move on, you don't need the grief. Or go into the station and tell them what's happened, preparing yourself mentally for further hostilities. Go to a defensible position and call the police. Avoid a confrontation at all costs. See what the other guy does before you do anything. Decide to take another course in how to handle volatile situations and difficult people. And realize that the fact that you have a CHL and some training doesn't solve any problems or reduce your risks in life.

THE NOBLE USES OF FIREARMS

In the great din of the national firearms debate it's easy to lose sight of the noble and respectable place firearms hold and have always held in American life. While some gun use in America is criminal and despicable, other applications appeal to the highest ideals our society cherishes, and are enshrined in and ensured by the statutes on the books:

- Protecting your family in emergencies
- Personal self-defense
- Preventing and deterring crimes
- Detaining criminals for arrest
- Guarding our national borders
- Preserving our interests abroad
- Helping defend our allies
- Overcoming tyranny
- Emergency preparedness
- Obtaining food by hunting
- Historical preservation and study
- Olympic competition
- Sporting pursuits
- Target practice
- Recreational shooting

RECOMMENDED READING

Knowledge is power, and the more you have the better off you are likely to be. Some CHL trainers will require that you read important books on personal safety, crime avoidance, self-defense and the use of deadly force. **Whether your instructor requires it or not, decide to read about this critical subject.** A selection of some of the most highly regarded books on these topics appears at the back of *The Texas Gun Owner's Guide* and are easily available directly from the publisher. If your instructor doesn't include these in your course, get them yourself. The single best book on the subject is probably *In The Gravest Extreme*, by Massad Ayoob.

You may also choose to obtain a complete copy of the Texas criminal code, since the laws reproduced in *The Texas Gun Owner's Guide* are a selected excerpt of gun laws only. Remember that no published edition of the law is complete without the legislation passed during the most recent session of the state congress, and that new federal laws may be passed at any time. An annotated edition of the law, available in major libraries, provides critical information in the form of court cases which clarify and expand on the meaning of the actual statutes.

APPENDIX A
GLOSSARY OF TERMS

Words, when used in the law, often have special meanings you wouldn't expect from simply knowing the English language. For the complete legal description of these and other important terms, see each chapter of the criminal code and other legal texts dealing with language. The following plain English descriptions are provided for your convenience only.

ACT = A bodily movement, including speech.

ACTION = Single action, revolver, or semi-automatic action.

ACTOR = A person who may be criminally responsible in a criminal action, sometimes referred to as the "suspect."

AMUSEMENT PARK = A permanent indoor or outdoor facility with rides, in a county with a population of more than one million, on at least 75 acres, open to the public at least 120 days annually, with full time security guards and controlled access.

ARMOR-PIERCING AMMUNITION = Handgun ammunition designed primarily for penetrating metal or body armor.

BENEFIT = Anything of economic value to a person or someone associated with that person.

BODILY INJURY = Physical pain, illness or impairment.

CHEMICAL DISPENSING DEVICE = A device that can cause an adverse psychological or physiological effect on a person. Small chemical dispensers sold commercially for personal protection are not included.

CHEMICALLY DEPENDENT PERSON = Someone who frequently or repeatedly drinks to excess or is a habitual drug user. SB60 §1-2 A person who has been convicted two times in the 10 years prior to application for a CHL license for a class B misdemeanor or greater involving the use of alcohol or a controlled substance is considered chemically dependent and automatically disqualifies the applicant.

CLUB = An instrument that can inflict serious bodily injury or death by striking a person. This includes, but isn't limited to, a blackjack, nightstick, tomahawk and mace.

CONDUCT = The actions you take or refrain from, and your thoughts about them.

CONCEALED HANDGUN = A handgun that can't be seen through ordinary observation.

CONVICTED = Found guilty of an offense by a court, even if the sentence is probation, the offender is discharged from community supervision, or the offender is pardoned, unless the pardon is granted for proof of innocence.

CRIMINAL INSTRUMENT = Anything which is normally legal but which is put to illegal use.

CRIMINAL NEGLIGENCE = A complex legal concept related to personal responsibility, determined in a court of law, covered in §6.01 through §6.04, and §8.07.

CULPABLE MENTAL STATE = An accountable state of mind. Specifically and in decreasing order of seriousness: intentionally, knowingly, recklessly or with criminal negligence, in the sense described by law.

DEADLY FORCE = Force which you know can cause death or serious physical injury.

DEADLY WEAPON = Anything made or adapted for lethal use or for inflicting serious bodily injury, including a firearm.

EXPLOSIVE WEAPON = An explosive or incendiary bomb, grenade, rocket or mine that can inflict serious bodily injury, death, substantial property damage, or a noise loud enough to cause public alarm or terror. Also included is any device for delivering or shooting an explosive weapon.

FELONY = A serious crime. An offense that carries a prison term of from six months to life. A Capital Felony (capital murder) is the most serious, and has a possible sentence of death. Texas uses lethal injection to inflict the penalty of death. A State Jail Felony is the least serious, and carries a possible sentence of six months. Felony fines may be up to $10,000 for an individual, and up to $20,000 for an enterprise.

FIREARM = A device that can (or can be readily converted to) expel a projectile through a barrel by using the energy of an explosion or burning substance. Antique or curio firearms made before 1899 and that may have an integral folding knife, are not firearms.

FIREARM SILENCER = Any device that can muffle the sound of a firearm.

GOVERNMENT = The recognized political structure within the state.

HANDGUN = A firearm designed, made or adapted for firing with one hand.

HARM = Loss, disadvantage or injury to a person or someone that person is responsible for.

HOAX BOMB = A device that reasonably appears to be an explosive or incendiary device. A device that, by its design, causes alarm or reaction of any type by a public safety agency official or emergency volunteer agency is a hoax bomb.

ILLEGAL KNIFE = A knife with a blade over five and a half inches, a hand instrument designed to cut or stab by being thrown, a dagger (which includes but isn't limited to a dirk, stiletto and poniard), a bowie knife, a sword or a spear.

INDIVIDUAL = A living human being.

INTOXICATED = Having an alcohol concentration of 0.10 or more, or being unable to function normally physically or mentally due to the use of alcohol or a controlled substance or drug or a combination of these.

KNIFE = Any bladed hand instrument that can inflict serious bodily injury or death by cutting or stabbing.

KNUCKLES = A hard substance that can be worn on a fist and can inflict serious bodily injury or death by striking.

LAW = Formal rules by which society controls itself. In Texas, the law means the Texas State Statutes, the state Constitution, the U.S. Constitution and statutes, city ordinances, county commissioners court orders, official court decisions, and rules adopted by law.

MACHINE GUN = A firearm capable of shooting more than two shots, without manually reloading, by a single pull of the trigger.

MISDEMEANOR = A crime less serious than a felony. An offense against the law that carries a sentence of imprisonment of up to 1 year. Misdemeanor fines can run up to $4,000 for an individual, and up to $10,000 for an enterprise.

PEACE OFFICER = Anyone duly appointed with legal authority to maintain public order and make arrests. Includes more than 26 categories (listed in Article 2.12 of the Code of Criminal Procedure, included in Appendix D), such as sheriffs, their deputies, an officer employed by the Texas Dept. of Health, and more.

PERSON = An individual, corporation, or association.

POSSESSION = Care, custody, control, or management.

PUBLIC PLACE = Anywhere the public can go.

PUBLIC SERVANT = Any officer or employee of any branch of government, either elected, appointed, or hired. Jurors, grand jurors, arbitrators, referees, attorneys or notary publics working for the government, candidates for public office, and a person performing government work under a claim of right even if not qualified.

QUALIFIED HANDGUN INSTRUCTOR = Someone certified by the Dept. of Public Safety to teach a concealed handgun course for a concealed-handgun license, and who may issue a Handgun Proficiency Certificate.

REASONABLE BELIEF = A belief that an ordinary and prudent person would have in the same circumstances.

RECKLESS = Acting with an awareness of and conscious disregard for a risk so dangerous that it is a gross deviation from the standard of care that a reasonable person would follow.

SERIOUS BODILY INJURY = Injury that creates a reasonable risk of death or death itself. Also, injury that causes serious and permanent disfigurement, or loss or impairment of any bodily member or organ.

SHORT-BARREL FIREARM = A rifle with a barrel less than 16 inches, a shotgun with a barrel less than 18 inches, or any weapon made from a rifle or shotgun and less than 26 inches overall.

SWITCHBLADE KNIFE = A knife with a blade that comes out of its handle automatically by centrifugal force, by gravity, or by pressing a button or other device on the handle.

UNLAWFUL = Anything that's criminal or a tort.

UNSOUND MIND = The mental condition of someone who has been judged mentally incompetent or mentally ill, who has been found not guilty of a crime by reason of insanity, or who has been diagnosed by a licensed physician as being unable to manage themselves or their personal affairs, or as suffering from depression, manic depression, or post-traumatic stress syndrome.

ZIP GUN = A device not originally a firearm, which has been adapted to function like one.

APPENDIX B
Crime and Punishment Chart

EXPLANATIONS

Type of Crime: Illegal activities are divided into these eight categories, to match the punishment to the crime. The category may be affected by how the crime is committed.

Jail Term: These are the ranges for a first offense involving a gun; many crimes have special sentences. A capital felony, in addition to life imprisonment, carries a possible death penalty for first degree murder, which is administered by lethal injection (CCP Art. 43.14).

Fines: These are maximums, which may be lowered at court discretion. Fines can be payable immediately or a court may grant permission to pay by a certain date or in installments.

Statute of Limitations: The period of time, from the discovery of an offense (or from the time when an offense should have been discovered with the exercise of reasonable diligence), within which a prosecution may begin (CCP Art. 12.01). There is no limitation on murder or manslaughter; 10 years for some kinds of theft, forgery, indecency with a child, and most forms of sexual assault; 7 years for misapplication of funds; 5 years for some kinds of theft, burglary, robbery, arson and some forms of sexual assault

Offenses: The chart provides a partial list of offenses in each category, and exceptions often apply.

CRIME AND PUNISHMENT

Type of Crime	Max. Sent. 1st Offense	Max. Fine for Person	Max. Fine for Business	Statute of Limitation
Capital Felony	Death or Life in Jail	None	$20,000	None

Capital murder, which includes murder of a peace officer or firefighter while on duty.

1st Degree Felony	5 Yrs.–Life	$10,000	$20,000	—

Murder, aggravated sexual assault, armed robbery, felony burglary of a habitation, shooting at a train and causing damage of $200,000 or more,

2nd Degree Felony	2-20 Yrs.	$10,000	$20,000	—

Murder triggered by passion, manslaughter, aggravated assault, armed kidnapping, shooting at a train and causing damage of $100,000-$200,000.

3rd Degree Felony	2-10 Yrs.	$10,000	$20,000	—

Deadly conduct with a firearm, unlawful possession of a firearm by a felon, carrying in a prohibited place, carrying a gun in a penal institution, most prohibited weapons offenses, shooting at a train causing damage $20,000-$100,000.

State Jail Felony	6 Mos.	$10,000	$20,000	—

Criminally negligent homicide, reckless injury to a child or an elderly or disabled person, aiding suicide where injury occurs, taking or trying to take a gun from a peace officer, shooting at a train causing damage $1,500-$20,000.

Class A Misdemeanor	1 Year	$4,000	$10,000	—

Unlawful carrying of a handgun, possessing, making, transporting or selling a prohibited weapon or hoax bomb, allowing child access to a loaded firearm who causes injury or death, possession of knuckles, deliberately letting a concealed handgun show, intoxicated CHL holder while armed, causing bodily injury, unlawful discharge in a city of 100,000 population, shooting at a train causing damage $500-$1500.

Class B Misdemeanor	6 Mos.	$2,000	$10,000	—

Disorderly conduct with a firearm, failing to carry CHL while armed, refusing to show CHL and ID to officer when asked, shooting at a train causing damage $20-$500.

Class C Misdemeanor	None	$500	$2,000	—

Disorderly conduct, assisting a suicide if no injury occurs, reckless damage or destruction, allowing a child access to a loaded firearm, threatening bodily injury.

THE PROPER AUTHORITIES C

Regulations on guns and their use come from a lot of places. Listed with each authority are the addresses and phones of the nearest offices. All cities are in Texas (TX) unless indicated.

Attorney General (800) 252-8011, (512) 463-2080 P.O. Box 12548, Austin 78711

Bureau of Alcohol, Tobacco and Firearms (202) 566-7591 Dept. of the Treasury; Washington, DC 20226

Bureau of Indian Affairs (202) 343-5116, 7163 U.S. Dept. of Interior; Washington, DC 20240

Coastal Water Authority (713) 658-9020 1200 Smith Street, Two Allen Center, Suite 2260, Houston 77002

National Forests

    Angeline National Forest , Angelina Ranger District (409) 639-8620 1907 Atkinson Drive, Lufkin 75901

    Davy Crockett National Forest, Neches Ranger District (409) 544-2046 or -2047, 1240 East Loop 304, Crockett 75835; Trinity Ranger District, (409) 831-2246 or -2247, Hwy. #94, Apple Springs 75926

    Sabine National Forest, Tenaha District (409) 275-2632 or 275-2635, 101 S. Blivar, San Augustine 75972; Yellowpine District (409) 787-3870 and 787-2791, 201 South Palm Street, Hemphill 75948

    Sam Houston National Forest, San Jacinto Ranger District (713) 592-6461, 308 N. Belcher St., Cleveland 77327; Raven Ranger District (409) 344-6205, FM #1275, New Waverly 77358

    Caddo & Lyndon B. Johnson National Grasslands (817) 627-5475, FM Road 730 South, Decatur 76234

    Rita Blanca National Grassland (806) 362-4254, P.O. Box 38, Texline 79087

National Park Service Recreation Areas Regional Office (505) 988-6100 National Park Service, P.O. Box 728, Santa Fe, NM 87504-0728

    Amistad Recreation Area, (512) 775-7491 Superintendent, National Park Service, P.O. Box 420367, Del Rio 78842-0367

    Lake Meredith Recreation Area (806) 857-3151 Superintendent, National Park Service, Box 1460, Fritch 79036

National Parks, Seashore and Preserve Regional Office (505) 988-6011
   National Parks Service, P.O. Box 728 Sante Fe, NM 87504-0728
   Big Bend National Park (915) 477-2251 TX 79834
   Big Thicket National Preserve (409) 839-2691, 3785 Milam,
      Beaumont 77701
   Guiadalupe Mountains National Park (915) 828-3251, HC 60, Box
      400, Salt Flat 79847-9400
   Lyndon B. Johnson National Historical Park (512) 868-7128, P.O. Box
      329, Johnson City 78636
   Padre Island National Seashore (512) 949-8173, 9405 South Padre
      Island Drive, Corpus Christi 78418
   San Antonia Missions National Historical Park (210) 229-5701, 2202
      Roosevelt Avenue, San Antonio 78210
National Rifle Association (800) 336-7402, 11250 Waples Mill Rd., Fairfax,
   VA 22030. Locally, call the Texas State Rifle Assoc., (214) 369-8772
River Authorities:
   Brazos River Authority (817) 776-1441 P.O. Box 7555, Waco 76714
   Central Colorado River Authority (915) 636-4373 P.O. Box 964,
      Coleman 76834
   Guadalupe-Blanco River Authority (210) 379-5822 933 East Court
      Street P.O. Box 271, Seguin 78156
   Lavaca-Navidad River Authority (512) 782-5229 P.O. Box 429,
      Edna 77957
   Lower Colorado River Authority (512) 473-3200 P.O. Box 220,
      Austin 78767
   Nueces River Authority (210) 278-6810 First State Bank Building, Suite
      206, P.O. Box 349, Uvalde 78802
   Sabine River Authority (409) 746-3780 P.O. Box 579, Orange 77630
   San Antonio River Authority (512) 227-1373 100 East Guenther Street,
      P.O. Box 830027
   San Jacinto River Authority (409) 588-1111 P.O. Box 329,
      Conroe 77305
   Trinity River Authority (817) 467-4343
   Upper Colorado River Authority (915) 655-6505 30 West Beauregard,
      P.O. Box 1482, San Angelo 76902
   Upper Guadalupe River Authority (210) 896-5445 215 W. Water
      Street, P.O. Box 1278, Kerrville 78029
Secretary of State (512) 463-5701, 5561 State Capitol Room 1E.8, P.O.
   Box 12697, Austin 78711
Texas Bureau of Indian Affairs Field Office (210) 773-1209 P.O. Box 972,
   Eagle Pass 78853
   Alabama-Coushatta Reservation (409) 563-4391 Route 3, Box 640,
      Livingston 77351
   Tigua (Ysleta del Sur Pueblo) (915) 859-7913 P.O. Box 17579,
      El Paso 79917
   Kickapoo Traditional Tribe of Texas (210) 773-2105 P.O. Box 972,
      Eagle Pass 78853

Texas Dept. of Public Safety Headquarters (512) 465-2000 5805 N. Lamar Blvd., P.O. Box 4087, Austin 78773

DPS Concealed-Handgun Hotline (512) 706-7293, 7294

DPS Concealed-Handgun Mailing Address: Texas DPS, Concealed-Handgun Licensing Unit, P.O. Box 15888, Austin, TX 78761-5888

DPS Region 1 Dallas: (214) 226-7611, 350 W. IH-30, Garland 75043

DPS Region 2 Houston: (713) 681-1761, 10110 Northwest Freeway, Houston 77092

DPS Region 3 Corpus Christi: (512) 854-2681, 1922 S. Padre Island Dr., Box 5277, Corpus Christi 78465

DPS Region 4 Midland: (915) 697-2211, 2405 S. Loop 250 West, Midland 79703

DPS Region 5 Lubbock: (806) 747-4491, 1302 W. 6th St., Box 420, Lubbock 79408

DPS Region 6 Waco: (817) 867-4600, 1617 E. Crest Dr., Waco 76705

Texas General Land Office (512) 463-5277 1700 N. Congress Ave., Austin 78701

Texas Gun Dealers Association (512) 472-3532

Texas Parks and Wildlife Department (512) 389-4800; 800-792-1112 4200 Smith School Road, Austin 78744

    Hunter Education Section (512) 389-4999

    Operation Game Thief (800) 792-GAME

Texas State Rifle Association (214) 369-8772 4600 Greenville Ave. #215, P.O. Box 710549, Dallas 75371

U.S. Army Corps of Engineers, Southwestern Division (214) 767-2510 1114 Commerce Street, Dallas 75242

U.S. Forest Service P.O. Box 96090, Washington, DC 20090

APPENDIX D
THE TEXAS GUN LAWS

On the following pages are excerpts from official Texas state law:

1–Firearms-related Texas Codes in alphabetical order;

2–The Code of Criminal Procedure;

3–Senate Bill 60, popularly known as the Right to Carry Law, the law which created the concealed-handgun license. This will eventually be codified in the laws as Texas Civil Statute 4413(29ee), and as modifications to several other statutes. It is presented here in its complete form as enacted. The parts of Senate Bill 60 that update the Penal Code have also been incorporated into the Penal Code text in this book (in effect, they appear twice).

Texas law covers a broad spectrum of subjects and fills more than 100 thick books, but **only gun laws for private citizens are included in this appendix**. A complete copy of the state law is available in major libraries, but keep in mind that those copies are incomplete (and in many instances inaccurate) without the new material from the last legislative session (which this book includes).

The laws reproduced here are *excerpts*. Only material related to bearing arms has been included. In some cases this means substantial portions of laws may have been edited. **For official legal procedings do not rely on these excerpts**—obtain unedited texts and competent professional assistance.

In Texas, the legislature meets only during odd-numbered years. More than 1,000 laws were enacted during the 1995 session. Many new gun laws were included, making some distinct changes. As examples, Penal Code §46.02—one of the most key gun laws—was amended four separate times; §46.03 was amended three times, and new weapons laws were introduced as §46.11, 46.12,

46.13 and 46.15. The laws provided here are effective as of Sep. 1, 1995; offenses that occured prior may be governed by earlier versions of the statutes.

How State Law Is Arranged

Each numbered part of a Texas state code is called a "section," represented by a "§" sign. This makes it easy to refer to any particular statute—just call it by its title and section numbers. For instance, Penal Code §46.02 is the part about unlawful carrying of weapons. You say it like this, "Texas Penal Code, section forty six oh two," or simply, "forty six oh two." The Code of Criminal Procedure is similar, except a section is called an "article," which is abbreviated "Art.".

Excerpt from the Constitution of the State of Texas
Article 1, Section 23:
RIGHT TO KEEP AND BEAR ARMS

Every citizen shall have the right to keep and bear arms in the lawful defense of himself or the State; but the Legislature shall have power, by law, to regulate the wearing of arms, with a view to prevent crime.

A Note About The Official Law Books

Law books can be confusing because one book can be known by several different names. For example, here is the name of the book that holds the Right-to-Carry law:

ON THE SPINE:
Vernon's Texas Civil Statutes

ON THE COVER:
Vernon's Civil Statutes of the State of Texas Annotated

ON THE TITLE PAGE:
Vernon's Annotated Revised Civil Statutes of the State of Texas

ON THE "CITE THIS BOOK THUS" PAGE:
Vernon's Ann.Civ.St.

IN SENATE BILL 60, THE RIGHT-TO-CARRY LAW:
Title 70, Revised Statutes

IN PENAL CODE §46.035:
Revised Statutes

ON THE DPS CHL-LAWS AFFIDAVIT:
V.C.S.

TEXAS GUN LAWS

EXCERPTS FROM VERNON'S TEXAS CODE ANNOTATED

Alcoholic Beverage Code § 11.61. Cancellation or Suspension of Permit

(e) Except as provided by Subsection (f), the commission or administrator shall cancel an original or renewal permit if it is found, after notice and hearing, that the permittee knowingly allowed a person to possess a firearm in a building on the licensed premises. This subsection does not apply to a person:

(1) who holds a security officer commission issued by the Texas Board of Private Investigators and Private Security Agencies, if:

(A) the person is engaged in the performance of the person's duties as a security officer;

(B) the person is wearing a distinctive uniform; and

(C) the weapon is in plain view;

(2) who is a peace officer; or

(3) who is a permittee or an employee of a permittee if the person is supervising the operation of the premises.

(f) The commission may adopt a rule allowing:

(1) a gun or firearm show on the premises of a permit holder, if the premises is owned or leased by a governmental entity or a nonprofit civic, religious, charitable, fraternal, or veterans' organization;

(2) the holder of a permit for the sale of alcoholic beverages for off-premises consumption to also hold a federal firearms license; or

(3) the ceremonial display of firearms on the premises of the permit holder.

Alcoholic Beverage Code § 61.71. Grounds for Cancellation or Suspension: Retail Dealer

(f) Except as provided by Subsection (g), the commission or administrator shall cancel an original or renewal dealer's on-premises or off-premises license if it is found, after notice and hearing, that the licensee knowingly allowed a person to possess a firearm in a building on the licensed premises. This subsection does not apply to a person:

(1) who holds a security officer commission issued by the Texas Board of Private Investigators and Private Security Agencies, if:

(A) the person is engaged in the performance of the person's duties as a security officer;

(B) the person is wearing a distinctive uniform; and

(C) the weapon is in plain view;

(2) who is a peace officer; or

(3) who is a licensee or an employee of a licensee if the person is supervising the operation of the premises.

(g) The commission may adopt a rule allowing:

(1) a gun or firearm show on the premises of a license holder, if the premises is owned or leased by a governmental entity or a nonprofit civic, religious, charitable, fraternal, or veterans' organization;

(2) the holder of a license for the sale of alcoholic beverages for off-premises consumption to also hold a federal firearms license; or

(3) the ceremonial display of firearms on the premises of the license holder.

Business and Commerce Code § 16.09. Classes of Goods and Services

(a) An applicant may include in a single application for registration of a mark all goods or services in connection with which the mark is actually being used and which are in a single class. An applicant may not include in a single application for registration goods or services which are not in a single class.

(b) The classes of goods are:
(9) Class 9: explosives, firearms, equipments, and projectiles;

Civil Practices and Remedies Code § 82.006. Firearms and Ammunition

(a) In a products liability action brought against a manufacturer or seller of a firearm or ammunition that alleges a design defect in the firearm or ammunition, the burden is on the claimant to prove, in addition to any other elements that the claimant must prove, that:
(1) the actual design of the firearm or ammunition was defective, causing the firearm or ammunition not to function in a manner reasonably expected by an ordinary consumer of firearms or ammunition; and
(2) the defective design was a producing cause of the personal injury, property damage, or death.
(b) The claimant may not prove the existence of the defective design by a comparison or weighing of the benefits of the firearm or ammunition against the risk of personal injury, property damage, or death posed by its potential to cause such injury, damage, or death when discharged.

Civil Practice and Remedies Code § 83.001. Affirmative Defense

It is an affirmative defense to a civil action for damages for personal injury or death that the defendant, at the time the cause of action arose, was justified in using deadly force under Section 9.32, Penal Code, against a person who at the time of the use of force was committing an offense of unlawful entry in the habitation of the defendant.

Civil Practice and Remedies Code § 125.001. Common Nuisance.

A person who knowingly maintains a place to which persons habitually go for the purpose of prostitution or gambling in violation of the Penal Code, for the purpose of discharge of a firearm in a public place in violation of Section 42.01(a)(9), Penal Code, for the purpose of reckless discharge of a firearm as described by Section 42.12, Penal Code, for the purpose of engaging in organized criminal activity as a member of a combination as described by Section 71.02, Penal Code, or for the delivery or use of a controlled substance in violation of Chapter 481, Health and Safety Code, maintains a common nuisance.

Civil Practice and Remedies Code § 125.004.

(a) Proof that prostitution or gambling in violation of the Penal Code, that discharge of a firearm in a public place in violation of Section 42.01(a)(9), Penal Code, that reckless discharge of a firearm as described by Section 42.12 , Penal Code, or that the delivery or use of a controlled substance in violation of Chapter 481, Health and Safety Code, is frequently committed at the place involved or that the place is frequently used for reckless discharge of a firearm as described by Section 42.12, Penal Code, is prima facie evidence that the proprietor knowingly permitted the act.

Civil Practice and Remedies Code § 125.004.

(b) Evidence that persons have been convicted of gambling, committing prostitution, discharge of a firearm in a public place in violation of Section 42.01(a)(9), Penal Code, reckless discharge of a firearm as described by Section 42.12, Penal Code, engaging in organized criminal activity as a member of a combination as described by Section 71.02, Penal Code, or delivering or using a controlled substance in violation of Chapter 481, Health and Safety Code, in the place involved is admissible to show knowledge on the part of the defendant that the act occurred. The originals or certified copies of the papers and judgments of those convictions are admissible in the suit for injunction, and oral evidence is admissible to show that the offense for which a person was convicted was committed at the place involved.

Civil Practice and Remedies Code § 125.021. Public Nuisance.

The habitual use or the threatened or contemplated habitual use of any place for any of the following purposes is a public nuisance:
(1) gambling, gambling promotion, or communicating gambling information prohibited by law;
(2) promotion or aggravated promotion of prostitution;
(3) compelling prostitution;
(4) commercial manufacture, commercial distribution, or commercial exhibition of obscene material;
(5) commercial exhibition of live dances or other acts depicting real or simulated sexual intercourse or deviate sexual intercourse;
(6) engaging in a voluntary fight between a man and a bull if the fight is for a thing of value or a championship, if a thing of value is wagered on the fight, or if an admission fee for the fight is directly or indirectly charged, as prohibited by law;
(7) discharge of a firearm in a public place in violation of Section 42.01(a)(9), Penal Code;

(8) reckless discharge of a firearm as described by Section 42.12 , Penal Code;
(9) engaging in organized criminal activity as a member of a combination as described by Section 71.02, Penal Code; or
(10) delivering or using a controlled substance in violation of Chapter 481, Health and Safety Code.

Civil Practice and Remedies Code § 125.041. Public Nuisance.

For the purposes of this subchapter, a public nuisance is considered to exist at a place if one or more of the following acts occurs at that place on a regular basis:

(1) gambling, gambling promotion, or communication of gambling information, as prohibited by Chapter 47, Penal Code;
(2) promotion or aggravated promotion of prostitution, as prohibited by Chapter 43, Penal Code;
(3) compelling prostitution, as prohibited by Chapter 43, Penal Code;
(4) commercial manufacture, commercial distribution, or commercial exhibition of material that is obscene, as defined by Section 43.21, Penal Code;
(5) commercial exhibition of a live dance or other act in which a person engages in real or simulated sexual intercourse or deviate sexual intercourse, as defined by Section 43.01, Penal Code;
(6) discharge of a firearm in violation of Section 42.01(a)(9), Penal Code;
(7) reckless discharge of a firearm as described by Section 42.12, Penal Code;
(8) engaging in organized criminal activity as a member of a combination as described by Section 71.02, Penal Code; or
(9) manufacture, delivery, or use of a controlled substance in violation of Chapter 481, Health and Safety Code.

Education Code § 4.31. Exhibition of Firearms

(a) It shall be unlawful to interfere with the normal activities, the normal occupancy, or normal use of any building or portion of a campus, or of any school bus engaged in the transportation of children to and from school sponsored activities, of any private or public school or institution of higher education or public vocational and technical school or institute by exhibiting or using or threatening to exhibit or use a firearm.
(b) A person who violates this section is guilty of a felony and upon conviction is punishable by a fine of up to $1,000 or by imprisonment in jail for a period not to exceed six months, or by both fine and imprisonment, or by imprisonment in the state penitentiary for a period not to exceed five years.

Education Code § 21.118. Firearms Safety Program.

(a) A school district may, and is strongly encouraged to, provide or participate in a firearms safety program for students in grades kindergarten through 12. A school district that provides a firearms safety program shall consult with a certified firearms instructor before establishing the curriculum for the program.
(b) A school district may not require a student to participate in a firearms safety program if the district receives written notice from a parent of the student to exempt the student from the program. A school district that provides or participates in a firearms safety program may not permit a student participating in the program, while the student is on district property, to handle a readily dischargeable firearm.
(c) The firearms safety program will meet the standards of the National Rifle Association Eddie Eagle Children's Gun Safety Course.

Family Code § 51.16

(m) On request of the Department of Public Safety, a juvenile court shall reopen and allow the department to inspect the files and records of the juvenile court relating to an applicant for a license to carry a concealed handgun under Article 4413 (29ee), Revised Statutes.

Family Code § 71.10

(c) On receipt of a request for law enforcement information system record check of a prospective transferee by a licensed firearms dealer under the Brady Handgun Violence Prevention Act, 18 U.S.C. Section 922, the chief law enforcement officer shall determine whether the Department of Public Safety has in the department's law enforcement information system a record indicating the existence of an active protective order directed to the prospective transferee. If the department's law enforcement information system indicates the existence of an active protective order directed to the prospective transferee, the chief law enforcement officer shall immediately advise the dealer that the transfer is prohibited.

Government Code § 411.047. Reporting Related To Concealed Handgun Incidents.

(a) The department shall maintain statistics related to responses by law enforcement agencies to incidents in which a person licensed to carry a handgun under Article 4413 (29ee), Revised Statutes, is arrested for an offense under Section 46.035, Penal Code, or discharges a handgun.
(b) The department by rule shall adopt procedures for local law enforcement to make reports to the department described by Subsection (a).

Government Code § 418.019. Restricted Sale and Transportation of Materials

The governor may suspend or limit the sale, dispensing, or transportation of alcoholic beverages, firearms, explosives, and combustibles.
<Applies when an official state of disaster has been declared, see Government Code § 418.001 et seq.>

Government Code § 431.114. Sale of Arms

The commanding officer of forces called to enforce law may order the closing of any place where arms, ammunition, or explosives are sold and forbid the sale, barter, loan, or gift of arms, ammunition, or explosives while forces are on duty in or near that place.

Health and Safety Code § 161.041. Mandatory Reporting

A physician who attends or treats, or who is requested to attend or treat, a bullet or gunshot wound, or the administrator, superintendent, or other person in charge of a hospital, sanitarium, or other institution in which a bullet or gunshot wound is attended or treated or in which the attention or treatment is requested shall report the case at once to the law enforcement authority of the municipality or county in which the physician practices or in which the institution is located.

Health and Safety Code § 161.042. Criminal Penalty

(a) A person commits an offense if the person is required to report under this subchapter and intentionally fails to report.
(b) An offense under this section is a misdemeanor punishable by confinement in jail for not more than six months or by a fine of not more than $100.

Health and Safety Code § 756.041. Applicability

This subchapter applies only to an outdoor shooting range located in a county with a population of more than 150,000.

Health and Safety Code § 756.0411. Definition

In this subchapter, "outdoor shooting range" means an outdoor shooting range, outdoor firing range, or other open property on which persons may fire a weapon for a fee or other remuneration but does not include a deer lease or other similar leases of property for the purpose of hunting or an archery range.

Health and Safety Code § 756.042. Construction Standards

The owner of an outdoor shooting range shall construct and maintain the range according to standards that are at least as stringent as the standards printed in the National Rifle Association range manual.

Health and Safety Code § 756.043. Civil Penalty

(a) The owner of an outdoor shooting range who fails to comply with Section 756.042 is liable within 60 days after a finding of noncompliance for a civil penalty of $50 for each day of noncompliance; the aggregate amount not to exceed $500.
(b) The attorney general or the appropriate district attorney, criminal district attorney, or county attorney shall recover the civil penalty in a suit on behalf of the state. If the attorney general brings the suit, the penalty shall be deposited in the state treasury to the credit of the general revenue fund. If another attorney brings the suit, the penalty shall be deposited in the general fund of the county in which the violation occurred.

Health and Safety Code § 756.044. Criminal Penalties

(a) The owner of an outdoor shooting range commits an offense if the owner intentionally or recklessly fails to comply with Section 756.042 and that failure results in injury to another person.

(b) An offense under this section is a Class C misdemeanor, except that if it is shown on the trial of the defendant that the defendant has previously been convicted of an offense under this section, the offense is a Class A misdemeanor.

Health and Safety Code § 756.045. Insurance Required

(a) The owner of an outdoor shooting range shall purchase and maintain an insurance policy that provides coverage of at least $500,000 for bodily injuries or death and another policy that provides that level of coverage for property damage resulting from firing any weapon while on the shooting range.

(b) The owner of an outdoor shooting range shall prominently display a sign at the shooting range stating that the owner has purchased insurance to cover bodily injury, death, or property damage occurring from activities at the shooting range.

Local Government Code § 215.001. Firearms; Explosives

(a) A municipality may not adopt regulations relating to the transfer, private ownership, keeping, transportation, licensing, or registration of firearms, ammunition, or firearm supplies.

(b) Subsection (a) does not affect the authority a municipality has under another law to:

(1) require residents or public employees to be armed for personal or national defense, law enforcement, or other lawful purpose;

(2) regulate the discharge of firearms within the limits of the municipality;

(3) regulate the use of property, the location of a business, or uses at a business under the municipality's fire code, zoning ordinance, or land-use regulations as long as the code, ordinance, or regulations are not used to circumvent the intent of Subsection (a) or Subdivision (5) of this subsection;

(4) regulate the use of firearms in the case of an insurrection, riot, or natural disaster if the municipality finds the regulations necessary to protect public health and safety;

(5) regulate the storage or transportation of explosives to protect public health and safety, except that 25 pounds or less of black powder for each private residence and 50 pounds or less of black powder for each retail dealer are not subject to regulation; or

(6) regulate the carrying of a firearm by a person other than a person licensed to carry a concealed handgun under Article 4413 (29ee), Revised Statutes, at a:

(A) public park;

(B) public meeting of a municipality, county, or other governmental body;

(C) political rally, parade, or official political meeting; or

(D) nonfirearms-related school, college, or professional athletic event.

(c) The exception provided by Subsection (b)(6) does not apply if the firearm is in or is carried to or from an area designated for use in a lawful hunting, fishing, or other sporting event and the firearm is of the type commonly used in the activity.

Local Government Code § 240.021. Subdivisions Covered by Subchapter

This subchapter applies only to a subdivision all or a part of which is located in the unincorporated area of a county and for which a plat is required to be prepared and filed under Chapter 232.

Local Government Code § 240.022. Authority to Regulate

To promote the public safety, the commissioners court of a county by order may prohibit or otherwise regulate the discharge of firearms on lots that are 10 acres or smaller and are located in the unincorporated area of the county in a subdivision.

Local Government Code § 240.023. Prohibited Regulations

This subchapter does not authorize the commissioners court to regulate the transfer, ownership, possession, or transportation of firearms and does not authorize the court to require the registration of firearms.

Local Government Code § 240.025. Criminal Penalty

A person commits an offense if the person intentionally or knowingly engages in conduct that is a violation of a regulation adopted under this subchapter by the commissioners court. An offense under this section is a Class C misdemeanor. If it is shown on the trial of an offense under this section that the person has previously been convicted of an offense under this section, the offense is a Class B misdemeanor.

Local Government Code § 250.001. Restriction on Regulation of Sport Shooting Ranges

(a) In this section, "sport shooting range" means a business establishment that is in existence on or before the effective date of this Act and operating an area for the discharge or other use of firearms for silhouette, skeet, trap, black powder, target, self-defense, or similar recreational shooting.

(b) A governmental official may not seek a civil or criminal penalty against a sport shooting range or its owner or operator based on the violation of a municipal or county ordinance, order, or rule regulating noise, if the sport shooting range is in compliance with the applicable ordinance, order, or rule.

(c) A person may not bring a nuisance or similar cause of action against a sport shooting range based on noise, if the sport shooting range is in compliance with all applicable municipal and county ordinances, orders, and rules regulating noise.

Local Government Code § 342.003. Fire Regulations

(a) The governing body of the municipality may:

(8) prohibit or otherwise regulate the use of fireworks and firearms;

(9) prohibit, direct, or otherwise regulate the keeping and management of buildings within the city that are used to store gunpowder or other combustible, explosive, or dangerous materials, and regulate the keeping and conveying of those materials;

(b) Subsection (a)(8) or (9) does not authorize a municipality to adopt any prohibition or other regulation in violation of Section 215.001.

Parks and Wildlife Code § 13.101. Authorization

The commission may promulgate regulations governing the health, safety, and protection of persons and property in state parks, historic sites, scientific areas, or forts under the control of the department, including public water within state parks, historic sites, scientific areas, and forts.

Parks and Wildlife Code § 13.108. Removal From Park

(a) Any person directly or indirectly responsible for disruptive, destructive, or violent conduct which endangers property or the health, safety, or lives of persons or animals may be removed from a park, historic site, scientific area, or fort for a period not to exceed 48 hours.

(b) Prior to removal under this section, the person must be given notice of the provisions of this section and an opportunity to correct the conduct justifying removal.

(c) A court of competent jurisdiction may enjoin a person from reentry to the park, scientific area, site, or fort, on cause shown, for any period set by the court.

Parks and Wildlife Code § 13.201. Authorization

The commission may make regulations prohibiting the use of firearms or certain types of firearms on state property adjacent to state parks and within 200 yards of the boundary of the state park.

Parks and Wildlife Code § 13.202. Application Limited

The regulations of the commission under Section 13.201 of this code apply only to state parks located within one mile of coastal water of this state.

Parks and Wildlife Code § 43.112. Confiscation and Disposition of Aircraft, Vehicles, Guns, and Other Devices; Immunity

(a) A game warden or other authorized employee of the department may seize and hold as evidence an aircraft, vehicle, gun, or other device used by a person if:

(1) the person is charged with a violation of this subchapter or a proclamation or regulation adopted under this subchapter; and

(2) The person used the aircraft, vehicle, gun, or other device in committing the violation with which the person is charged.

(b) The department may sell an aircraft, vehicle, gun, or other device seized under this section to the highest bidder if:

(1) the person who used the aircraft, vehicle, gun, or other device to commit a violation is convicted of the violation or enters a plea of nolo contendere to the violation;

(2) the department receives at least three written bids; and

(3) the highest bid is not less than the appraised value of the aircraft, vehicle, gun, or other device.

(c) The department shall release an aircraft, vehicle, gun, or other device seized under this section to the owner if the person charged with a violation is acquitted or the charge against the person is dismissed.

(d) If the department is not authorized to sell or required to release the aircraft, vehicle, gun, or other device, the department may keep and use the aircraft, vehicle, gun, or other device to protect the wildlife resources of this state.

(e) A game warden or authorized employee of the department is not liable for any damages arising from the seizure of an aircraft, vehicle, gun, or other device under this section unless the damages are caused by an act that was intentional or grossly negligent.

(f) The department shall deposit money received under this section in the state treasury to the credit of the game, fish, and water safety fund for the enforcement of fish, shrimp, and oyster laws, game laws, and laws pertaining to sand, shell, and gravel.

Parks and Wildlife Code § 62.012. Written Consent to Hunt or Target Shoot Required

(a) This section applies only to a county having a population of 2,000,000 or more. This section does not apply to a person hunting or target shooting on a public or private shooting range.

(b) Except as provided by Subsection (d) of this section, no person possessing a firearm may hunt a wild animal or wild bird, or engage in target shooting on land owned by another unless the person has in his immediate possession the written consent of the owner of the land to hunt or engage in target shooting on the land.

(c) To be valid, the written consent required by Subsection (b) of this section must:

(1) contain the name of the person permitted to hunt or engage in target shooting on the land;

(2) identify the land on which hunting or target shooting is permitted;

(3) be signed by the owner of the land or by an agent, lessee, or legal representative of the owner; and

(4) show the address and phone number of the person signing the consent.

(d) The owner of the land on which hunting or target shooting occurs, the landowner's lessee, agent, or legal representative, and a person hunting or target shooting with the landowner or the landowner's lessee, agent, or legal representative are not required to have in their possession the written consent required by Subsection (b) of this section.

Parks and Wildlife Code § 62.081. Weapons Prohibited

Except as provided in Section 62.082 of this code, no person may hunt with, possess, or shoot a firearm, bow, crossbow, slingshot, or any other weapon on or across the land of the Lower Colorado River Authority.

Parks and Wildlife Code § 62.082. Target Ranges

(a) The Board of Directors of the Lower Colorado River Authority may lease river authority land to be used on a nonprofit basis for a target rifle or archery range only and not for hunting.

(b) A member of the boy scouts or the girl scouts or other nonprofit public service group or organization may possess and shoot a firearm, bow, and crossbow for target or instructional purposes under the supervision of a qualified instructor registered with and approved by the Lower Colorado River Authority on ranges designated by the Lower Colorado River Authority. This subsection does not permit hunting by any person.

Parks and Wildlife Code § 143.023. Discharge of Firearm

(a) Except as provided in Subsections (b) and (c) of this section, no person may shoot, fire, or discharge any firearm in, on, along, or across Lake Lavon in Collin County.

(b) This section does not apply to peace officers, game wardens, or other representatives of the department in the lawful discharge of their duties.

(c) This section does not apply to a person hunting with a shotgun during an open season or when it is lawful to hunt in or on Lake Lavon.

(d) A person who violates this section is guilty of a misdemeanor and on conviction is punishable by a fine of not less than $10 nor more than $200 plus costs, or confinement in the county jail for not more than one year, or both.

EXCERPTS FROM THE TEXAS PENAL CODE

CHAPTER 1 • GENERAL PROVISIONS

Penal Code §1.01. Short Title
This code shall be known and may be cited as the Penal Code.

Penal Code §1.02. Objectives of the Code
The general purposes of this code are to establish a system of prohibitions, penalties, and correctional measures to deal with conduct that unjustifiably and inexcusably causes or threatens harm to those individual or public interests for which state protection is appropriate. To this end, the provisions of this code are intended, and shall be construed, to achieve the following objectives:
1. to insure the public safety through:
A. the deterrent influence of the penalties hereinafter provided;
B. the rehabilitation of those convicted of violations of this code; and
C. such punishment as may be necessary to prevent likely recurrence of criminal behavior;
2. by definition and grading of offenses to give fair warning of what is prohibited and of the consequences of violation;
3. to prescribe penalties that are proportionate to the seriousness of offenses and that permit recognition of differences in rehabilitation possibilities among individual offenders;
4. to safeguard conduct that is without guilt from condemnation as criminal;
5. to guide and limit the exercise of official discretion in law enforcement to prevent arbitrary or oppressive treatment of persons suspected, accused, or convicted of offenses; and
6. to define the scope of state interest in law enforcement against specific offenses and to systematize the exercise of state criminal jurisdiction.

Penal Code §1.07. Definitions
(a) In this code:
1. "Act" means a bodily movement, whether voluntary or involuntary, and includes speech.
2. "Actor" means a person whose criminal responsibility is in issue in a criminal action. Whenever the term "suspect" is used in this code, it means "actor."
3. "Agency" includes authority, board, bureau, commission, committee, council, department, district, division, and office.
4. "Alcoholic beverage" has the meaning assigned by Section 1-04, Alcoholic Beverage Code.
5. "Another" means a person other than the actor.
6. "Association" means a government or governmental subdivision or agency, trust, partnership, or two or more persons having a joint or common economic interest.
7. "Benefit" means anything reasonably regarded as economic gain or advantage, including benefit to any other person in whose welfare the beneficiary is interested.
8. "Bodily injury" means physical pain, illness, or any impairment of physical condition.
9. "Coercion" means a threat, however communicated:
A. to commit an offense;
B. to inflict bodily injury in the future on the person threatened or another;
C. to accuse a person of any offense
D. to expose a person to hatred, contempt, or ridicule;
E. to harm the credit or business repute of any person; or
F. to take or withhold action as a public servant, or to cause a public servant to take or withhold action.
10. "Conduct" means an act or omission and its accompanying mental state.
11. "Consent" means assent in fact, whether express or apparent.
12. "Controlled substance" has the meaning assigned by Section 481.002, Health and Safety Code.
13. "Corporation" includes nonprofit corporations, professional associations created pursuant to statute, and joint stock companies.
14. "Correctional facility" means a place designated by law for the confinement of a person arrested for, charged with, or convicted of a criminal offense. The term includes:

A. a municipal or county jail;
B. a confinement facility operated by the Texas Department of Criminal Justice;
C. a confinement facility operated under contract with any division of the Texas Department of Criminal Justice; and
D. a community corrections facility operated by a community supervision and corrections department.
15. "Criminal negligence" is defined in Section 6.03 (Culpable Mental States).
16. "Dangerous drug" has the meaning assigned by Section 483.001, Health and Safety Code.
17. "Deadly weapon" means:
A. a firearm or anything manifestly designed, made, or adapted for the purpose of inflicting death or serious bodily injury; or
B. anything that in the manner of its use or intended use is capable of causing death or serious bodily injury.
18. "Drug" has the meaning assigned by Section 481.002, Health and Safety Code.
19. "Effective consent" includes consent by a person legally authorized to act for the owner. Consent is not effective if:
A. induced by force, threat, or fraud;
B. given by a person the actor knows is not legally authorized to act for the owner;
C. given by a person who by reason of youth, mental disease or defect, or intoxication is known by the actor to be unable to make reasonable decisions; or
D. given solely to detect the commission of an offense.
20. "Electric generating plant" means a facility that generates electric energy for distribution to the public.
21. "Electric utility substation" means a facility used to switch or change voltage in connection with the transmission of electric energy for distribution to the public.
22. "Element of offense" means:
A. the forbidden conduct;
B. the required culpability;
C. any required result; and
D. the negation of any exception to the offense.
23. "Felony" means an offense so designated by law or punishable by death or confinement in a penitentiary.
24. "Government" means:
A. the state;
B. a county, municipality, or political subdivision of the state; or
C. any branch or agency of the state, a county, municipality, or political subdivision.
25. "Harm" means anything reasonably regarded as loss, disadvantage, or injury. including harm to another person in whose welfare the person affected is interested.
26. "Individual" means a human being who has been born and is alive.
27. "Institutional division" means the institutional division of the Texas Department of Criminal Justice.
28. "Intentional" is defined in Section 6.03 (Culpable Mental States).
29. "Knowing" is defined in Section 6.03 (Culpable Mental States).
30. "Law" means the constitution or a statute of this state or of the United States, a written opinion of a court of record, a municipal ordinance, an order of a county commissioners court, or a rule authorized by and lawfully adopted under a statute.
31. "Misdemeanor" means an offense so designated by law or punishable by fine, by confinement in jail, or by both fine and confinement in jail.
32. "Oath" includes affirmation.
33. "Official proceeding" means any type of administrative, executive, legislative, or judicial proceeding that may be conducted before a public servant.
34. "Omission" means failure to act.
35. "Owner" means a person who:
A. has title to the property, possession of the property, whether lawful or not, or a greater right to possession of the property than the actor; or
B. is a holder in due course of a negotiable instrument.
36. "Peace officer" means a person elected, employed, or appointed as a peace officer under Article 2.12, Code of Criminal Procedure, Section 51.212 or 51.214, Education Code, or other law.
37. "Penal institution" means a place designated by law for confinement of persons arrested for, charged with, or convicted of an offense.
38. "Person" means an individual, corporation, or association.
39. "Possession" means actual care, custody, control, or management.
40. "Public place" means any place to which the public or a substantial group of the public has access and includes, but is not limited to, streets, highways, and the common areas of schools, hospitals, apartment houses, office buildings, transport facilities, and shops.
41. "Public servant" means a person elected, selected, appointed, employed, or otherwise designated as one of the following, even if he has not yet qualified for office or assumed his duties:
A. an officer, employee, or agent of government;
B. a juror or grand juror; or

C. an arbitrator, referee, or other person who is authorized by law or private written agreement to hear or determine a cause or controversy; or

D. an attorney at law or notary public when participating in the performance of a governmental function; or

E. a candidate for nomination or election to public office; or

F. a person who is performing a governmental function under a claim of right although he is not legally qualified to do so.

42. "Reasonable belief" means a belief that would be held by an ordinary and prudent man in the same circumstances as the actor.

43. "Reckless" is defined in Section 6.03 (Culpable Mental States).

44. "Rule" includes regulation.

45. "Secure correctional facility" means:

A. a municipal or county jail; or

B. a confinement facility operated by or under a contract with any division of the Texas Department of Criminal Justice.

46. "Serious bodily injury" means bodily injury that creates a substantial risk of death or that causes death, serious permanent disfigurement, or protracted loss or impairment of the function of any bodily member or organ.

47. "Swear" includes affirm.

48. "Unlawful" means criminal or tortious or both and includes what would be criminal or tortious but for a defense not amounting to justification or privilege.

(b) The definition of a term in this code applies to each grammatical variation of the term.

Penal Code §1.08. Preemption

No governmental subdivision or agency may enact or enforce a law that makes any conduct covered by this code an offense subject to a criminal penalty. This section shall apply only as long as the law governing the conduct proscribed by this code is legally enforceable.

CHAPTER 2 • BURDEN OF PROOF

Penal Code §2.01. Proof Beyond a Reasonable Doubt

All persons are presumed to be innocent and no person may be convicted of an offense unless each element of the offense is proved beyond a reasonable doubt. The fact that he has been arrested, confined, or indicted for, or otherwise charged with, the offense gives rise to no inference of guilt at his trial.

Penal Code §2.02. Exception

(a) An exception to an offense in this code is so labeled by the phrase: "It is an exception to the application of ...."

(b) The prosecuting attorney must negate the existence of an exception in the accusation charging commission of the offense and prove beyond a reasonable doubt that the defendant or defendant's conduct does not fall within the exception.

(c) This section does not affect exceptions applicable to offenses enacted prior to the effective date of this code.

Penal Code §2.03. Defense

(a) A defense to prosecution for an offense in this code is so labeled by the phrase: "It is a defense to prosecution ...."

(b) The prosecuting attorney is not required to negate the existence of a defense in the accusation charging commission of the offense.

(c) The issue of the existence of a defense is not submitted to the jury unless evidence is admitted supporting the defense.

(d) If the issue of the existence of a defense is submitted to the jury, the court shall charge that a reasonable doubt on the issue requires that the defendant be acquitted.

(e) A ground of defense in a penal law that is not plainly labeled in accordance with this chapter has the procedural and evidentiary consequences of a defense.

Penal Code §2.04. Affirmative Defense

(a) An affirmative defense in this code Is so labeled by the phrase: "It is an affirmative defense to prosecution ...."
(b) The prosecuting attorney is not required to negate the existence of an affirmative defense in the accusation charging commission of the offense.
(c) The issue of the existence of an affirmative defense is not submitted to the jury unless evidence is admitted supporting the defense.
(d) If the issue of the existence of an affirmative defense is submitted to the jury, the court shall charge that the defendant must prove the affirmative defense by a preponderance of evidence

Penal Code §2.05. Presumption

When this code or another penal law establishes a presumption with respect to any fact, it has the following consequences:
1. if there is sufficient evidence of the facts that give rise to the presumption, the issue of the existence of the presumed fact must be submitted to the jury, unless the court is satisfied that the evidence as a whole clearly precludes a finding beyond a reasonable doubt of the presumed fact; and
2. if the existence of the presumed fact is submitted to the jury, the court shall charge the jury, in terms of the presumption and the specific element to which it applies, as follows:
A. that the facts giving rise to the presumption must be proven beyond a reasonable doubt;
B. that if such facts are proven beyond a reasonable doubt the jury may find that the element of the offense sought to be presumed exists, but it is not bound to so find;
C. that even though the jury may find the existence of such element, the state must prove beyond a reasonable doubt each of the other elements of the offense charged; and
D. if the jury has a reasonable doubt as to the existence of a fact or facts giving rise to the presumption, the presumption fails and the jury shall not consider the presumption for any purpose.

CHAPTER 6 • CULPABILITY GENERALLY

Penal Code §6.01. Requirement of Voluntary Act or Omission

(a) A person commits an offense only if he voluntarily engages in conduct, including an act, an omission, or possession.
b) Possession is a voluntary act if the possessor knowingly obtains or receives the thing possessed or is aware of his control of the thing for a sufficient time to permit him to terminate his control.
(c) A person who omits to perform an act does not commit an offense unless a law as defined by Section 1.07 provides that the omission is an offense or otherwise provides that he has a duty to perform the act.

Penal Code §6.02. Requirement of Culpability

(a) Except as provided in Subsection (b), a person does not commit an offense unless he intentionally, knowingly, recklessly, or with criminal negligence engages in conduct as the definition of the offense requires.
(b) If the definition of an offense does not prescribe a culpable mental state, a culpable mental state is nevertheless required unless the definition plainly dispenses with any mental element.
(c) If the definition of an offense does not prescribe a culpable mental state, but one is nevertheless required under Subsection (b), intent, knowledge, or recklessness suffices to establish criminal responsibility.
(d) Culpable mental states are classified according to relative degrees, from highest to lowest, as follows:
1. intentional;
2. knowing;
3. reckless;
4. criminal negligence.
(e) Proof of a higher degree of culpability than that charged constitutes proof of the culpability charged.

Penal Code §6.03. Definitions of Culpable Mental States

(a) A person acts intentionally, or with intent, with respect to the nature of his conduct or to a result of his conduct when it is his conscious objective or desire to engage in the conduct or cause the result.

(b) A person acts knowingly, or with knowledge, with respect to the nature of his conduct or to circumstances surrounding his conduct when he is aware of the nature of his conduct or that the circumstances exist. A person acts knowingly, or with knowledge, with respect to a result of his conduct when he is aware that his conduct is reasonably certain to cause the result.
(c) A person acts recklessly, or is reckless, with respect to circumstances surrounding his conduct or the result of his conduct when he is aware of but consciously disregards a substantial and unjustifiable risk that the circumstances exist or the result will occur. The risk must be of such a nature and degree that its disregard constitutes a gross deviation from the standard of care that an ordinary person would exercise under all the circumstances as viewed from the actor's standpoint.
(d) A person acts with criminal negligence, or is criminally negligent, with respect to circumstances surrounding his conduct or the result of his conduct when he ought to be aware of a substantial and unjustifiable risk that the circumstances exist or the result will occur. The risk must be of such a nature and degree that the failure to perceive it constitutes a gross deviation from the standard of care that an ordinary person would exercise under all the circumstances as viewed from the actor's standpoint.

Penal Code §6.04. Causation: Conduct and Results

(a) A person is criminally responsible if the result would not have occurred but for his conduct, operating either alone or concurrently with another cause, unless the concurrent cause was clearly sufficient to produce the result and the conduct of the actor clearly insufficient.
(b) A person is nevertheless criminally responsible for causing a result if the only difference between what actually occurred and what he desired. contemplated, or risked is that:
1. a different offense was committed; or
2. a different person or property was injured, harmed, or otherwise affected.

CHAPTER 8 • GENERAL DEFENSES TO CRIMINAL RESPONSIBILITY

Penal Code §8.03. Mistake of Law

(a) It is no defense to prosecution that the actor was ignorant of the provisions of any law after the law has taken effect.

Penal Code §8.07. Age Affecting Criminal Responsibility

(a) A person may not be prosecuted for or convicted of any offense that he committed when younger than 15 years of age except:
1. perjury and aggravated perjury when it appears by proof that he had sufficient discretion to understand the nature and obligation of an oath;
2. a violation of a penal statute cognizable under Chapter 302, Acts of the 55th Legislature, Regular Session, 1957 (Article 67011-4, Vernon's Texas Civil Statutes), except conduct which violates the laws of this state prohibiting driving while intoxicated or under the influence of intoxicating liquor (first or subsequent offense) or driving while under the influence of any narcotic drug or of any other drug to a degree which renders him incapable of safely driving a vehicle (first or subsequent offense);
3. a violation of a motor vehicle traffic ordinance of an incorporated city or town in this state;
4. a misdemeanor punishable by fine only other than public intoxication; or
5. violation of a penal ordinance of a political subdivision.
(b) Unless the juvenile court waives jurisdiction and certifies the individual for criminal prosecution, a person may not be prosecuted for or convicted of any offense committed before reaching 17 years of age except:
1. perjury and aggravated perjury when it appears by proof that he had sufficient discretion to understand the nature and obligation of an oath;
2. violation of a penal statute cognizable under Chapter 302, Acts of the 55th Legislature, Regular Session, 1957 (Article 67011-4, Vernon's Texas Civil Statutes), except conduct which violates the laws of this state prohibiting driving while intoxicated or under the influence of intoxicating liquor (first or subsequent offense) or driving while under the influence of any narcotic drug or of any other drug to a degree which renders him incapable of safely driving a vehicle (first or subsequent offense);
3. violation of a motor vehicle traffic ordinance of an incorporated city or town in this state;
4. misdemeanor punishable by fine only other than public intoxication; or
5. a violation of a penal ordinance of a political subdivision.
(c) Unless the juvenile court waives jurisdiction and certifies the individual for criminal prosecution, a person who has been alleged in a petition for an adjudication hearing to have engaged in delinquent conduct or conduct indicating a need for supervision may not be

prosecuted for or convicted of any offense alleged in the juvenile court petition or any offense within the knowledge of the juvenile court judge as evidenced by anything in the record of the juvenile court proceedings.

(d) No person may, in any case, be punished by death for an offense committed while he was younger than 17 years.

CHAPTER 9 • JUSTIFICATION EXCLUDING CRIMINAL RESPONSIBILITY

SUBCHAPTER A. GENERAL PROVISIONS

Penal Code §9.01. Definitions
In this chapter:
1. "Custody" means:
A. under arrest by a peace officer; or
B. under restraint by a public servant pursuant to an order of a court.
2. "Escape" means unauthorized departure from custody or failure to return to custody following temporary leave for a specific purpose or limited period, but does not include a violation of conditions of community supervision or parole, or following leave that is part of an intermittent sentence.
3. "Deadly force" means force that is intended or known by the actor to cause, or in the manner of its use or intended use is capable of causing, death or serious bodily injury.

Penal Code §9.02. Justification as a Defense
It is a defense to prosecution that the conduct in question is justified under this chapter.

Penal Code §9.03. Confinement as Justifiable Force
Confinement is justified when force is justified by this chapter if the actor takes reasonable measures to terminate the confinement as soon as he knows he safely can unless the person confined has been arrested for an offense.

Penal Code §9.04. Threats as Justifiable Force
The threat of force is justified when the use of force is justified by this chapter. For purposes of this section, a threat to cause death or serious bodily injury by the production of a weapon or otherwise, as long as the actor's purpose is limited to creating an apprehension that he will use deadly force if necessary, does not constitute the use of deadly force.

Penal Code §9.05. Reckless Injury of Innocent Third Person
Even though an actor is justified under this chapter in threatening or using force or deadly force against another, if in doing so he also recklessly injures or kills an innocent third person, the justification afforded by this chapter is unavailable in a prosecution for the reckless in jury or killing of the innocent third person.

Penal Code §9.06. Civil Remedies Unaffected
The fact that conduct is justified under this chapter does not abolish or impair any remedy for the conduct that is available in a civil suit.

SUBCHAPTER B. JUSTIFICATION GENERALLY

Penal Code §9.21. Public Duty

(a) Except as qualified by Subsections (b) and (c), conduct is justified if the actor reasonably believes the conduct is required or authorized by law, by the judgment or order of a competent court or other governmental tribunal, or in the execution of legal process.

(b) The other sections of this chapter control when force is used against a person to protect persons (subchapter C), to protect property (Subchapter D), for law enforcement (Subchapter E), or by virtue of a special relationship (Subchapter F).

(c) The use of deadly force is not justified under this section unless the actor reasonably believes the deadly force is specifically required by statute or unless it occurs in the lawful conduct of war. If deadly force is so justified, there is no duty to retreat before using it.

(d) The justification afforded by this section is available if the actor reasonably believes:

1. the court or governmental tribunal has jurisdiction or the process is lawful, even though the court or governmental tribunal lacks jurisdiction or the process is unlawful; or

2. his conduct is required or authorized to assist a public servant in the performance of his official duty, even though the servant exceeds his lawful authority.

Penal Code §9.22. Necessity

Conduct is justified if:

1. the actor reasonably believes the conduct is immediately necessary to avoid imminent harm;

2. the desirability and urgency of avoiding the harm clearly outweigh, according to ordinary standards of reasonableness, the harm sought to be prevented by the law proscribing the conduct; and

3. a legislative purpose to exclude the justification claimed for the conduct does not otherwise plainly appear.

SUBCHAPTER C. PROTECTION OF PERSONS

Penal Code §9.31. Self-Defense

(a) Except as provided in Subsection (b), a person is justified in using force against another when and to the degree he reasonably believes the force is immediately necessary to protect himself against the other's use or attempted use of unlawful force.

(b) The use of force against another is not justified:

(1) in response to verbal provocation alone;

(2) to resist an arrest or search that the actor knows is being made by a peace officer, or by a person acting in a peace officer's presence and at his direction, even though the arrest or search is unlawful, unless the resistance is justified under Subsection (c);

(3) if the actor consented to the exact force used or attempted by the other;

(4) if the actor provoked the other's use or attempted use of unlawful force, unless:

(A) the actor abandons the encounter, or clearly communicates to the other his intent to do so reasonably believing he cannot safely abandon the encounter; and

(B) the other nevertheless continues or attempts to use unlawful force against the actor; or

(5) if the actor sought an explanation from or discussion with the other person concerning the actor's differences with the other person while the actor was:

(A) carrying a weapon in violation of Section 46.02; or

(B) possessing or transporting a weapon in violation of Section 46.05.

(c) The use of force to resist an arrest or search is justified:

1. if, before the actor offers any resistance, the peace officer (or person acting at his direction) uses or attempts to use greater force than necessary to make the arrest or search; and
2. when and to the degree the actor reasonably believes the force is immediately necessary to protect himself against the peace officer's (or other person's) use or attempted use of greater force than necessary.

(d) The use of deadly force is not justified under this subchapter except as provided in Sections 9.32, 9.33, and 9.34.

Penal Code § 9.32. Deadly Force in Defense of Person

(a) A person is justified in using deadly force against another:

(1) if he would be justified in using force against the other under Section 9.31;
(2) if a reasonable person in the actor's situation would not have retreated; and
(3) when and to the degree he reasonably believes the deadly force is immediately necessary:

(A) to protect himself against the other's use or attempted use of unlawful deadly force; or
(B) to prevent the other's imminent commission of aggravated kidnapping, murder, sexual assault, aggravated sexual assault, robbery, or aggravated robbery.

(b) The requirement imposed by Subsection (a)(2) does not apply to an actor who uses force against a person who is at the time of the use of force committing an offense of unlawful entry in the habitation of the actor.

Penal Code §9.33. Defense of a Third Person

A person is justified in using force or deadly force against another to protect a third person if:

1. under the circumstances as the actor reasonably believes them to be, the actor would be justified under Section 9.31 or 9.32 in using force or deadly force to protect himself against the unlawful force or unlawful deadly force he reasonably believes to be threatening the third person he seeks to protect; and
2. the actor reasonably believes that his intervention is immediately necessary to protect the third person.

Penal Code §9.34. Protection of Life or Health

(a) A person is justified in using force, but not deadly force, against another when and to the degree he reasonably believes the force is immediately necessary to prevent the other from committing suicide or inflicting serious bodily injury to himself.

(b) A person is justified in using both force and deadly force against another when and to the degree he reasonably believes the force or deadly force is immediately necessary to preserve the other's life in an emergency.

SUBCHAPTER D. PROTECTION OF PROPERTY

Penal Code §9.41. Protection of One's Own Property

(a) A person in lawful possession of land or tangible, movable property is justified in using force against another when and to the degree the actor reasonably believes the force is immediately necessary to prevent or terminate the other's trespass on the land or unlawful interference with the property.

(b) A person unlawfully dispossessed of land or tangible, movable property by another is justified in using force against the other when and to the degree the actor reasonably believes the force is immediately necessary to reenter the land or recover the property if the actor uses the force immediately or in fresh pursuit after the dispossession and:

1. the actor reasonably believes the other had no claim of right when he dispossessed the actor; or
2. the other accomplished the dispossession by using force, threat, or fraud against the actor.

Penal Code §9.42. Deadly Force to Protect Property

A person is justified in using deadly force against another to protect land or tangible, movable property:

1. if he would be justified in using force against the other under Section 9.41; and
2. when and to the degree he reasonably believes the deadly force is immediately necessary:
A. to prevent the other's imminent commission of arson, burglary, robbery, aggravated robbery, theft during the nighttime, or criminal mischief during the nighttime; or
B. to prevent the other who is fleeing immediately after committing burglary, robbery, aggravated robbery, or theft during the nighttime from escaping with the property; and
3. he reasonably believes that:
A. the land or property cannot be protected or recovered by any other means; or
B. the use of force other than deadly force to protect or recover the land or property would expose the actor or another to a substantial risk of death or serious bodily injury.

Penal Code §9.43. Protection of Third Person's Property

A person is justified in using force or deadly force against another to protect land or tangible, movable property of a third person if, under the circumstances as he reasonably believes them to be, the actor would be justified under Section 9.41 or 9.42 in using force or deadly force to protect his own land or property and:

1. the actor reasonably believes the unlawful interference constitutes attempted or consummated theft of or criminal mischief to the tangible, movable property; or
2. the actor reasonably believes that:
A. the third person has requested his protection of the land or property;
B. he has a legal duty to protect the third person's land or property; or
C. the third person whose land or property he uses force or deadly force to protect is the actor's spouse, parent, or child, resides with the actor, or is under the actor's care.

Penal Code §9.44. Use of Device to Protect Property

The justification afforded by Sections 9.41 and 9.43 applies to the use of a device to protect land or tangible, movable property if:

1. the device is not designed to cause, or known by the actor to create a substantial risk of causing, death or serious bodily injury; and
2. use of the device is reasonable under all the circumstances as the actor reasonably believes them to be when he installs the device.

SUBCHAPTER E. LAW ENFORCEMENT

Penal Code §9.51. Arrest and Search

(a) A peace officer, or a person acting in a peace officer's presence and at his direction, is justified in using force against another when and to the degree the actor reasonably believes the force is immediately necessary to make or assist in making an arrest or search, or to prevent or assist in preventing escape after arrest, if:

1. the actor reasonably believes the arrest or search is lawful or, if the arrest or search is made under a warrant, he reasonably believes the warrant is valid; and

2. before using force, the actor manifests his purpose to arrest or search and identifies himself as a peace officer or as one acting at a peace officer's direction, unless he reasonably believes his purpose and identity are already known by or cannot reasonably be made known to the person to be arrested.

(b) A person other than a peace officer (or one acting at his direction) is justified in using force against another when and to the degree the actor reasonably believes the force is immediately necessary to make or assist in making a lawful arrest, or to prevent or assist in preventing escape after lawful arrest if, before using force, the actor manifests his purpose to and the reason for the arrest or reasonably believes his purpose and the reason are already known by or cannot reasonably be made known to the person to be arrested.

(c) A peace officer is justified in using deadly force against another when and to the degree the peace officer reasonably believes the deadly force is immediately necessary to make an arrest, or to prevent escape after arrest, if the use of force would have been justified under Subsection (a) and:

1. the actor reasonably believes the conduct for which arrest is authorized Included the use or attempted use of deadly force; or

2. the actor reasonably believes there is a substantial risk that the person to be arrested will cause death or serious bodily injury to the actor or another if the arrest is delayed.

(d) A person other than a peace officer acting in a peace officer's presence and at his direction is justified in using deadly force against another when and to the degree the person reasonably believes the deadly force is immediately necessary to make a lawful arrest, or to prevent escape after a lawful arrest, if the use of force would have been justified under Subsection (b) and:

1. the actor reasonably believes the felony or offense against the public peace for which arrest is authorized included the use or attempted use of deadly force: or

2. the actor reasonably believes there is a substantial risk that the person to be arrested will cause death or serious bodily injury to another if the arrest is delayed.

(e) There is no duty to retreat before using deadly force justified by Subsection (c) or (d).

(f) Nothing in this section relating to the actor's manifestation of purpose or identity shall be construed as conflicting with any other law relating to the issuance, service, and execution of an arrest or search warrant either under the laws of this state or the United States.

(g) Deadly force may only be used under the circumstances enumerated in Subsections (c) and (d).

Penal Code §9.52. Prevention of Escape From Custody

The use of force to prevent the escape of an arrested person from custody is justifiable when the force could have been employed to effect the arrest under which the person is in custody, except that a guard employed by a correctional facility or a peace officer is justified in using any force, including deadly force, that he reasonably believes to be immediately necessary to prevent the escape of a person from the correctional facility.

Penal Code §9.53. Maintaining Security in Correctional Facility

An officer or employee of a correctional facility is justified in using force against a person in custody when and to the degree the officer or employee reasonably believes the force is necessary to maintain the security of the correctional facility, the safety or security of other persons in custody or employed by the correctional facility, or his own safety or security.

CHAPTER 12 • PUNISHMENTS

SUBCHAPTER A. GENERAL PROVISIONS

Penal Code §12.01. Punishment in Accordance with Code
(a) A person adjudged guilty of an offense under this code shall be punished in accordance with this chapter and the Code of Criminal Procedure.
(b) Penal laws enacted after the effective date of this code shall be classified for punishment purposes in accordance with this chapter.
(c) This chapter does not deprive a court of authority conferred by law to forfeit property, dissolve a corporation, suspend or cancel a license or permit, remove a person from office, cite for contempt, or impose any other civil penalty. The civil penalty may be included in the sentence.

Penal Code §12.02. Classification of Offenses
Offenses are designated as felonies or misdemeanors.

Penal Code §12.03. Classification of Misdemeanors
(a) Misdemeanors are classified according to the relative seriousness of the offense into three categories:
1. Class A misdemeanors;
2. Class B misdemeanors;
3. Class C misdemeanors.
(b) An offense designated a misdemeanor in this code without specification as to punishment or category is a Class C misdemeanor.
(c) Conviction of a Class C misdemeanor does not impose any legal disability or disadvantage.

Penal Code §12.04. Classification of Felonies
(a) Felonies are classified according to the relative seriousness of the offense into five categories:
1. capital felonies;
2. felonies of the first degree;
3. felonies of the second degree;
4. felonies of the third degree; and
5. state jail felonies.
(b) An offense designated a felony in this code without specification as to category is a state jail felony.

SUBCHAPTER B. ORDINARY MISDEMEANOR PUNISHMENTS

Penal Code §12.21. Class A Misdemeanor
An individual adjudged guilty of a Class A misdemeanor shall be punished by:
1. a fine not to exceed $4,000;
2. confinement in jail for a term not to exceed one year; or
3. both such fine and confinement.

Penal Code §12.22. Class B Misdemeanor
An individual adjudged guilty of a Class B misdemeanor shall be punished by:
1. a fine not to exceed $2,000;
2. confinement in jail for a term not to exceed 180 days; or
3. both such fine and confinement.

Penal Code §12.23. Class C Misdemeanor

An individual adjudged guilty of a Class C misdemeanor shall be punished by a fine not to exceed $500.

SUBCHAPTER C. ORDINARY FELONY PUNISHMENTS

Penal Code §12.31. Capital Felony

(a) An individual adjudged guilty of a capital felony in a case in which the state seeks the death penalty shall be punished by imprisonment in the institutional division for life or by death. An individual adjudged guilty of a capital felony in a case in which the state does not seek the death penalty shall be punished by imprisonment in the institutional division for life.

(b) In a capital felony trial in which the state seeks the death penalty, prospective jurors shall be informed that a sentence of life imprisonment or death is mandatory on conviction of a capital felony. In a capital felony trial in which the state does not seek the death penalty, prospective jurors shall be informed that the state is not seeking the death penalty and that a sentence of life imprisonment is mandatory on conviction of the capital felony.

Penal Code §12.32. First Degree Felony Punishment

(a) An individual adjudged guilty of a felony of the first degree shall be punished by imprisonment in the institutional division for life or for any term of not more than 99 years or less than 5 years.

(b) In addition to imprisonment, an individual adjudged guilty of a felony of the first degree may be punished by a fine not to exceed $10,000.

Penal Code §12.33. Second Degree Felony Punishment

(a) An individual adjudged guilty of a felony of the second degree shall be punished by imprisonment in the institutional division for any term of not more than 20 years or less than 2 years.

(b) In addition to imprisonment, an individual adjudged guilty of a felony of the second degree may be punished by a fine not to exceed $10,000.

Penal Code §12.34. Third Degree Felony Punishment

(a) An individual adjudged guilty of a felony of the third degree shall be punished by imprisonment in the institutional division for any term of not more than 10 years or less than 2 years.

(b) In addition to imprisonment, an individual adjudged guilty of a felony of the third degree may be punished by a fine not to exceed $10,000.

Penal Code §12.35. State Jail Felony Punishment

(a) Except as provided by Subsection (c), an individual adjudged guilty of a state jail felony shall be punished by confinement in a state jail for any term of not more than two years or less than 180 days.

(b) In addition to confinement, an individual adjudged guilty of a state jail felony may be punished by a fine not to exceed $10,000.

(c) An individual adjudged guilty of a state jail felony shall be punished for a third degree felony if it is shown on the trial of the offense that:

1. a deadly weapon as defined by Section 1.07 was used or exhibited during the commission of the offense or during immediate flight following the commission of the offense, and that the individual used or exhibited the deadly weapon or was a party to the offense and knew that a deadly weapon would be used or exhibited; or

2. the individual has previously been finally convicted of any felony:

A. listed in Section 3g(a)(1), Article 42.12, Code of Criminal Procedure; or

B. for which the judgment contains an affirmative finding under Section 3g(a)(2), Article 42.12, Code of Criminal Procedure.

SUBCHAPTER E. CORPORATIONS AND ASSOCIATIONS

Penal Code §12.51. Authorized Punishments for Corporations and Associations

(a) If a corporation or association is adjudged guilty of an offense that provides a penalty consisting of a fine only, a court may sentence the corporation or association to pay a fine in an amount fixed by the court, not to exceed the fine provided by the offense.

(b) If a corporation or association is adjudged guilty of an offense that provides a penalty including imprisonment, or that provides no specific penalty, a court may sentence the corporation or association to pay a fine in an amount fixed by the court, not to exceed:

1. $20,000 if the offense is a felony of any category;
2. $10,000 if the offense is a Class A or Class B misdemeanor;
3. $2,000 if the offense is a Class C misdemeanor; or
4. $50,000 if, as a result of an offense classified as a felony or Class A misdemeanor, an individual suffers serious bodily injury or death.

(c) In lieu of the fines authorized by Subsections (a), (b)(1), (b)(2), and (b)(4), if a court finds that the corporation or association gained money or property or caused personal injury or death, property damage, or other loss through the commission of a felony or Class A or Class B misdemeanor, the court may sentence the corporation or association to pay a fine in an amount fixed by the court, not to exceed double the amount gained or caused by the corporation or association to be lost or damaged, whichever is greater.

(d) In addition to any sentence that may be imposed by this section, a corporation or association that has been adjudged guilty of an offense may be ordered by the court to give notice of the conviction to any person the court deems appropriate.

(e) On conviction of a corporation or association, the court shall notify the attorney general of that fact.

CHAPTER 16 • CRIMINAL INSTRUMENTS AND OFFENSES INVOLVING CERTAIN COMMUNICATIONS

Penal Code §16.01. Unlawful Use Of Criminal Instrument

(a) A person commits an offense if:
1. he possesses a criminal instrument with intent to use it in the commission of an offense; or
2. with knowledge of its character and with intent to use or aid or permit another to use in the commission of an offense, he manufactures, adapts, sells, installs, or sets up a criminal instrument.

(b) For the purpose of this section, "criminal instrument" means anything, the possession, manufacture, or sale of which is not otherwise an offense, that is specially designed, made, or adapted for use in the commission of an offense.

(c) An offense under Subsection (a)(1) is one category lower than the offense intended. An offense under Subsection (a)(2) is a state jail felony.

CHAPTER 19 • CRIMINAL HOMICIDE

Penal Code §19.01. Types Of Criminal Homicide

(a) A person commits criminal homicide if he intentionally, knowingly, recklessly, or with criminal negligence causes the death of an individual.

(b) Criminal homicide is murder, capital murder, manslaughter, or criminally negligent homicide.

Penal Code §19.02. Murder

(a) In this section:
1. "Adequate cause" means cause that would commonly produce a degree of anger, rage, resentment, or terror in a person of ordinary temper, sufficient to render the mind incapable of cool reflection.

2. "Sudden passion" means passion directly caused by and arising out of provocation by the individual killed or another acting with the person killed which passion arises at the time of the offense and is not solely the result of former provocation.

(b) A person commits an offense if he:

1. intentionally or knowingly causes the death of an individual;
2. Intends to cause serious bodily injury and commits an act clearly dangerous to human life that causes the death of an individual; or
3. commits or attempts to commit a felony, other than manslaughter, and in the course of and in furtherance of the commission or attempt, or in immediate flight from the commission or attempt, he commits or attempts to commit an act clearly dangerous to human life that causes the death of an individual.

(c) Except as provided by Subsection (d), an offense under this section is a felony of the first degree.

(d) At the punishment stage of a trial, the defendant may raise the issue as to whether he caused the death under the immediate influence of sudden passion arising from an adequate cause. If the defendant proves the issue in the affirmative by a preponderance of the evidence, the offense is a felony of the second degree.

Penal Code §19.03. Capital Murder.

(a) A person commits an offense if he commits murder as defined under Section 19.02(b)(1) and:

1. the person murders a peace officer or fireman who is acting in the lawful discharge of an official duty and who the person knows is a peace officer or fireman;
2. the person intentionally commits the murder in the course of committing or attempting to commit kidnapping, burglary, robbery, aggravated sexual assault, arson, or obstruction or retaliation;
3. the person commits the murder for remuneration or the promise of remuneration or employs another to commit the murder for remuneration or the promise of remuneration;
4. the person commits the murder while escaping or attempting to escape from a penal institution;
5. the person, while incarcerated in a penal institution, murders another:
A. who is employed in the operation of the penal institution; or
B. with the intent to establish, maintain, or participate in a combination or in the profits of a combination;
6. the person:
A. while incarcerated for an offense under this section or Section 19.02, murders another; or
B. while serving a sentence of life imprisonment or a term of 99 years for an offense under Section 20.04, 22.021, or 29.03, murders another;
7. the person murders more than one person:
A. during the same criminal transaction; or
B. during different criminal transactions but the murders are committed pursuant to the same scheme or course of conduct; or
8. the person murders an individual under six years of age.

(b) An offense under this section is a capital felony.

(c) If the jury or, when authorized by law, the judge does not find beyond a reasonable doubt that the defendant is guilty of an offense under this section, he may be convicted of murder or of any other lesser included offense.

Penal Code §19.04. Manslaughter

(a) A person commits an offense if he recklessly causes the death of an individual.

(b) An offense under this section is a felony of the second degree.

Penal Code §19.05. Criminally Negligent Homicide

(a) A person commits an offense if he causes the death of an individual by criminal negligence.

(b) An offense under this section is a state jail felony.

CHAPTER 20 • KIDNAPPING AND FALSE IMPRISONMENT

Penal Code §20.01. Definitions

In this chapter:

1. "Restrain" means to restrict a person's movements without consent, so as to interfere substantially with his liberty, by moving him from one place to another or by confining him. Restraint is "without consent" if it is accomplished by:
A. force, intimidation, or deception; or

B. any means, including acquiescence of the victim, if he is a child less than 14 years of age or an incompetent person and the parent, guardian, or person or institution acting in loco parentis has not acquiesced in the movement or confinement.
2. "Abduct" means to restrain a person with intent to prevent his liberation by:
A. secreting or holding him in a place where he is not likely to be found; or
B. using or threatening to use deadly force.
3. "Relative" means a parent or stepparent, ancestor, sibling, or uncle or aunt, including an adoptive relative of the same degree through marriage or adoption.

Penal Code §20.02. False Imprisonment

(a) A person commits an offense if he intentionally or knowingly restrains another person.
(b) It is an affirmative defense to prosecution under this section that:
1. the person restrained was a child younger than 14 years of age;
2. the actor was a relative of the child; and
3. the actor's sole intent was to assume lawful control of the child.
(c) An offense under this section is a Class B misdemeanor unless the actor recklessly exposes the victim to a substantial risk of serious bodily injury, in which event it is a felony of the third degree.
(d) It is no offense to detain or move another under this section when it is for the purpose of effecting a lawful arrest or detaining an individual lawfully arrested.

Penal Code §20.03. Kidnapping

(a) A person commits an offense if he intentionally or knowingly abducts another person.
(b) It is an affirmative defense to prosecution under this section that:
1. the abduction was not coupled with intent to use or to threaten to use deadly force;
2. the actor was a relative of the person abducted; and
3. the actor's sole intent was to assume lawful control of the victim.
(c) An offense under this section is a felony of the third degree.

Penal Code §20.04. Aggravated Kidnapping

(a) A person commits an offense if he intentionally or knowingly abducts another person with the intent to:
(1) hold him for ransom or reward;
(2) use him as a shield or hostage;
(3) facilitate the commission of a felony or the flight after the attempt or commission of a felony;
(4) inflict bodily injury on him or violate or abuse him sexually;
(5) terrorize him or a third person; or
(6) interfere with the performance of any governmental or political function.
(b) A person commits an offense if the person intentionally or knowingly abducts another person and uses or exhibits a deadly weapon during the commission of the offense.
(c) Except as provided by Subsection (d), an offense under this section is a felony of the first degree.
(d) At the punishment stage of a trial, the defendant may raise the issue as to whether he voluntarily released the victim in a safe place. If the defendant proves the issue in the affirmative by a preponderance of the evidence, the offense is a felony of the second degree.

CHAPTER 22 • ASSAULTIVE OFFENSES

Penal Code §22.01. Assault

(a) A person commits an offense if the person:
1. intentionally, knowingly, or recklessly causes bodily injury to another, including the person's spouse;
2. intentionally or knowingly threatens another with imminent bodily injury, including the person's spouse; or
3. intentionally or knowingly causes physical contact with another when the person knows or should reasonably believe that the other will regard the contact as offensive or provocative.
(b) An offense under Subsection (a)(1) is a Class A misdemeanor, except that the offense is a felony of the third degree if the offense is committed against a person the actor knows is a public servant while the public servant is lawfully discharging an official duty, or in retaliation or on account of an exercise of official power or performance of an official duty as a public servant.

(c) An offense under Subsection (a)(2) or (3) is a Class C misdemeanor, except that an offense under Subsection (a)(3) is a Class A misdemeanor if the offense was committed against an elderly individual or disabled individual, as those terms are defined by Section 22.04.

(d) For purposes of Subsection (b), the actor is presumed to have known the person assaulted was a public servant if the person was wearing a distinctive uniform or badge indicating the person's employment as a public servant.

Penal Code §22.02. Aggravated Assault

(a) A person commits an offense if the person commits assault as defined in Section 22.01 and the person:

1. causes serious bodily injury to another, including the person's spouse; or
2. uses or exhibits a deadly weapon during the commission of the assault.

(b) An offense under this section is a felony of the second degree, except that the offense is a felony of the first degree if the offense is committed:

1. by a public servant acting under color of the servant's office or employment;
2. against a person the actor knows is a public servant while the public servant is lawfully discharging an official duty, or in retaliation or on account of an exercise of official power or performance of an official duty as a public servant; or
3. in retaliation against or on account of the service of another as a witness, prospective witness, informant, or person who has reported the occurrence of a crime.

(c) The actor is presumed to have known the person assaulted was a public servant if the person was wearing a distinctive uniform or badge indicating the person's employment as a public servant.

Penal Code §22.05. Deadly Conduct

(a) A person commits an offense if he recklessly engages in conduct that places another in imminent danger of serious bodily injury.

(b) A person commits an offense if he knowingly discharges a firearm at or in the direction of:

1. one or more individuals; or
2. a habitation, building, or vehicle and is reckless as to whether the habitation, building, or vehicle is occupied.

(c) Recklessness and danger are presumed if the actor knowingly pointed a firearm at or in the direction of another whether or not the actor believed the firearm to be loaded.

(d) For purposes of this section, "building," "habitation," and "vehicle" have the meanings assigned those terms by Section 30.01.

(e) An offense under Subsection (a) is a Class A misdemeanor. An offense under Subsection (b) is a felony of the third degree.

Penal Code §22.08. Aiding Suicide

(a) A person commits an offense if, with intent to promote or assist the commission of suicide by another, he aids or attempts to aid the other to commit or attempt to commit suicide.

(b) An offense under this section is a Class C misdemeanor unless the actor's conduct causes suicide or attempted suicide that results in serious bodily injury, in which event the offense is a state jail felony.

CHAPTER 28 • ARSON, CRIMINAL MISCHIEF, AND OTHER PROPERTY DAMAGE OR DESTRUCTION

Penal Code §28.01. Definitions

In this chapter:

1. "Habitation" means a structure or vehicle that is adapted for the overnight accommodation of persons and includes:
A. each separately secured or occupied portion of the structure or vehicle; and
B. each structure appurtenant to or connected with the structure or vehicle.
2. "Building" means any structure or enclosure intended for use or occupation as a habitation or for some purpose of trade, manufacture, ornament, or use.
3. "Property" means:
A. real property
B. tangible or intangible personal property, including anything severed from land; or
C. a document, including money, that represents or embodies anything of value.
4. "Vehicle" includes any device in, on, or by which any person or property is or may be propelled, moved, or drawn in the normal course of commerce or transportation.

5. "Open-space land" means real property that is undeveloped for the purpose of human habitation.
6. "Controlled burning" means the burning of unwanted vegetation with the consent of the owner of the property on which the vegetation is located and in such a manner that the fire is controlled and limited to a designated area.

Penal Code §28.02. Arson

(a) A person commits an offense if he starts a fire or causes an explosion with intent to destroy or damage:
1. any vegetation, fence, or structure on open-space land; or
2. any building, habitation, or vehicle:
A. knowing that it is within the limits of an incorporated city or town;
B. knowing that it is insured against damage or destruction;
C. knowing that it is subject to a mortgage or other security interest;
D. knowing that it is located on property belonging to another;
E. knowing that it has located within it property belonging to another; or
F. when he is reckless about whether the burning or explosion will endanger the life of some individual or the safety of the property of another.
(b) It is an exception to the application of Subsection (a)(1) that the fire or explosion was a part of the controlled burning of open-space land.
(c) It is a defense to prosecution under Subsection (a)(2)(A) that prior to starting the fire or causing the explosion, the actor obtained a permit or other written authorization granted in accordance with a city ordinance, if any, regulating fires and explosions.
(d) An offense under this section is a felony of the second degree, unless bodily injury or death is suffered by any person by reason of the commission of the offense, in which event it is a felony of the first degree.

Penal Code §28.03. Criminal Mischief

(a) A person commits an offense if, without the effective consent of the owner:
1. he intentionally or knowingly damages or destroys the tangible property of the owner;
2. he intentionally or knowingly tampers with the tangible property of the owner and causes pecuniary loss or substantial inconvenience to the owner or a third person; or
3. he intentionally or knowingly makes markings, including inscriptions, slogans, drawings, or paintings, on the tangible property of the owner.
(b) Except as provided by Subsection (f), an offense under this section is:
1. a Class C misdemeanor if:
A. the amount of pecuniary loss is less than $20; or
B. except as provided in Subdivision (3)(B), it causes substantial inconvenience to others;
2. a Class B misdemeanor if the amount of pecuniary loss is $20 or more but less than $500;
3. a Class A misdemeanor if the amount of pecuniary loss is:
A. $500 or more but less than $1,500; or
B. less than $1,500 and the actor causes in whole or in part impairment or interruption of public communications, public transportation, public water, gas, or power supply, or other public service, or causes to be diverted in whole, in part, or in any manner, including installation or removal of any device for any such purpose, any public communications, public water, gas, or power supply;
4. a state jail felony if the amount of pecuniary loss is $1,500 or more but less than $20,000;
5. a felony of the third degree if the amount of the pecuniary loss is $20,000 or more but less than $100,000;
6. a felony of the second degree if the amount of pecuniary loss is $100,000 or more but less than $200,000; or
7. a felony of the first degree if the amount of pecuniary loss is $200,000 or more.

Penal Code §28.04. Reckless Damage Or Destruction

(a) A person commits an offense if, without the effective consent of the owner, he recklessly damages or destroys property of the owner.
(b) An offense under this section is a Class C misdemeanor.

Penal Code §28.05. Actor's Interest In Property

It is no defense to prosecution under this chapter that the actor has an interest in the property damaged or destroyed if another person also has an interest that the actor is not entitled to infringe.

Penal Code §28.07. Interference With Railroad Property

(b) A person commits an offense if the person:

1. throws an object or discharges a firearm or weapon at a train or railmounted work equipment

(c) An offense under Subsection (b)(1) is a Class B misdemeanor unless the person causes bodily injury to another, in which event the offense is a felony of the third degree.

CHAPTER 29 • ROBBERY

Penal Code §29.02. Robbery

(a) A person commits an offense if, in the course of committing theft as defined in Chapter 31 and with intent to obtain or maintain control of the property, he:

1. intentionally, knowingly, or recklessly causes bodily injury to another; or

2. intentionally or knowingly threatens or places another in fear of imminent bodily injury or death.

(b) An offense under this section is a felony of the second degree.

Penal Code §29.03. Aggravated Robbery

(a) A person commits an offense if he commits robbery as defined in Section 29.02, and he:

1. causes serious bodily injury to another;

2. uses or exhibits a deadly weapon; or

3. causes bodily injury to another person or threatens or places another person in fear of imminent bodily injury or death, if the other person is:

A. 65 years of age or older; or

B. a disabled person.

(b) An offense under this section is a felony of the first degree.

(c) In this section, "disabled person" means an individual with a mental, physical, or developmental disability who is substantially unable to protect himself from harm.

CHAPTER 30 • BURGLARY AND CRIMINAL TRESPASS

Penal Code §30.02. Burglary

(a) A person commits an offense if, without the effective consent of the owner, he:

1. enters a habitation, or a building (or any portion of a building) not then open to the public, with intent to commit a felony or theft; or

2. remains concealed, with intent to commit a felony or theft, in a building or habitation; or

3. enters a building or habitation and commits or attempts to commit a felony or theft.

(b) For purposes of this section, "enter" means to intrude:

1. any part of the body; or

2. any physical object connected with the body.

(c) Except as provided in Subsection (d), an offense under this section is a:

1. state jail felony if committed in a building other than a habitation; or

2. felony of the second degree if committed in a habitation.

(d) An offense under this section is a felony of the first degree if:

(1) the premises are a habitation; and

(2) any party to the offense entered the habitation with intent to commit a felony other than felony theft or committed or attempted to commit a felony other than felony theft.

Penal Code §30.04. Burglary Of Vehicles

(a) A person commits an offense if, without the effective consent of the owner, he breaks into or enters a vehicle or any part of a vehicle with intent to commit any felony or theft.

(b) For purposes of this section, "enter" means to intrude:

1. any part of the body; or

2. any physical object connected with the body.

(c) An offense under this section is a Class A misdemeanor.

Penal Code §30.05. Criminal Trespass

(a) A person commits an offense if he enters or remains on property or in a building of another without effective consent and he:
1. had notice that the entry was forbidden; or
2. received notice to depart but failed to do so.
(b) For purposes of this section:
1. "Entry" means the intrusion of the entire body.
2. "Notice" means:
A. oral or written communication by the owner or someone with apparent authority to act for the owner;
B. fencing or other enclosure obviously designed to exclude intruders or to contain livestock;
C. a sign or signs posted on the property or at the entrance to the building, reasonably likely to come to the attention of intruders, indicating that entry is forbidden; or
D. the visible presence on the property of a crop grown for human consumption that is under cultivation, in the process of being harvested, or marketable if harvested at the time of entry.
3. "Shelter center" has the meaning assigned by Section 51.002(1), Human Resources Code.
(c) It is a defense to prosecution under this section that the actor at the time of the offense was a fire fighter or emergency medical services personnel, as that term is defined by Section 773.003, Health and Safety Code, acting in the lawful discharge of an official duty under exigent circumstances.
(d) An offense under this section is a Class B misdemeanor unless it is committed in a habitation or a shelter center or unless the actor carries a deadly weapon on or about his person during the commission of the offense, in which event it is a Class A misdemeanor.

CHAPTER 37 • PERJURY AND OTHER FALSIFICATION

Penal Code §37.02. Perjury

(a) A person commits an offense if, with intent to deceive and with knowledge of the statement's meaning:
1. he makes a false statement under oath or swears to the truth of a false statement previously made and the statement is required or authorized by law to be made under oath; or
2. he makes a false unsworn declaration under Chapter 132, Civil Practice and Remedies Code.
(b) An offense under this section is a Class A misdemeanor.

Penal Code §37.03. Aggravated Perjury

(a) A person commits an offense if he commits perjury as defined in Section 37.02, and the false statement:
1. is made during or in connection with an official proceeding; and
2. is material.
(b) An offense under this section Is a felony of the third degree.

Penal Code §37.08. False Report To Peace Officer

(a) A person commits an offense if, with intent to deceive, he knowingly makes a false statement to a peace officer conducting a criminal investigation and the statement is material to the investigation.
(b) An offense under this section is a Class B misdemeanor.

Penal Code §37.09. Tampering With Or Fabricating Physical Evidence

(a) A person commits an offense if, knowing that an investigation or official proceeding is pending or in progress, he:
1. alters, destroys, or conceals any record, document, or thing with intent to impair its verity, legibility, or availability as evidence in the investigation or official proceeding; or
2. makes, presents, or uses any record, document, or thing with knowledge of its falsity and with intent to affect the course or outcome of the investigation or official proceeding.
(b) This section shall not apply if the record, document, or thing concealed is privileged or is the work product of the parties to the investigation or official proceeding.
(c) An offense under this section is a felony of the third degree.

Penal Code §38.03. Resisting Arrest, Search, Or Transportation

(a) A person commits an offense if he intentionally prevents or obstructs a person he knows is a peace officer or a person acting in a peace officer's presence and at his direction from effecting an arrest, search, or transportation of the actor or another by using force against the peace officer or another.

(b) It is no defense to prosecution under this section that the arrest or search was unlawful.

(c) Except as provided in Subsection (d), an offense under this section is a Class A misdemeanor.

(d) An offense under this section is a felony of the third degree if the actor uses a deadly weapon to resist the arrest or search.

Penal Code §38.06. Escape

(a) A person commits an offense if he escapes from custody when he is:

1. under arrest for, charged with, or convicted of an offense; or
2. in custody pursuant to a lawful order of a court.

(b) Except as provided in Subsections (c), (d), and (e), an offense under this section is a Class A misdemeanor.

(c) An offense under this section is a felony of the third degree if the actor:

1. is under arrest for, charged with, or convicted of a felony; or
2. is confined in a secure correctional facility.

(d) An offense under this section is a felony of the second degree if the actor to effect his escape causes bodily injury.

(e) An offense under this section is a felony of the first degree if to effect his escape the actor:

1. causes serious bodily injury; or
2. uses or threatens to use a deadly weapon.

Penal Code §38.07. Permitting Or Facilitating Escape

(a) An official or employee of a correctional facility commits an offense if he knowingly permits or facilitates the escape of a person in custody.

(b) A person commits an offense if he knowingly causes or facilitates the escape of one who is in custody pursuant to:

1. an allegation or adjudication of delinquency; or
2. involuntary commitment for mental illness under Subtitle C, Title 7, Health and Safety Code, or for chemical dependency under Chapter 462, Health and Safety Code.

(c) Except as provided in Subsections (d) and (e), an offense under this section is a Class A misdemeanor.

(d) An offense under this section is a felony of the third degree if the person in custody:

1. was under arrest for, charged with, or convicted of a felony; or
2. was confined in a correctional facility other than a secure correctional facility after conviction of a felony.

(e) An offense under this section is a felony of the second degree if:

1. the actor or the person in custody used or threatened to use a deadly weapon to effect the escape; or
2. the person in custody was confined in a secure correctional facility after conviction of a felony.

Penal Code §38.09. Implements For Escape

(a) A person commits an offense if, with intent to facilitate escape, he introduces into a correctional facility, or provides a person in custody or an inmate with, a deadly weapon or anything that may be useful for escape.

(b) An offense under this section is a felony of the third degree unless the actor introduced or provided a deadly weapon, in which event the offense is a felony of the second degree.

Penal Code §38.14. Taking Or Attempting To Take Weapon From Peace Officer

(a) In this section, "firearm" has the meanings assigned by Section 46.01.

(b) A person commits an offense if the person intentionally or knowingly and with force takes or attempts to take from a peace officer the officer's firearm, nightstick, or personal protection chemical dispensing device with the intention of harming the officer or a third person.

(c) The actor is presumed to have known that the peace officer was a peace officer if the officer was wearing a distinctive uniform or badge indicating his employment, or if the officer identified himself as a peace officer.

(d) It is a defense to prosecution under this section that the defendant took or attempted to take the weapon from a peace officer who was using force against the defendant or another in excess of the amount of force permitted by law.

(e) An offense under this section is a state jail felony.

Penal Code §38.15. Interference With Public Duties

(a) A person commits an offense if the person with criminal negligence interrupts, disrupts, impedes, or otherwise interferes with:

1. a peace officer while the peace officer is performing a duty or exercising authority imposed or granted by law;
(b) An offense under this section is a Class B misdemeanor.

CHAPTER 42 • DISORDERLY CONDUCT AND RELATED OFFENSES

Penal Code §42.01. Disorderly Conduct
(a) A person commits an offense if he intentionally or knowingly:
1. uses abusive, indecent, profane, or vulgar language in a public place, and the language by its very utterance tends to incite an immediate breach of the peace;
2. makes an offensive gesture or display in a public place, and the gesture or display tends to incite an immediate breach of the peace;
3. creates, by chemical means, a noxious and unreasonable odor in a public place;
4. abuses or threatens a person in a public place in an obviously offensive manner;
5. makes unreasonable noise in a public place other than a sport shooting range, as defined by Section 250.001, Local Government Code, or in or near a private residence that he has no right to occupy;
6. fights with another in a public place;
7. enters on the property of another and for a lewd or unlawful purpose looks into a dwelling on the property through any window or other opening in the dwelling;
8. while on the premises of a hotel or comparable establishment, for a lewd or unlawful purpose looks into a guest room not his own through a window or other opening in the room;
9. discharges a firearm in a public place other than a public road or a sport shooting range, as defined by Section 250.001, Local Government Code;
10. displays a firearm or other deadly weapon in a public place in a manner calculated to alarm;
11. discharges a firearm on or across a public road; or
12. exposes his anus or genitals in a public place and is reckless about whether another may be present who will be offended or alarmed by his act.
(b) It is a defense to prosecution under Subsection (a)(4) that the actor had significant provocation for his abusive or threatening conduct.
(c) For purposes of this section:
(1) an act is deemed to occur in a public place or near a private residence if it produces its offensive or proscribed consequences in the public place or near a private residence; and
(2) a noise is presumed to be unreasonable if the noise exceeds a decibel level of 85 after the person making the noise receives notice from a magistrate or peace officer that the noise is a public nuisance.
(d) An offense under this section is a Class C misdemeanor unless committed under Subsection (a)(9) or (a)(10), in which event it is a Class B misdemeanor.

Penal Code § 42.12. Discharge Of Firearm In Certain Municipalities.
(a) A person commits an offense if the person recklessly discharges a firearm inside the corporate limits of a municipality having a population of 100,000 or more.
(b) An offense under this section is a Class A misdemeanor.
(c) If conduct constituting an offense under this section also constitutes an offense under another section of this code, the person may be prosecuted under either section.
(d) Subsection (a) does not affect the authority of a municipality to enact an ordinance which prohibits the discharge of a firearm.

NOTES

NOTES

CHAPTER 46 • WEAPONS

Penal Code §46.01. Definitions

In this chapter:
1. "Club" means an instrument that is specially designed, made, or adapted for the purpose of inflicting serious bodily injury or death by striking a person with the instrument, and includes but is not limited to the following:
A. blackjack;
B. nightstick;
C. mace;
D. tomahawk.
2. "Explosive weapon" means any explosive or incendiary bomb, grenade, rocket, or mine, that is designed, made, or adapted for the purpose of inflicting serious bodily injury, death, or substantial property damage, or for the principal purpose of causing such a loud report as to cause undue public alarm or terror, and includes a device designed, made, or adapted for delivery or shooting an explosive weapon.
3. "Firearm" means any device designed, made, or adapted to expel a projectile through a barrel by using the energy generated by an explosion or burning substance or any device readily convertible to that use. Firearm does not include antique or curio firearms that were manufactured prior to 1899 and that may have, as an integral part, a folding knife blade or other characteristics of weapons made illegal by this chapter.
4. "Firearm silencer" means any device designed, made, or adapted to muffle the report of a firearm.
5. "Handgun" means any firearm that is designed, made, or adapted to be fired with one hand.
6. "Illegal knife" means a:
A. knife with a blade over five and one-half inches;
B. hand instrument designed to cut or stab another by being thrown;
C. dagger, including but not limited to a dirk, stiletto, and poniard;
D. bowie knife;
E. sword; or
F. spear.
7. "Knife" means any bladed hand instrument that Is capable of inflicting serious bodily injury or death by cutting or stabbing a person with the instrument.
8. "Knuckles" means any instrument that consists of finger rings or guards made of a hard substance and that is designed, made, or adapted for the purpose of inflicting serious bodily injury or death by striking a person with a fist enclosed In the knuckles.
9. "Machine gun" means any firearm that is capable of shooting more than two shots automatically, without manual reloading, by a single function of the trigger.
10. "Short-barrel firearm" means a rifle with a barrel length of less than 16 Inches or a shotgun with a barrel length of less than 18 Inches, or any weapon made from a shotgun or rifle If, as altered, it has an overall length of less than 26 inches.
11. "Switchblade knife" means any knife that has a blade that folds, closes, or retracts into the handle or sheath, and that:
A. opens automatically by pressure applied to a button or other device located on the handle; or
B. opens or releases a blade from the handle or sheath by the force of gravity or by the application of centrifugal force.
12. "Armor-piercing ammunition" means handgun ammunition that is designed primarily for the purpose of penetrating metal or body armor and to be used principally in pistols and revolvers.
13. "Hoax bomb" means a device that:

A. reasonably appears to be an explosive or incendiary device; or (B) by its design causes alarm or reaction of any type by an official of a public safety agency or a volunteer agency organized to deal with emergencies.

14. "Chemical dispensing device" means a device, other than a small chemical dispenser sold commercially for personal protection, that is designed, made, or adapted for the purpose of dispensing a substance capable of causing an adverse psychological or physiological effect on a human being.

15. "Racetrack" has the meaning assigned that term by the Texas Racing Act (Article 179e, Vernon's Texas Civil Statutes).

16. "Zip gun" means a device or combination of devices that was not originally a firearm and is adapted to expel a projectile through a smooth-bore or rifled-bore barrel by using the energy generated by an explosion or burning substance.

Penal Code §46.02. Unlawful Carrying Weapons.

(a) A person commits an offense if he intentionally, knowingly, or recklessly carries on or about his person a handgun, illegal knife, or club.

(b) It is a defense to prosecution under this section that the actor was, at the time of the commission of the offense:

(1) in the actual discharge of his official duties as a member of the armed forces or state military forces as defined by Section 431.001, Government Code, or as a guard employed by a penal institution;

(2) on his own premises or premises under his control unless he is an employee or agent of the owner of the premises and his primary responsibility is to act in the capacity of a security guard to protect persons or property, in which event he must comply with Subdivision (5);

(3) traveling;

(4) engaging in lawful hunting, fishing, or other sporting activity on the immediate premises where the activity is conducted, or was directly en route between the premises and the actor's residence, if the weapon is a type commonly used in the activity; or

(5) a person who holds a security officer commission issued by the Texas Board of Private Investigators and Private Security Agencies, if:

(A) he is engaged in the performance of his duties as a security officer or traveling to and from his place of assignment;

(B) he is wearing a distinctive uniform; and

(C) the weapon is in plain view; or

<Note: There is no paragraph (6). It was deleted by SB 15 in 1995.>

<Note: Three paragraphs numbered (7) were enacted in 1995:>

(7) <from SB 60> carrying a concealed handgun and a valid license issued under Article 4413 (29ee), Revised Statutes, to carry a concealed handgun of the same category as the handgun the person is carrying.

(7) <from SB 538> a holder of an alcoholic beverage permit or license or an employee of a holder of an alcoholic beverage permit or license if the actor is supervising the operation of the permitted or licensed premises.

(7) <from HB 713> a person who holds a security officer commission and a personal protection authorization issued by the Texas Board of Private Investigators and Private Security Agencies and who is providing personal protection under the Private Investigators and Private Security Agencies Act (Article 4413(29bb), Vernon's Texas Civil Statutes).

(c) It is a defense to prosecution under this section for the offense of carrying a club that the actor was, at the time of the commission of the offense, a noncommissioned security guard at an institution of higher education who carried a nightstick or similar club, and who had undergone 15 hours of training in the proper use of the club, including at least seven hours of training in the use of the club for nonviolent restraint. For the purposes of this section, "nonviolent restraint" means the use of reasonable force, not intended and not likely to inflict bodily injury.

(d) It is a defense to prosecution under this section for the offense of carrying a firearm or carrying a club that the actor was, at the time of the commission of the offense, a public security officer employed by the adjutant general under Section 431.029, Government Code, and was performing official duties or traveling to or from a place of duty.

(e) Except as provided by Subsection (f), an offense under this section is a Class A misdemeanor.

(f) An offense under this section is a felony of the third degree if the offense is committed on any premises licensed or issued a permit by this state for the sale of alcoholic beverages.

Penal Code §46.03. Places Weapons Prohibited

(a) A person commits an offense if, with a firearm, illegal knife, club, or prohibited weapon listed in Section 46.05a), he intentionally, knowingly, or recklessly goes:

1. on the physical premises of a school, an educational institution, or a passenger transportation vehicle of a school or an educational institution, whether the school or educational institution is public or private, unless pursuant to written regulations or written authorization of the Institution;
2. on the premises of a polling place on the day of an election or while early voting is in progress;
3. in any government court or offices utilized by the court, unless pursuant to written regulations or written authorization of the court;
4. on the premises of a racetrack; or
5. into a secured area of an airport.

(b) It is a defense to prosecution under Subsections (a)(1)-(4) that the actor possessed a firearm while in the actual discharge of his official duties as a peace officer or a member of the armed forces or national guard or a guard employed by a penal institution, or an officer of the court.

(c) In this section "secured area" means an area of an airport terminal building to which access is controlled by the inspection of persons and property under federal law.

(d) It is a defense to prosecution under Subsection (a) that the actor possessed a firearm or club while traveling to or from the actor's place of assignment or in the actual discharge of duties as:

(1) a member of the armed forces or national guard;
(2) a guard employed by a penal institution;
(3) a security officer commissioned by the Texas Board of Private Investigators and Private Security Agencies if:
(A) the actor is wearing a distinctive uniform; and
(B) the firearm or club is in plain view; or
(5) a security officer who holds a personal protection authorization under the Private Investigators and Private Security Agencies Act (Article 4413(29bb), Vernon's Texas Civil Statutes).

(e) It is a defense to prosecution under Subsection (a)(5) that the actor checked all firearms as baggage in accordance with federal or state law or regulations before entering a secured area.

(f) It is not a defense to prosecution under this section that the actor possessed a handgun and was licensed to carry a concealed handgun under Article 4413 (29ee), Revised Statutes.

(g) An offense under this section is a third degree felony.

Penal Code § 46.035. Unlawful Carrying Of Handgun By License Holder.

(a) A license holder commits an offense if the license holder carries a handgun on or about the license holder's person under the authority of Article 4413 (29ee), Revised Statutes, and intentionally fails to conceal the handgun.

(b) A license holder commits an offense if the license holder intentionally, knowingly, or recklessly carries a handgun under the authority of Article 4413 (29ee), Revised Statutes, regardless of whether the handgun is concealed, on or about the license holder's person:

(1) on the premises of a business that has a permit or license issued under Chapter 25, 28, 32, or 69, Alcoholic Beverage Code, if the business derives 51 percent or more of its income from the sale of alcoholic beverages for on-premises consumption;
(2) on the premises where a high school, collegiate, or professional sporting event or interscholastic event is taking place, unless the license holder is a participant in the event and a handgun is used in the event;
(3) on the premises of a correctional facility;

(4) on the premises of a hospital licensed under Chapter 241, Health and Safety Code, or on the premises of a nursing home licensed under Chapter 242, Health and Safety Code, unless the license holder has written authorization of the hospital or nursing home administration, as appropriate;

(5) in an amusement park; or

(6) on the premises of a church, synagogue, or other established place of religious worship.

(c) A license holder commits an offense if the license holder intentionally, knowingly, or recklessly carries a handgun under the authority of Article 4413 (29ee), Revised Statutes, regardless of whether the handgun is concealed, at any meeting of a governmental entity.

(d) A license holder commits an offense if, while intoxicated, the license holder carries a handgun under the authority of Article 4413 (29ee), Revised Statutes, regardless of whether the handgun is concealed.

(e) A license holder who is licensed as a security officer under the Private Investigators and Private Security Agencies Act (Article 4413 (29bb), Vernon's Texas Civil Statutes) and employed as a security officer commits an offense if, while in the course and scope of the security officer's employment, the security officer violates a provision of Article 4413 (29ee), Revised Statutes.

(f) In this section:

(1) "Amusement park" means a permanent indoor or outdoor facility or park where amusement rides are available for use by the public that is located in a county with a population of more than 1 million, encompasses at least 75 acres in surface area, is enclosed with access only through controlled entries, is open for operation more than 120 days in each calendar year, and has security guards on the premises at all times. The term does not include any public or private driveway, street, sidewalk or walkway, parking lot, parking garage, or other parking area.

(2) "License holder" means a person licensed to carry a handgun under Article 4413 (29ee), Revised Statutes.

(3) "Premises" means a building or a portion of a building. The term does not include any public or private driveway, street, sidewalk or walkway, parking lot, parking garage, or other parking area.

(g) An offense under Subsection (a), (b), (c), (d), or (e) is a Class A misdemeanor, unless the offense is committed under Subsection (b) (1) or (b) (3), in which event the offense is a felony of the third degree.

(h) It is a defense to prosecution under Subsection (a) that the actor, at the time of the commission of the offense, displayed the handgun under circumstances in which the actor would have been justified in the use of deadly force under Chapter 9.

Penal Code §46.04. Unlawful Possession Of Firearm By Felon

(a) A person who has been convicted of a felony commits an offense if he possesses a firearm:

1. after conviction and before the fifth anniversary of the person's release from confinement following conviction of the felony or the person's release from supervision under community supervision, parole, or mandatory supervision, whichever date is later; or

2. after the period described by Subdivision (1), at any location other than the premises at which the person lives.

(b) An offense under this section is a felony of the third degree.

Penal Code §46.05. Prohibited Weapons

(a) A person commits an offense if he intentionally or knowingly possesses, manufactures, transports, repairs, or sells:

1. an explosive weapon;
2. a machine gun;
3. a short-barrel firearm;
4. a firearm silencer;
5. a switchblade knife;
6. knuckles;
7. armor-piercing ammunition;

8. a chemical dispensing device; or
9. a zip gun.
(b) It is a defense to prosecution under this section that the actor's conduct was incidental to the performance of official duty by the armed forces or national guard, a governmental law enforcement agency, or a correctional facility.
(c) It is a defense to prosecution under this section that the actor's possession was pursuant to registration pursuant to the National Firearms Act, as amended.
(d) It is an affirmative defense to prosecution under this section that the actor's conduct:
1. was incidental to dealing with a switchblade knife, springblade knife, or short-barrel firearm solely as an antique or curio; or
2. was incidental to dealing with armor-piercing ammunition solely for the purpose of making the ammunition available to an organization, agency, or institution listed in Subsection (b).
(e) An offense under this section is a felony of the third degree unless it is committed under Subsection (a)(5) or (a)(6), in which event, it is a Class A misdemeanor.

Penal Code §46.06. Unlawful Transfer Of Certain Weapons

(a) A person commits an offense if the person:
(1) sells, rents, leases, loans, or gives a handgun to any person knowing that the person to whom the handgun is to be delivered intends to use it unlawfully or in the commission of an unlawful act;
(2) intentionally or knowingly sells, rents, leases, or gives or offers to sell, rent, lease, or give to any child younger than 18 years any firearm, club, or illegal knife;
(3) intentionally, knowingly, or recklessly sells a firearm or ammunition for a firearm to any person who is intoxicated;
(4) knowingly sells a firearm or ammunition for a firearm to any person who has been convicted of a felony before the fifth anniversary of the later of the following dates:
(A) the person's release from confinement following conviction of the felony; or
(B) the person's release from supervision under community supervision, parole, or mandatory supervision following conviction of the felony; or
(5) sells, rents, leases, loans, or gives a handgun to any person knowing that an active protective order is directed to the person to whom the handgun is to be delivered.
(b) In this section:
(1) "Intoxicated" means substantial impairment of mental or physical capacity resulting from introduction of any substance into the body.
(2) "Active protective order" means a protective order issued under Chapter 71, Family Code, that is in effect. The term does not include a temporary protective order issued before the court holds a hearing on the matter.

(c) It is an affirmative defense to prosecution under Subsection (a)(2) that the transfer was to a minor whose parent or the person having legal custody of the minor had given written permission for the sale or, if the transfer was other than a sale, the parent or person having legal custody had given effective consent.
(d) An offense under this section is a Class A misdemeanor.

Penal Code §46.07. Interstate Purchase

A resident of this state may, if not otherwise precluded by law, purchase firearms, ammunition, reloading components, or firearm accessories in contiguous states. This authorization is enacted in conformance with Section 922(b)(3)(A), Public Law 90-618, 90th Congress.

Penal Code §46.08. Hoax Bombs

(a) A person commits an offense if the person knowingly manufactures, sells, purchases, transports, or possesses a hoax bomb with intent to use the hoax bomb to:
1. make another believe that the hoax bomb is an explosive or incendiary device; or

2. cause alarm or reaction of any type by an official of a public safety agency or volunteer agency organized to deal with emergencies.
(b) An offense under this section is a Class A misdemeanor.

Penal Code §46.09. Components Of Explosives

(a) A person commits an offense if the person knowingly possesses components of an explosive weapon with the intent to combine the components into an explosive weapon for use in a criminal endeavor.
(b) An offense under this section is a felony of the third degree.

Penal Code §46.10. Deadly Weapon In Penal Institution

(a) A person commits an offense if, while confined in a penal institution, he intentionally, knowingly, or recklessly:
1. carries on or about his person a deadly weapon; or
2. possesses or conceals a deadly weapon in the penal institution.
(b) It is an affirmative defense to prosecution under this section that at the time of the offense the actor was engaged in conduct authorized by an employee of the penal institution.
(c) A person who is subject to prosecution under both this section and another section under this chapter may be prosecuted under either section.
(d) An offense under this section is a felony of the third degree.

Penal Code § 46.11. Penalty If Offense Committed Within Weapon-Free School Zone.

(a) Except as provided by Subsection (b), the punishment prescribed for an offense under this chapter is increased to the punishment prescribed for the next highest category of offense if it is shown beyond a reasonable doubt on the trial of the offense that the actor committed the offense in a place that the actor knew was:
(1) within 300 feet of the premises of a school; or
(2) on premises where:
(A) an official school function is taking place; or
(B) an event sponsored or sanctioned by the University Interscholastic League is taking place.
(b) This section does not apply to an offense under Section 46.03(a)(1).
(c) In this section, "institution of higher education," "premises," and "school" have the meanings assigned by Section 481.134, Health and Safety Code.

Penal Code § 46.12. Maps As Evidence Of Location Or Area.

(a) In a prosecution of an offense for which punishment is increased under Section 46.11, a map produced or reproduced by a municipal or county engineer for the purpose of showing the location and boundaries of weapon-free zones is admissible in evidence and is prima facie evidence of the location or boundaries of those areas if the governing body of the municipality or county adopts a resolution or ordinance approving the map as an official finding and record of the location or boundaries of those areas.
(b) A municipal or county engineer may, on request of the governing body of the municipality or county, revise a map that has been approved by the governing body of the municipality or county as provided by Subsection (a).
(c) A municipal or county engineer shall file the original or a copy of every approved or revised map approved as provided by Subsection (a) with the county clerk of each county in which the area is located.
(d) This section does not prevent the prosecution from:
(1) introducing or relying on any other evidence or testimony to establish any element of an offense for which punishment is increased under Section 46.11; or
(2) using or introducing any other map or diagram otherwise admissible under the Texas Rules of Criminal Evidence.

Penal Code § 46.13. Making A Firearm Accessible To A Child.

(a) in this section:
(1) "Child" means a person younger than 17 years of age.

(2) "Readily dischargeable firearm" means a firearm that is loaded with ammunition, whether or not a round is in the chamber.

(3) "Secure" means to take steps that a reasonable person would take to prevent the access to a readily dischargeable firearm by a child, including but not limited to placing a firearm in a locked container or temporarily rendering the firearm inoperable by a trigger lock or other means.

(b) A person commits an offense if a child gains access to a readily dischargeable firearm and the person with criminal negligence:

(1) failed to secure the firearm; or

(2) left the firearm in a place to which the person knew or should have known the child would gain access.

(c) It is an affirmative defense to prosecution under this section that the child's access to the firearm:

(1) was supervised by a person older than 18 years of age and was for hunting, sporting, or other lawful purposes;

(2) consisted of lawful defense by the child of people or property;

(3) was gained by entering property in violation of this code; or

(4) occurred during a time when the actor was engaged in an agricultural enterprise.

(d) Except as provided by Subsection (e), an offense under this section is a Class C misdemeanor.

(e) An offense under this section is a Class A misdemeanor if the child discharges the firearm and causes death or serious bodily injury to himself or another person.

(f) A peace officer or other person may not arrest the actor before the seventh day after the date on which the offense is committed if:

(1) the actor is a member of the family, as defined by Section 71.01, Family Code, of the child who discharged the firearm; and

(2) the child in discharging the firearm caused the death of or serious injury to the child.

(g) A dealer of firearms shall post in a conspicuous position on the premises where the dealer conducts business a sign that contains the following warning in block letters not less than one inch in height:

"IT IS UNLAWFUL TO STORE, TRANSPORT, OR ABANDON AN UNSECURED FIREARM IN A PLACE WHERE CHILDREN ARE LIKELY TO BE AND CAN OBTAIN ACCESS TO THE FIREARM."

Penal Code §46.15. Nonapplicability To Peace Officers.

Sections 46.02 and 46.03 do not apply to peace officers and neither section prohibits a peace officer from carrying a weapon in this state, regardless of whether the officer is engaged in the actual discharge of the officer's duties while carrying the weapon.

CHAPTER 71 • ORGANIZED CRIME AND CRIMINAL STREET GANGS

Penal Code §71.01. Definitions

In this chapter,

(a) "Combination" means three or more persons who collaborate in carrying on criminal activities, although:

1. participants may not know each other's identity;

2. membership in the combination may change from time to time; and

3. participants may stand in a wholesaler-retailer or other arm's-length relationship in illicit distribution operations.

(b) "Conspires to commit" means that a person agrees with one or more persons that they or one or more of them engage in conduct that would constitute the offense and that person and one or more of them perform an overt act in pursuance of the agreement. An agreement constituting conspiring to commit may be inferred from the acts of the parties.

(c) "Profits" means property constituting or derived from any proceeds obtained, directly or indirectly, from an offense listed in Section 71.02.

Penal Code §71.02. Engaging In Organized Criminal Activity

(a) A person commits an offense if, with the intent to establish, maintain, or participate in a combination or in the profits of a combination, he commits or conspires to commit one or more of the following:
1. murder, capital murder, arson, aggravated robbery, robbery, burglary, theft, aggravated kidnapping, kidnapping, aggravated assault, aggravated sexual assault, sexual assault, forgery, deadly conduct, assault punishable as a Class A misdemeanor, burglary of a motor vehicle, or unauthorized use of a motor vehicle;
2. any gambling offense punishable as a Class A misdemeanor;
3. promotion of prostitution, aggravated promotion of prostitution, or compelling prostitution;
4. unlawful manufacture, transportation, repair, or sale of firearms or prohibited weapons;
5. unlawful manufacture, delivery, dispensation, or distribution of a controlled substance or dangerous drug, or unlawful possession of a controlled substance or dangerous drug through forgery, fraud, misrepresentation, or deception;
6. any unlawful wholesale promotion or possession of any obscene material or obscene device with the intent to wholesale promote the same;
7. any unlawful employment, authorization, or inducing of a child younger than 17 years of age in an obscene sexual performance;
8. any felony offense under Chapter 32, Penal Code; or
9. any offense under Chapter 36, Penal Code.
(b) Except as provided in Subsections (c) and (d), an offense under this section is one category higher than the most serious offense listed in Subsection (a) that was committed, and if the most serious offense is a Class A misdemeanor, the offense is a state jail felony, except that if the most serious offense is a felony of the first degree, the offense is a felony of the first degree.
(c) Conspiring to commit an offense under this section is of the same degree as the most serious offense listed In Subsection (a) that the person conspired to commit.
(d) At the punishment stage of a trial, the defendant may raise the issue as to whether in voluntary and complete renunciation of the offense he withdrew from the combination before commission of an offense listed in Subsection (a) and made substantial effort to prevent the commission of the offense. If the defendant proves the issue in the affirmative by a preponderance of the evidence the offense is the same category of offense as the most serious offense listed in Subsection (a) that is committed, unless the defendant is convicted of conspiring to commit the offense, in which event the offense is one category lower than the most serious offense that the defendant conspired to commit.

Property Code § 42.002. Personal Property Eligible for Exemption

The following personal property is eligible for the exemption:
(D) two firearms;
<Relates to bankruptcy>

Civil Statutes Article 5069-51.16. Prohibited Practices

A pawnbroker shall not:
(h) Display for sale in storefront windows or sidewalk display case so that same may be viewed from the street, any pistol, dirk, dagger, blackjack, hand chain, sword cane, knuckles made of any metal or any hard substance, switchblade knife, springblade knife, or throwblade knife, or depict same on any sign or advertisement which may be viewed from the street.

EXCERPTS FROM

VERNON'S TEXAS STATUTES ANNOTATED

CODE OF CRIMINAL PROCEDURE (CCP)

CHAPTER 1 • GENERAL PROVISIONS

CCP Article 1.01. Short Title
This Act shall be known, and may be cited, as the "Code of Criminal Procedure."

CCP Article 1.02. Effective Date
This Code shall take effect and be in force on and after January 1, 1966. The procedure herein prescribed shall govern all criminal proceedings instituted after the effective date of this Act and all proceedings pending upon the effective date hereof insofar as are applicable.

CCP Article 1.03. Objects Of This Code
This Code is intended to embrace rules applicable to the prevention and prosecution of offenses against the laws of this State, and to make the rules of procedure in respect to the prevention and punishment of offenses intelligible to the officers who are to act under them, and to all persons whose rights are to be affected by them. It seeks:
1. To adopt measures for preventing the commission of crime;
2. To exclude the offender from all hope of escape;
3. To insure a trial with as little delay as is consistent with the ends of justice;
4. To bring to the investigation of each offense on the trial all the evidence tending to produce conviction or acquittal;
5. To insure a fair and impartial trial; and
6. The certain execution of the sentence of the law when declared.

CCP Article 1.04. Due Course Of Law
No citizen of this State shall be deprived of life, liberty, property, privileges or immunities, or in any manner disfranchised, except by the due course of the law of the land.

CCP Article 1.05. Rights Of Accused
In all criminal prosecutions the accused shall have a speedy public trial by an impartial jury. He shall have the right to demand the nature and cause of the accusation against him, and to have a copy thereof. He shall not be compelled to give evidence against himself. He shall have

the right of being heard by himself, or counsel, or both; shall be confronted with the witnesses against him, and shall have compulsory process for obtaining witnesses in his favor. No person shall be held to answer for a felony unless on Indictment of a grand jury.

CCP Article 1.06. Searches and Seizures

The people shall be secure in their persons, houses, papers and possessions from all unreasonable seizures or searches. No warrant to search any place or to seize any person or thing shall issue without describing them as near as may be, nor without probable cause supported by oath or affirmation.

CCP Article 1.24. Public Trial

The proceedings and trials in all courts shall be Public.

CCP Article 1.25. Confronted By Witnesses

The defendant, upon a trial, shall be confronted with the witnesses, except in certain cases provided for in this code where depositions have been taken.

CCP Article 1.26. Construction Of This Code

The provisions of this Code shall be liberally construed, so as to attain the objects intended by the Legislature: The prevention, suppression and punishment of crime.

CCP Article 1.27. Common Law Governs

If this code fails to provide a rule of procedure in any procedure in any particular state of case which may arise, the rules of the common law shall be applied and govern.

CHAPTER 2 • GENERAL DUTIES OF OFFICERS

CCP Article 2.12. Who Are Peace Officers.

The following are peace officers:
(1) sheriffs and their deputies;
(2) constables and deputy constables;
(3) marshals or police officers of an incorporated city, town, or village;
(4) rangers and officers commissioned by the Public Safety Commission and the Director of the Department of Public Safety;
(5) investigators of the district attorneys', criminal district attorneys', and county attorneys' offices;
(6) law enforcement agents of the Texas Alcoholic Beverage Commission;
(7) each member of an arson investigating unit commissioned by a city, a county, or the state;
(8) officers commissioned under Section 21.483, Education Code, or Subchapter E, Chapter 51, Education Code;
(9) officers commissioned by the General Services Commission;
(10) law enforcement officers commissioned by the Parks and Wildlife Commission;
(11) airport police officers commissioned by a city with a population of more than one million, according to the most recent federal census, that operates an airport that serves commercial air carriers;
(12) airport security personnel commissioned as peace officers by the governing body of any political subdivision of this state, other than a city described by Subdivision (11), that operates an airport that serves commercial air carriers;
(13) municipal park and recreational patrolmen and security officers;
(14) security officers commissioned as peace officers by the State Treasurer;
(15) officers commissioned by a water control and improvement district under Section 51.132, Water Code;
(16) officers commissioned by a board of trustees under Chapter 341, Acts of the 57th Legislature, Regular Session, 1961 (Article 1187f, Vernon's Texas Civil Statutes);
(17) investigators commissioned by the Texas State Board of Medical Examiners;
(18) officers commissioned by the board of managers of the Dallas County Hospital District, the Tarrant County Hospital District, or the Bexar County Hospital District under Section 281.057, Health and Safety Code;
(19) county park rangers commissioned under Subchapter E, Chapter 351, Local Government Code;
(20) investigators employed by the Texas Racing Commission;
(21) officers commissioned by the State Board of Pharmacy;

(22) officers commissioned by the governing body of a metropolitan rapid transit authority under Section 13, Chapter 141, Acts of the 63rd Legislature, Regular Session, 1973 (Article 1118x, Vernon's Texas Civil Statutes), or by a regional transportation authority under Section 10, Chapter 683, Acts of the 66th Legislature, Regular Session, 1979 (Article 1118y, Vernon's Texas Civil Statutes);
(23) officers commissioned by the Texas High-Speed Rail Authority;
(24) investigators commissioned by the attorney general under Section 402.009, Government Code;
(25) security officers and investigators commissioned as peace officers under Chapter 466, Government Code;
(26) an officer employed by the Texas Department of Health under Section 431.2471, Health and Safety Code;
(27) officers appointed by an appellate court under Subchapter F, Chapter 53, Government Code;
(28) officers commissioned by the state fire marshal under Chapter 417, Government Code; and
(29) apprehension specialists commissioned by the Texas Youth Commission as officers under Section 61.0931, Human Resources Code.

CCP Article 2.122. Special Investigators

(a) The following named criminal investigators of the United States shall not be deemed peace officers, but shall have the powers of arrest, search and seizure as to felony offenses only under the laws of the State of Texas:
1. Special Agents of the Federal Bureau of Investigation;
2. Special Agents of the Secret Service;
3. Special Agents of United States Customs, excluding border patrolmen and custom inspectors;
4. Special Agents of Alcohol, Tobacco and Firearms;
5. Special Agents of Federal Drug Enforcement Agency;
6. Inspectors of the United States Postal Service;
7. Special Agents and Law Enforcement Officers of the United States Forest Service;
8. Special Agents of the Criminal Investigation Division and Inspectors of the Internal Revenue Service; and
9. Civilian Special Agents of the United States Naval Investigative Service.
(b) A person designated as a special policeman by the Federal Protective Services division of the General Services Administration under 40 U.S.C. Section 318 or 318d is not a peace officer but has the powers of arrest and search and seizure as to any offense under the laws of this state.

CCP Article 2.14. May Summon Aid

Whenever a peace officer meets with resistance in discharging any duty imposed upon him by law, he shall summon a sufficient number of citizens of his county to overcome the resistance; and all persons summoned are bound to obey.

CCP Article 2.15. Person Refusing To Aid

The peace officer who has summoned any person to assist him in performing any duty shall report such person, if he refuse to obey, to the proper district or county attorney, in order that he may be prosecuted for the offense.* *[was Art. 348 in the "old" Penal Code which was repealed in 1974. No offense remains today.]

CCP Article 2.20. Deputy

Wherever a duty is imposed by this Code upon the sheriff, the same duty may lawfully be performed by his deputy. When there is no sheriff in a county, the duties of that office, as to all proceedings under the criminal law, devolve upon the officer who, under the law, is empowered to discharge the duties of sheriff, in case of vacancy of the office.
[How do you become a deputy?]

CCP Article 2.21. Duty Of Clerks

(a) Each clerk of the district or county court shall receive and file all papers and exhibits in respect to criminal proceedings, issue all process in such cases, and perform all other duties imposed upon them by law.
(b) Any firearm or contraband received by a court as an exhibit in any criminal proceeding shall be placed in the hands of the sheriff for safekeeping at any time during the pendency of such proceeding or thereafter.
(c) The sheriff shall receive and hold exhibits consisting of firearms or contraband and release them only to the person or persons authorized by the court in which such exhibits have been received or dispose of them as provided by Chapter 18 of this code.
(d) In this article, "eligible exhibit" means an exhibit filed with the clerk that:

1. is not a firearm or contraband;
2. has not been ordered by the court to be returned to its owner; and
3. is not an exhibit in another pending criminal action.
(e) An eligible exhibit may be disposed of as provided by this article:
1. on or after the first anniversary of the date on which a conviction becomes final in the case, if the case is a misdemeanor or a felony for which the sentence imposed by the court is five years or less; or
2. on or after the second anniversary of the date on which a conviction becomes final in the case, if the case is a non-capital felony for which the sentence imposed by the court is greater than five years.
(f) A clerk in a county with a population of 1.7 million or more may dispose of an eligible exhibit on the date provided by Subsection (e) of this article if on that date the clerk has not received a request for the exhibit from either the attorney representing the state in the case or the attorney representing the defendant.
(g) A clerk in a county with a population of less than 1.7 million must provide written notice by mail to the attorney representing the state in the case and the attorney representing the defendant before disposing of an eligible exhibit.
(h) The notice under Subsection (g) of this article must:
1. describe the eligible exhibit;
2. give the name and address of the court holding the exhibit; and
3. state that the eligible exhibit will be disposed of unless a written request is received by the clerk before the 31st day after the date of notice.
(i) If a request is not received by a clerk covered by Subsection (g) of this article before the 31st day after the date of notice, the clerk may dispose of the eligible exhibit.
(j) If a request is timely received, the clerk shall deliver the eligible exhibit to the person making the request if the court determines the requestor is the owner of the eligible exhibit.

CCP Article 3.01. Words And Phrases

All words, phrases and terms used in this Code are to be taken and understood in their usual acceptation in common language, except where specially defined.

CHAPTER 8 • SUPPRESSION OF RIOTS AND OTHER DISTURBANCES

CCP Article 8.01. Officer May Require Aid

When any officer authorized to execute process is resited, or when he has sufficient reason to believe that he will meet with resistance in executing the same, he may command as many of the citizens of his county as he may think proper; and the sheriff may call any military company in the county to aid him in overcoming the resistance, and if necessary, in seizing and arresting the persons engaged in such resistance.

CHAPTER 12 • LIMITATION

CCP Article12.01. Felonies

Except as provided in Article 12.03, felony indictments may be presented within these limits, and not afterward:
1. no limitation; murder and manslaughter;
2. ten years from the date of the commission of the offense:
A. theft of any estate, real, personal or mixed, by an executor, administrator, guardian or trustee, with intent to defraud any creditor, heir, legatee, ward, distributee, beneficiary or settlor of a trust interested in such estate;
B. theft by a public servant of government property over which he exercises control in his official capacity;
C. forgery or the uttering, using or passing of forged instruments;
D. sexual assault under Section 22.011(a)(2) of the Penal Code; indecency with a child;
3. seven years from the date of the commission of the offense: misapplication of fiduciary property or property of a financial institution;
4. five years from the date of the commission of the offense:
A. theft, burglary, robbery;

B. arson;
C. sexual assault, except as provided in Subsection (2)(D) of this article;
5. three years from the date of the commission of the offense; all other felonies.

CCP Article 12.02. Misdemeanors

An indictment or information for any misdemeanor may be presented within two years from the date of the commission of the offense, and not afterward.

CCP Article 12.03. Aggravated Offenses, Attempt, Conspiracy, Solicitation, Organized Criminal Activity

(a) The limitation period for criminal attempt is the same as that of the offense attempted.
(b) The limitation period for criminal conspiracy or organized criminal activity is the same as that of the most serious offense that is the object of the conspiracy or the organized criminal activity.
(c) The limitation period for criminal solicitation is the same as that of the felony solicited.
(d) Any offense that bears the title "aggravated" shall carry the same limitation period as the primary crime.

CCP Article12.04. Computation

The day on which the offense was committed and the day on which the indictment or information is presented shall be excluded from the computation of time.

CCP Article12.05. Absence From State And Time Of Pendency Of Indictment, Etc., Not Computed

(a) The time during which the accused is absent from the state shall not be computed in the period of limitation.
(b) The time during the pendency of an indictment, information, or complaint shall not be computed in the period of limitation.
(c) The term "during the pendency," as used herein, means that period of time beginning with the day the indictment, information, or complaint is filed in a court of competent jurisdiction, and ending with the day such accusation is, by an order of a trial court having jurisdiction thereof, determined to be invalid for any reason.

CHAPTER 15 • ARREST UNDER WARRANT

CCP Article 15.27. Notification To Schools Required

(a) A law enforcement agency that arrests or takes into custody as provided by Chapter 52, Family Code, an individual who the agency knows or believes is enrolled as a student in a public primary or secondary school, for an offense listed in Subsection (h) of this article, shall orally notify the superintendent or a person designated by the superintendent in the school district in which the student is enrolled or believed to be enrolled of that arrest or detention within 24 hours after the arrest or detention, or on the next school day. Within seven days after the date the oral notice is given, the law enforcement agency shall mail written notification, marked "PERSONAL and CONFIDENTIAL" on the mailing envelope, to the superintendent or the person designated by the superintendent. The written notification must have the following printed on its face in large, bold letters:
"WARNING: The information contained in this notice is intended only to inform appropriate school personnel of an arrest or detention of a student believed to be enrolled in this school. An arrest or detention should not be construed as proof that the student is guilty. Guilt is determined in a court of law. THE INFORMATION CONTAINED IN THIS NOTICE IS CONFIDENTIAL!"
(b) On conviction or on an adjudication of delinquent conduct of an individual enrolled as a student in a public primary or secondary school, for an offense or for any conduct listed in Subsection (h) of this article, the office of the prosecuting attorney acting in the case shall notify the superintendent or a person designated by the superintendent in the school district in which the student is enrolled of the conviction or adjudication. Oral notification must be given within 24 hours of the time of the determination of guilt, or on the next school day. Within seven days after the date the oral notice is given, the office of the prosecuting attorney shall mail written notice, which must contain a statement of the offense of which the individual is convicted or on which the adjudication is grounded.
(c) A parole or probation office having jurisdiction over a student described by Subsection (a), (b), or (e) of this article who transfers from a school or is subsequently removed from a

school and later returned to a school or school district other than the one the student was enrolled in when the arrest, detention, conviction, or adjudication occurred shall notify the new school officials of the arrest or detention in a manner similar to that provided for by Subsection (a) or (e)(1) of this article, or of the conviction or delinquent adjudication in a manner similar to that provided for by Subsection (b) or (e)(2) of this article.

(d) The superintendent or a person designated by the superintendent in the school district may send to a school district employee having direct supervisory responsibility over the student the information contained in the confidential notice if the superintendent or the person designated by the superintendent determines that the school district employee needs the information for educational purposes or for the protection of the person informed or others.

(e) 1. A law enforcement agency that arrests or detains an individual that the law enforcement agency knows or believes is enrolled as a student in a private primary or secondary school shall make the oral and written notifications described by Subsection (a) of this article to the principal or a school employee designated by the principal of the school in which the student is enrolled.

2. On conviction or an adjudication of delinquent conduct of an individual enrolled as a student in a private primary or secondary school, the office of prosecuting attorney shall make the oral and written notifications described by Subsection (b) of this article to the principal or a school employee designated by the principal of the school in which the student is enrolled.

3. The principal of a private school in which the student is enrolled or a school employee designated by the principal may send to a school employee having direct supervisory responsibility over the student the information contained in the confidential notice, for the same purposes as described by Subsection (d) of this article.

(f) A person who receives information under this article may not disclose the information except as specifically authorized by this article. A person who intentionally violates this article commits an offense. An offense under this subsection is a Class C misdemeanor.

(g) On receipt of a notice under this article, a school official may take the precautions necessary to prevent further violence in the school, on school property, or at school-sponsored or school-related activities on or off school property, but may not penalize a student solely because a notification is received about the student.

(h) This article applies to:

1. an offense listed in Section 8(c), Article 42.18, Code of Criminal Procedure; reckless conduct, as described by Section 22.05, Penal Code; or a terroristic threat, as described by Section 22.07, Penal Code;

2. the unlawful use, sale, or possession of a controlled substance, drug paraphernalia, or marihuana, as defined by Chapter 481, Health and Safety Code;

3. the unlawful possession of any of the weapons or devices listed in Sections 46.01(1)-(14) or (16), Penal Code; or a weapon listed as a prohibited weapon under Section 46.06, Penal Code; or

4. a criminal offense under Section 71.02, Penal Code.

CHAPTER 18 • SEARCHES AND SEARCH WARRANTS

CCP Article 18.18. Disposition Of Gambling Paraphernalia, Prohibited Weapon, Criminal Instrument, And Other Contraband

(a) Following the final conviction of a person for possession of a gambling device or equipment, altered gambling equipment, or gambling paraphernalia, for an offense involving a criminal instrument, for an offense involving an obscene device or material, the court entering the judgment of conviction shall order that the machine, device, gambling equipment or gambling paraphernalia, instrument, obscene device or material be destroyed or forfeited to the state. Not later than the 30th day after the final conviction of a person for an offense involving a prohibited weapon, the court entering the judgment of conviction on its own motion, on the motion of the prosecuting attorney in the case, or on the motion of the law enforcement agency initiating the complaint on notice to the prosecuting attorney in the case if the prosecutor fails to move for the order shall order that the prohibited weapon be destroyed or forfeited to law enforcement agency that initiated the complaint. If the court fails to enter the order within the time required by this subsection, any magistrate in the county in which the offense occurred may enter the order. Following the final conviction of a person for an offense involving dog fighting, the court entering the judgment of conviction shall order that any dog-fighting equipment be destroyed or forfeited to the state. Destruction of dogs, if necessary, must be carried out by a veterinarian licensed in this state or, if one is not available, by trained personnel of a humane society or an animal shelter. If forfeited, the court shall order the contraband delivered to the state, any political subdivision of the state, or to any state institution or agency. If gambling proceeds were seized, the court shall order them forfeited to the state and shall transmit them to the grand jury of the county in which they were seized for use in investigating alleged violations of the Penal Code, or to the state, any political subdivision of the state, or to any state institution or agency.

(b) If there is no prosecution or conviction following seizure, the magistrate to whom the return was made shall notify in writing the person found in possession of the alleged gambling device or equipment, altered gambling equipment or gambling paraphernalia, gambling proceeds, prohibited weapon, obscene device or material, criminal instrument, or dog-fighting equipment to show cause why the property seized should not be destroyed or the proceeds forfeited. The magistrate, on the motion of the law enforcement agency seizing a prohibited weapon, shall order the weapon destroyed or forfeited to the law enforcement agency seizing the weapon, unless a person shows cause as to why the prohibited weapon should not be destroyed or forfeited. A law enforcement agency shall make a motion under this section in a timely manner after the time at which the agency is informed in writing by the attorney representing the state that no prosecution will arise from the seizure.

(c) The magistrate shall include in the notice a detailed description of the property seized and the total amount of alleged gambling proceeds; the name of the person found in possession; the address where the property or proceeds were seized; and the date and time of the seizure.

(d) The magistrate shall send the notice by registered or certified mail, return receipt requested, to the person found in possession at the address where the property or proceeds were seized. If no one was found in possession, or the possessor's address is unknown, the magistrate shall post the notice on the courthouse door.

(e) Any person interested in the alleged gambling device or equipment, altered gambling equipment or gambling paraphernalia, gambling proceeds, prohibited weapon, obscene device or material, criminal instrument, or dog-fighting equipment seized must appear before the magistrate on the 20th day following the date the notice was mailed or posted. Failure to timely appear forfeits any interest the person may have in the property or proceeds seized, and no person after failing to timely appear may contest destruction or forfeiture.

(f) If a person timely appears to show cause why the property or proceeds should not be destroyed or forfeited, the magistrate shall conduct a hearing on the issue and determine the nature of property or proceeds and the person's interest therein. Unless the person proves by a preponderance of the evidence that the property or proceeds is not gambling equipment, altered gambling equipment, gambling paraphernalia, gambling device, gambling proceeds, prohibited weapon, criminal instrument, or dog-fighting equipment and that he is entitled to possession, the magistrate shall dispose of the property or proceeds in accordance with Paragraph (a) of this article.

(g) For purposes of this article:
1. "criminal instrument" has the meaning defined in the Penal Code;
2. "gambling device or equipment, altered gambling equipment or gambling paraphernalia" has the meaning defined in the Penal Code;
3. "prohibited weapon" has the meaning defined in the Penal Code; and
4. "dog-fighting equipment" means:
A. equipment used for training or handling a fighting dog, including a harness, treadmill, cage, decoy, pen, house for keeping a fighting dog, feeding apparatus, or training pen;
B. equipment used for transporting a fighting dog, including any automobile, or other vehicle, and its appurtenances which are intended to be used as a vehicle for transporting a fighting dog;
C. equipment used to promote or advertise an exhibition of dog fighting, including a printing press or similar equipment, paper, ink, or photography equipment; or
D. a dog trained, being trained, or intended to be used to fight with another dog.
6. "obscene device or material" means a device or material introduced into evidence and thereafter found obscene by virtue of a final judgment after all appellate remedies have been exhausted.

CCP Article 18.19. Disposition Of Seized Weapons

(a) Weapons seized in connection with an offense involving the use of a weapon or an offense under Penal Code Chapter 46 shall be held by the law enforcement agency making the seizure, subject to the following provisions, unless:
1. the weapon is a prohibited weapon identified in Penal Code Chapter 46, in which event Article 18.18 of this code applies; or
2. the weapon is alleged to be stolen property, in which event Chapter 47 of this code applies.

(b) When a weapon described in Paragraph (a) of this article is seized, and the seizure is not made pursuant to a search or arrest warrant, the person seizing the same shall prepare and deliver to a magistrate a written inventory of each weapon seized.

(c) If there is no prosecution or conviction for an offense involving the weapon seized, the magistrate to whom the seizure was reported shall notify in writing the person found in possession that he is entitled to the weapon upon request to the court in which he was convicted. If the weapon is not requested within 60 days after notification, the magistrate shall order the weapon destroyed or forfeited to the state for use by the law enforcement agency holding the weapon.

(d) A person either convicted or receiving deferred adjudication under Penal Code Chapter 46 is entitled to the weapon seized upon request to the law enforcement agency holding the weapon. However, the court entering the judgment shall order the weapon destroyed or forfeited to the state for use by the law enforcement agency holding the weapon if:

(1) the person does not request the weapon within 60 days after the date of the judgment of conviction;
(2) the person has been previously convicted under Penal Code Chapter 46;
(3) the weapon is one defined as a prohibited weapon under Penal Code Chapter 46;
(4) the offense for which the person is convicted or receives deferred adjudication was committed in or on the premises of a playground, school, video arcade facility, or youth center, as those terms are defined by Section 481.134, Health and Safety Code; or
(5) the court determines based on the prior criminal history of the defendant or based on the circumstances surrounding the commission of the offense that possession of the seized weapon would pose a threat to the community or one or more individuals.
(e) If the person found in possession of a weapon is convicted of an offense involving the use of the weapon, the court entering judgment of conviction shall order destruction of the weapon or forfeiture to the state for use by the law enforcement agency holding the weapon.

CCP Article 42.12. Adult Probation, Parole, and Mandatory Supervision Law
Sec. 13B. Community Supervision For Making A Firearm Accessible To A Child.

(a) A court granting community supervision to a defendant convicted of an offense under Section 46.13, Penal Code, may require as a condition of community supervision that the defendant:
(1) provide an appropriate public service activity designated by the court; or
(2) attend a firearms safety course which meets or exceeds the requirements set by the National Rifle Association as of January 1, 1995, for a firearms safety course that requires not more than 17 hours of instruction.
(b) The court shall require the defendant to pay the cost of attending the firearms safety course under Subsection (a)(2).

CHAPTER 59 • FORFEITURE OF CONTRABAND

CCP Article 59.01. Definitions

In this chapter:
1. "Attorney representing the state" means the prosecutor with felon) jurisdiction in the county in which a forfeiture proceeding is held under this chapter or, in a proceeding for forfeiture of contraband as defined under Subdivision (2)(B)(iv) of this article, the city attorney of a municipality if the property is seized in that municipality by a peace officer employed by that municipality and the governing body of the municipality has approved procedures for the city attorney acting in a forfeiture proceeding.
2. "Contraband" means property of any nature, including real, personal, tangible, or intangible, that is:
A. used in the commission of:
i. any first or second degree felony under the Penal Code;
ii. any felony under Chapters 29, 30, 31, or 32, Penal Code: or
iii. any felony under The Securities Act (Article 581-1 et seq., Vernon's Texas Civil Statutes);
B. used or intended to be used in the commission of:
i. any felony under Chapter 481, Health and Safety Code (Texas Controlled Substances Act.);
ii. any felony under Chapter 483, Health and Safety Code;
iii. a felony under Article 350, Revised Statutes; or
iv. [as added by ch. 828, 73rd Leg., 1993.] a Class A misdemeanor under Subchapter B, Chapter 365, Health and Safety Code, if the defendant has been grievously convicted twice of an offense under that subchapter;
iv. [sic—two clauses labelled "iv."][as added by ch. 761, 73rdLeg., 1993.] any felony under Chapter 34, Penal Code; or
v. any felony under The Sale of Checks Act (Article 489d, Vernon's Texas Civil Statutes);
C. the proceeds gained from the commission of a felony listed in Paragraph (A) or (B) of this subdivision or a crime of violence; or
D. acquired with proceeds gained from the commission of a felony listed in Paragraph (A) or (B) of this subdivision or a crime of violence.
3. "Crime of violence" has the meaning assigned by Section 3, Crime Victims Compensation Act (Article 8309-1, Vernon's Texas Civil Statutes).
4. "Interest holder" means the bona fide holder of a perfected lien or a perfected security interest in property.
5. "Law enforcement agency" means an agency of the state or an agency of a political subdivision of the state authorized by law to employ peace officers.

6. "Owner" means a person who claims an equitable or legal ownership interest in property.
7. "Proceeds" includes income a person accused or convicted of a crime or the person's representative or assignee receives from a movie, book, magazine article, tape recording, phonographic record, radio or television presentation, or live entertainment in which the crime was reenacted.
8. "Seizure" means the restraint of property by a peace officer under Article 59.03(a) or (b) of this code, whether the officer restrains the property by physical force or by a display of the officer's authority.

Complete Text Of Senate Bill 60
THE 1995 TEXAS RIGHT TO CARRY BILL

A BILL TO BE ENTITLED
AN ACT
relating to the issuance of a license to carry a concealed handgun; requiring of an applicant for the license a handgun proficiency and safety training course and a criminal background check; providing penalties.
BE IT ENACTED BY THE LEGISLATURE OF THE STATE OF TEXAS:

SECTION 1. Title 70, Revised Statutes, is amended by adding Article 4413 (29ee) to read as follows:

Art. 4413 (29ee). LICENSE TO CARRY A CONCEALED HANDGUN
Sec. 1. DEFINITIONS.
In this article:
(1) "Action" means single action, revolver, or semi-automatic action.
(2) "Chemically dependent person" means a person who frequently or repeatedly becomes intoxicated by excessive indulgence in alcohol or uses controlled substances or dangerous drugs so as to acquire a fixed habit and an involuntary tendency to become intoxicated or use those substances as often as the opportunity is presented.
(3) "Concealed handgun" means a handgun, the presence of which is not openly discernible to the ordinary observation of a reasonable person.
(4) "Convicted" means an adjudication of guilt or an order of deferred adjudication entered against a person by a court of competent jurisdiction whether or not:
(A) the imposition of the sentence is subsequently probated and the person is discharged from community supervision; or
(B) the person is pardoned for the offense, unless the pardon is expressly granted for subsequent proof of innocence.
(5) "Department" means the Department of Public Safety, including employees of the department.
(6) "Director" means the director of the Department of Public Safety or the director's designee.
(7) "Handgun" has the meaning assigned by Section 46.01, Penal Code.
(8) "Intoxicated" has the meaning assigned by Section 49.01, Penal Code.
(9) "Qualified handgun instructor" means a person who is certified to instruct in the use of handguns by the department.
(10) "Unsound mind" means the mental condition of a person who:
(A) has been adjudicated mentally incompetent, mentally ill, or not guilty of a criminal offense by reason of insanity;
(B) has been diagnosed by a licensed physician as being characterized by a mental disorder or infirmity that renders the person incapable of managing the person's self or the person's affairs, unless the person furnishes a certificate from a licensed physician stating that the person is no longer disabled or under any medication for the treatment of a mental or psychiatric disorder; or
(C) has been diagnosed by a licensed physician as suffering from depression, manic depression, or post-traumatic stress syndrome, unless the person furnishes a certificate from a licensed physician stating that the person is no longer disabled or under an medication for the treatment of a mental or psychiatric disorder.
Sec. 2. ELIGIBILITY.
(a) A person is eligible for a license to carry a concealed handgun if the person:

(1) is a legal resident of this state for the six-month period preceding the date of application under this article;

(2) is at least 21 years of age;

(3) has not been convicted of a felony;

(4) is not charged with the commission of a Class A or Class B misdemeanor or an offense under Section 42.01, Penal Code, or of a felony under an information or indictment;

(5) is not a fugitive from justice for a felony or a Class A or Class B misdemeanor;

(6) is not a chemically dependent person;

(7) is not a person of unsound mind;

(8) has not, in the five years preceding the date of application, been convicted of a Class A or Class B misdemeanor or an offense under Section 42.01, Penal Code;

(9) is fully qualified under applicable federal and state law to purchase a handgun;

(10) has not been finally determined to be delinquent in making a child support payment administered or collected by the attorney general;

(11) has not been finally determined to be delinquent in the payment of a tax or other money collected by the comptroller, state treasurer, tax collector of a political subdivision of the state, Texas Alcoholic Beverage Commission, or any other agency or subdivision of the state;

(12) has not been finally determined to be in default on a loan made under Chapter 57, Education Code;

(13) is not currently restricted under a court protective order or subject to a restraining order affecting the spousal relationship, not including a restraining order solely affecting property interests;

(14) has not, in the 10 years preceding the date of application, been adjudicated as having engaged in delinquent conduct violating a penal law of the grade of felony; and

(15) has not made any material misrepresentation, or failed to disclose any material fact, in an application submitted pursuant to Section 3 of this article or in a request for application submitted pursuant to Section 4 of this article.

(b) For the purposes of this section, an offense under the laws of this state, another state, or the United States is:

(1) a felony if the offense is so designated by law or if confinement for one year or more in a penitentiary is affixed to the offense as a possible punishment; and

(2) a Class A misdemeanor if the offense is not a felony and confinement in a jail other than a state jail felony facility is affixed as a possible punishment.

(c) An individual who has been convicted two times within the 10 year period preceding the date on which the person applies for a license of an offense of the grade of Class B misdemeanor or greater that involves the use of alcohol or a controlled substance as a statutory element of the offense is a chemically dependent person for purposes of this section and is not qualified to receive a license under this article. Nothing in this subsection shall preclude the disqualification of an individual for being a chemically dependent person if other evidence exists that the person is a chemically dependent person.

Sec. 3. APPLICATION.

(a) An applicant for a license to carry a concealed handgun must submit to the director's designee described by Section 5 of this article:

(1) a completed application on a form provided by the department that requires only the information listed in Subsection (b) of this section;

(2) two recent color passport photographs of the applicant;

(3) a certified copy of the applicant's birth certificate or certified proof of age;

(4) proof of residency in this state;

(5) two complete sets of legible and classifiable fingerprints of the applicant taken by a person employed by a law enforcement agency who is appropriately trained in recording fingerprints;(6) a nonrefundable application and license fee of $140 paid to the department;

(7) a handgun proficiency certificate described by Section 17 of this article;

(8) an affidavit signed by the applicant stating that the applicant:

(A) has read and understands each provision of this article that creates an offense under the laws of this state and each provision of the laws of this state related to use of deadly force; and

(B) fulfills all the eligibility requirements listed under Section 2 of this article; and

(9) a form executed by the applicant that authorizes the director to make an inquiry into any noncriminal history records that are necessary to determine the applicant's eligibility for a license under initial Section 2 (a) of this article.

(b) An applicant must provide on the application a statement of the applicant's:

(1) full name and place and date of birth;

(2) race and sex;

(3) residence and business addresses for the preceding five years;

(4) hair and eye color;

(5) height and weight;

(6) driver's license number or identification certificate number issued by the department;

(7) criminal history record information of the type maintained by the department under Chapter 411, Government Code, including a list of offenses for which the applicant was arrested, charged, or under an information or indictment and the disposition of the offenses; and

(8) history during the preceding five years, if any, of treatment received by, commitment to, or residence in:

(A) a drug or alcohol treatment center licensed to provide drug or alcohol treatment under the laws of this state or another state;or

(B) a psychiatric hospital.

(c) The department shall distribute on request a copy of this article and application materials.

Sec. 4. REQUEST FOR APPLICATION MATERIALS.

(a) A person applying for a license to carry a concealed handgun must apply by obtaining a request for application materials from a handgun dealer, the department, or any other person or entity approved by the department. This request for application materials shall include the applicant's full name, address, race, sex, height, date of birth, and driver's license number and such other identifying information as may be required by the department by rule. This request shall be in a form prescribed by the department and made available to interested parties by the department. An individual who desires to receive application materials shall complete the request for application materials and forward it to the department at its Austin address. The department shall review all such requests for application materials and make a preliminary determination as to whether or not the individual is qualified to receive a handgun license. If an individual is not disqualified to receive a handgun license, the department shall forward to the individual the appropriate application materials as described in this article. The applicant shall complete the application materials and forward the completed materials to the department at its Austin address.

(b) In the event that a preliminary review indicates that an individual will not be qualified to receive a handgun license, the department shall send written notification to that individual. The notice shall provide the reason that the preliminary review indicates that the individual is not entitled to receive a handgun license. The individual shall be given an opportunity to correct whatever defect may exist.

Sec. 5. REVIEW OF APPLICATION MATERIALS.

(a) Initial receipt of the application materials by the department at its initial Austin headquarters, the department shall conduct the appropriate criminal history record check of the applicant through its computerized criminal history system. Not later than the 30th day after the date the department receives the application materials, the department shall forward the materials to the director's designee in the geographical area of the applicant's residence so that the designee may conduct the investigation detailed in Subsection (b) of this section.

(b) The director's designee as needed shall conduct an additional criminal history record check of the applicant and an investigation of the applicant's local official records to verify the accuracy of the application materials. The scope of the record check and the investigation are at the sole discretion of the department. The department shall send a fingerprint card to the Federal Bureau of Investigation for a national criminal history check of the applicant. On completion of the investigation, the director's designee shall return all materials and the result of the investigation to the appropriate division of the department at its Austin headquarters. The director's designee may submit to the appropriate division of the department, at the department's Austin headquarters, along with the application materials a written recommendation for disapproval of the application, accompanied by an affidavit stating personal knowledge or naming persons with personal knowledge of a ground for denial under Section 2 of this article. The director's designee in the appropriate geographical area may also submit the application and the recommendation that the license be issued.

Sec. 6. LICENSE.

(a) The department shall issue a license to carry a concealed handgun to an applicant if the applicant meets all the eligibility requirements and submits all the application materials. The department may issue a license to carry handguns only of the categories indicated on the applicant's certificate of proficiency issued under Section 17 of this article. The department shall administer the licensing procedures in good faith so that any applicant who meets all the eligibility requirements and submits all the application materials shall receive a license. The department may not deny an application of the basis of a capricious or arbitrary decision by the department.

(b) (1) After January 1, 1997, the department, not later than the 60th day after the date of the receipt by the director's designee of the completed application materials, shall:

(A) issue the license; or

(B) notify the applicant in writing that the application was denied:

(i) on the grounds that the applicant failed to qualify under the criteria listed in Section 2 of this article;

(ii) based on the affidavit of the director's designee submitted to the department under Section 5 (b) of this article; or

(iii) based on the affidavit of the qualified handgun instructor submitted to the department under Section 17(c) of this article.

(2) Between the effective date of this article and December 31, 1996, the department shall perform the duties set out in this subsection not later than the 90th day after the date of the receipt by the director's designee of the completed application materials.

(c) If the department issues a license, the department shall notify the sheriff of the county in which the license holder resides that a license has been issued to the license holder. On request of a local law enforcement agency, the department shall notify the agency of the licenses that have been issued to license holders who reside in the county in which the agency is located.

(d) A license issued under this article is effective from the date of issuance.

(e) The department by rule shall adopt the form of the license. A license must include:

(1) a number assigned to the license holder by the department;

(2) a statement of the period for which the license is effective;

(3) a statement of the category or categories of handguns the license holder may carry as provided by Subsection (f) of this section;

(4) a color photograph of the license holder; and

(5) the license holder's full name, date of birth, residence address, hair and eye color, height, weight, signature, and the number of a driver's license or an identification certificate issued to the license holder by the department.

(f) A category of handguns contains handguns that are not prohibited by law and are of certain actions. The categories of handguns are as follows:

(1) SA: any handguns, whether semi-automatic or not; and

(2) NSA: handguns that are not semi-automatic.

(g) On a demand by a magistrate or a peace officer that a license holder display the license holder's handgun license, the license holder shall display both the license and the license holder's driver's license or identification certificate issued by the department.

(h) If a license holder is carrying a handgun on or about the license holder's person when a magistrate or a peace officer demands that the license holder display identification, the license holder shall display both the license holder's driver's license or identification certificate issued by the department and the license holder's handgun license.

(i) A person commits an offense if the person fails or refuses to display the license and identification as required by Subsection (g) or (h) of this section. An offense under this subsection is a Class B misdemeanor.

Sec. 7. NOTIFICATION OF DENIAL, REVOCATION, OR SUSPENSION OF LICENSE; REVIEW.

(a) The department shall give written notice to each applicant for a handgun license of any denial, revocation, or suspension of that license. Not later than the 30th day after the notice is received by the applicant, according to the records of the department, the applicant or license holder may request a hearing on the denial, revocation, or suspension. The applicant must make a written request for a hearing addressed to the department at its Austin address.   The request for hearing must reach the department in Austin prior to the 30th day after the date of receipt of the written notice. On receipt of a request for hearing from a license holder or applicant, the department shall promptly schedule a hearing in the appropriate justice court in the county of residence of the applicant or license holder. The justice court shall conduct a hearing to review the denial, revocation, or suspension of the license. In a proceeding under this section, a justice of the peace shall act as an administrative hearing officer. A hearing under this section is not subject to Chapter 2001, Government Code (Administrative Procedure Act). The department may be represented by a district attorney or county attorney, the attorney general, or a designated member of the department.

(b) The department, on receipt of a request for hearing, shall file the appropriate petition in the justice court selected for the hearing and send a copy of that petition to the applicant or license holder at the address contained in departmental records. A hearing under this section must be scheduled within 30 days of receipt of the request for a hearing. The hearing shall be held expeditiously but in no event more than 60 days after the date that the applicant or license holder requested the hearing. The date of the hearing may be reset on the motion of either party, by agreement of the parties, or by the court as necessary to accommodate the court's docket.

(c) On receipt of the application materials by the department at its Austin headquarters, the department will conduct the appropriate criminal history record check of the applicant through its computerized criminal history system. Within 30 days of receipt of the application materials, they will be forwarded to the director's designee in the geographical area of the applicant's residence to conduct the investigation detailed in Subsection (d) of this section.

(d) The director's designee in the appropriate geographical area shall, as needed, conduct an additional criminal history record check of the applicant and an investigation of the applicant's local official records to verify the accuracy of the application materials. The scope of the record check and the investigation are at the sole discretion of the department. On completion of the investigation, the director's designee shall return all materials and the result of the investigation to the appropriate division of the department at its Austin headquarters. The director's designee may submit to the appropriate division of the department, at the department's Austin headquarters, along with the application materials a written recommendation for disapproval of the application, accompanied by an affidavit stating personal knowledge or naming persons with personal knowledge of a ground for denial under Section 2 of this article. The director's designee in the appropriate geographical area may also submit the application and the recommendation that the license be issued.

(3) The justice court shall determine if the denial, revocation, or suspension is supported by a preponderance of the evidence. Both the applicant or license holder and the department may present evidence. The court shall affirm the denial, revocation, or suspension if the court determines that denial, revocation, or suspension was supported by a preponderance of the evidence. If the court determines that the denial, revocation, or suspension was not supported by a preponderance of the evidence, the court shall order the department to immediately issue or return the license to the applicant or license holder.

(d) A proceeding under this section is subject to Chapter 105, Civil Practice and Remedies Code, relating to fees, expenses, and attorney's fees.

(e) A party adversely affected by the court's ruling following a hearing under this section may appeal the ruling by filing within 30 days after the ruling a petition in a county court at law in the county in which the applicant or license holder resides or, if there is no county court at law in the county, in the county court of the county. A person who appeals under this section must send by certified mail a copy of the person's petition, certified by the clerk of the court in which the petition is filed, to the appropriate division of the department at its Austin headquarters. The trial on appeal shall be a trial de novo without a jury. The department may be represented by a district or county attorney or the attorney general.

(f) A suspension of a license may not be probated.

(g) If an applicant or a license holder does not petition the justice court, a denial becomes final and a revocation or suspension takes effect on the 30th day after receipt of written notice. Failure of the director to issue or deny a license as required under Section 6 (b) of this article for a period of more than 30 days after he is required to act under that section constitutes denial.

(h) The department is specifically authorized to utilize and to introduce into evidence certified copies of governmental records to establish the existence of certain events which could result in the denial, revocation, or suspension of a license under this article, including but not limited to records regarding convictions, judicial findings regarding mental competency, judicial findings regarding chemical dependency, or other matters that may be established by governmental records which have been properly authenticated.

Sec. 8. NOTICE OF CHANGE OF ADDRESS OR NAME.

(a) If a person who is a current license holder moves from the address stated on the license or if the name of the person is changed by marriage or otherwise, the person shall, not later than the 30th day after the date of the address or name change, notify the department and provide the department with the number of the person's license and the person's:

(1) former and new addresses; or

(2) former and new names.

(b) If the name of the license holder is changed by marriage or otherwise, the person shall apply for a duplicate license.

(c) If a license holder moved from the address on the license, the person shall apply for a duplicate license.

(d) The department shall charge a license holder a fee of $25 for a duplicate license.

(e) The department shall make the forms available on request.

(f) The department shall notify the sheriff of the county in which a license holder resides of a change made under Subsection (a) of this section by the license holder. On request of a local law enforcement agency, the department shall notify the agency of changes made under Subsection (a) of this section by license holders who reside in the county in which the agency is located.

(g) If a license is lost, stolen, or destroyed, the license holder shall apply for a duplicate license not later than the 30th day after the date of the loss, theft, or destruction of the license.

(h) If a license holder is required under this section to apply for a duplicate license and the license expires not later than the 60th day after the date of the loss, theft, or destruction of the license, the applicant may renew the license with the modified information included on the new license. The applicant shall pay only the nonrefundable renewal fee.

Sec. 9. EXPIRATION.

(a) A license issued under this article expires on the first birthday of the license holder occurring after the fourth anniversary of the date of issuance.

(b) A renewed license expires on the license holder's birthdate, four years after the date of the expiration of the previous license.

(c) A duplicate license expires on the date the license that was duplicated would have expired.

(d) A modified license expires on the date the license that was modified would have expired.

Sec. 10. MODIFICATION.

(a) To modify a license to allow a license holder to carry a handgun of a different category than the license indicates, the license holder must:

(1) complete a proficiency examination as provided by Section 16(e) of this article;

(2) obtain a handgun proficiency certificate under Section 17 of this article not more than six months before the date of application for a modified license; and

(3) submit to the department:

(A) an application for a modified license on a form provided by the department;

(B) a copy of the handgun proficiency certificate;

(C) payment of a modified license fee of $25; and
(D) two recent color passport photographs of the license holder.
(b) The director by rule shall adopt a modified license application form requiring an update of the information on the original completed application.
(c) The department may modify the license of a license holder who meets all the eligibility requirements and submits all the modification materials. Not later than the 45th day after receipt of the modification materials, the department shall issue the modified license or notify the license holder in writing that the modified license application was denied.
(d) On receipt of a modified license, the license holder shall return the previously issued license to the department.

Sec. 11. RENEWAL.
(a) To renew a license, a license holder must:
(1) complete a continuing education course in handgun proficiency under Section 16(c) of this article not more than six months before the date of application for renewal;
(2) obtain a handgun proficiency certificate under Section 17 of this article not more than six months before the date of application for renewal; and
(3) submit to the department:
(A) an application for renewal on a form provided by the department;
(B) a copy of the handgun proficiency certificate;
(C) payment of a nonrefundable renewal fee as set by the department; and
(D) two recent color passport photographs of the applicant.
(b) The director by rule shall adopt a renewal application form requiring an update of the information on the original completed application. The director by rule shall set the renewal fee in an amount that is sufficient to cover the actual cost to the department to renew a license. Not later than the 60th day before the expiration date of the license, the department shall mail to each license holder a written notice of the expiration of the license and a renewal form.
(c) The department shall renew the license of a license holder who meets all the eligibility requirements and submits all the renewal materials. Not later than the 45th day after receipt of the renewal materials, the department shall issue the renewal or notify the license holder in writing that the renewal application was denied.
(d) The director by rule shall adopt a procedure by which a license holder who satisfies the eligibility criteria may renew a license by mail. The materials for renewal by mail must include a form to be signed and returned to the department by the applicant that describes state law regarding:
(1) the use of deadly force; and
(2) the places where it is unlawful for the holder of a license issued under this article to carry a concealed handgun.

Sec. 12. REVOCATION.
(a) A license may be revoked under this section if the license holder:
(1) was not entitled to the license at the time it was issued;
(2) gave false information on the application;
(3) subsequently becomes ineligible for a license under Section 2 of this article; or
(4) is convicted of an offense under Section 46.035, Penal Code.
(b) If a peace officer believes a reason listed in Subsection (a) of this section to revoke a license exists, the peace officer shall prepare an affidavit on a form provided by the department stating the reason for the revocation of the license and giving the department all of the information available to the peace officer at the time of the preparation of the form. The officer shall attach the officer's reports relating to the license holder to the form and send the form and attachments to the appropriate division of the department at its Austin headquarters not later than the fifth working day after the date the form is prepared. The officer shall send a copy of the form and the attachments to the license holder. If the license holder has not surrendered the license or the license was not seized as evidence, the license holder shall surrender the license to the appropriate division of the department not later than the 10th day after the date the license holder receives the notice of revocation from the department, unless the license holder requests a hearing from the department. The license holder may request that the justice court in the justice court precinct in which the license holder resides review the revocation as provided by Section 7 of this

article. If a request is made for the justice court to review the revocation and hold a hearing, the license holder shall surrender the license on the date an order of revocation has been entered by the justice court.

(c) A license holder whose license has been revoked for a reason listed in this section may reapply as a new applicant for the issuance of a license under this article after the second anniversary of the date of the revocation if the cause for revocation does not exist on the date of the second anniversary. If the cause of revocation exists on the date of the second anniversary after the date of revocation, the license holder may not apply for a new license until the cause for the revocation no longer exists and has not existed for a period of two years.

Sec. 13. SUSPENSION OF LICENSE.

(a) A license may be suspended under this section if the license holder:

(1) is convicted of disorderly conduct punishable as a Class C misdemeanor under Section 42.01, Penal Code;

(2) fails to display a license as required by Section 6 of this article;

(3) fails to notify the department of a change of address or name as required by Section 8 of this article;

(4) carries a concealed handgun under the authority of this article of a different category than the license holder is licensed to carry;

(5) has been charged by indictment with the commission of an offense that would make the license holder ineligible for a license on conviction; or

(6) fails to return a previously issued license after a license is modified as required by Section 10(d) of this article.

(b) If any peace officer believes a reason listed in Subsection (a) of this section to suspend a license exists, the officer shall prepare an affidavit on a form provided by the department stating the reason for the suspension of the license and giving the department all of the information available to the officer at the time of the preparation of the form. The officer shall attach the officer's reports relating to the license holder to the form and send the form and the attachments to the appropriate division of the department at its Austin headquarters not later than the fifth working day after the date the form is prepared. The officer shall send a copy of the form and the attachments to the license holder. If the license holder has not surrendered the license or the license was not seized as evidence, the license holder shall surrender the license to the appropriate division of the department not later than the 10th day after the date the license holder receives the notice of suspension from the department unless the license holder requests a hearing from the department. The license holder may request that the justice court in the justice court precinct in which the license holder resides review the suspension as provided by Section 7 of this article. If a request is made for the justice court to review the suspension and hold a hearing, the license holder shall surrender the license on the date an order of suspension has been entered by the justice court.

(c) A license may be suspended under this section for not less than one year and not more than three years.

Sec. 14. SEIZURE OF HANDGUN AND LICENSE.

(a) If a peace officer arrests and takes into custody a license holder who is carrying a handgun under the authority of this article, the peace office shall seize the license holder's handgun and license as evidence.

(b) The provisions of Article 18.19, Code of Criminal Procedure, relating to the disposition of weapons seized in connection with criminal offenses, apply to a handgun seized under this subsection.

(c) Any judgment of conviction entered by any court for an offense under Section 46.035, Penal Code, shall contain the handgun license number of the convicted license holder. A certified copy of the judgment is conclusive and sufficient evidence to justify revocation of a license under Section 12(a)(4) of this article.

Sec. 15. LIMITATION OF LIABILITY.

(a) A court may not hold the state, an agency or subdivision of the state, an officer or employee of the state, a peace officer, or a qualified handgun instructor liable for damages caused by:

(1) an action authorized under this article or failure to perform a duty imposed by this article; or

(2) the actions of an applicant or license holder that occur after the applicant has received a license or been denied a license under this article.

(b) A cause of action in damages may not be brought against the state, an agency or subdivision of the state, an officer or employee of the state, a peace officer, or a qualified handgun instructor for any damage caused by the actions of an applicant or license holder under this article.

(c) The department is not responsible for any injury or damage inflicted on any person by an applicant or license holder arising or alleged to have arisen from an action taken by the department under this article.

(d) The immunities granted above under Subsections (a), (b), and (c) do not apply to acts or failures to act by the state, an agency or subdivision of the state, an officer of the state, or a peace officer when such acts or failures to act were capricious or arbitrary.

Sec. 16. HANDGUN PROFICIENCY REQUIREMENT.

(a) The director shall by rule establish minimum standards for handgun proficiency and shall develop a course to teach handgun proficiency and examinations to measure handgun proficiency. The course to teach handgun proficiency must contain training sessions divided into two parts. One part of the course must be classroom instruction and the other part must be range instruction and an actual demonstration by the applicant of the applicant's ability to safely and proficiently use the handgun for which the applicant seeks certification. An applicant may not be certified unless the applicant demonstrates, at a minimum, the degree of proficiency that is required to effectively operate a 9-millimeter or .38-caliber handgun. The department shall distribute the standards, course requirements, and examinations on request to any qualified handgun instructor.

(b) A handgun proficiency course must be administered by a qualified handgun instructor and must include at least 10 hours and not more than 15 hours of instruction on:

(1) the laws that relate to weapons and to the use of deadly force;

(2) handgun use, proficiency, and safety;

(3) nonviolent dispute resolution; and

(4) proper storage practices for handguns with an emphasis on storage practices that eliminate the possibility of accidental injury to a child.

(c) The department shall by rule develop a continuing education course in handgun proficiency for a license holder who wishes to renew a license. The continuing education course shall be administered by a qualified handgun instructor and must include at least four hours of instruction on one or more of the subjects listed in Subsection (b) of this section and include other information the director determines is appropriate.

(d) The proficiency examination to obtain or to renew a license must be administered by a qualified handgun instructor and must include:

(1) a written section on the subjects listed in Subsection (b) of this section; and

(2) a physical demonstration of proficiency in the use of one or more handguns of specific categories and in handgun safety procedures.

(e) The proficiency examination to modify a license must be administered by a qualified handgun instructor and must include a physical demonstration of the proficiency in the use of one or more handguns of specific categories and in handgun safety procedures.

(f) The department shall develop and distribute directions and materials for course instruction, test administration, and recordkeeping. All test results shall be sent to the department, and the department shall maintain a record of the results.

(g) A person who wishes to obtain or renew a license to carry a concealed handgun shall apply in person to a qualified handgun instructor to take the appropriate course in handgun proficiency, demonstrate handgun proficiency, and obtain a handgun proficiency certificate as described by Section 17 of this article.

(h) A license holder who wishes to modify a license to allow the license holder to carry a handgun of a different category than the license indicates shall apply in person to a qualified handgun instructor to demonstrate the required knowledge and proficiency to obtain a handgun proficiency certificate in that category as described by Section 17 of this article.

(i) A certified firearms instructor of the department may monitor any class or training presented by a qualified handgun instructor. A qualified handgun instructor shall cooperate with the department in the department's efforts to monitor the presentation of training by the qualified handgun instructor. A qualified handgun instructor shall make available for inspection to the department any and all records maintained by a qualified handgun instructor under this article. The qualified handgun instructor shall keep a record of all certificates of handgun proficiency issued by the qualified handgun instructor and other information required by the department by rule.

(j) The department shall conduct a study to determine the effectiveness and feasibility of allowing an applicant to take a written competency examination administered by a qualified handgun instructor in lieu of attending the classroom instruction required under this section as part of the handgun proficiency course. The department shall report the findings of the study to the legislature not later than January 31, 1997.

Sec. 17. HANDGUN PROFICIENCY CERTIFICATE.

(a) The department shall develop a sequentially numbered handgun proficiency certificate and distribute the certificate to qualified handgun instructors who administer the handgun proficiency examination described in Section 16 of this article. The department by rule may set a fee not to exceed $5 to cover the cost of their certificates.

(b) If a person successfully completes the proficiency requirements as described in Section 16 of this article, the instructor shall endorse a certificate of handgun proficiency provided by the department. An applicant must successfully complete both classroom and range instruction to receive a certificate. The certificate must indicate the category of any handgun for which the applicant demonstrated proficiency during the examination.

(c) A qualified handgun instructor may submit to the department a written recommendation for disapproval of the application for a license, renewal, or modification of a license, accompanied by an affidavit stating personal knowledge or naming persons with personal knowledge of facts that lead the instructor to believe that an applicant is not qualified for handgun proficiency certification.

Sec. 18. QUALIFIED HANDGUN INSTRUCTORS.

(a) The director may certify as a qualified handgun instructor a person who:

(1) is certified by the Commission on Law Enforcement Officer Standards and Education or the Texas Board of Private Investigators and Private Security Agencies to instruct others in the use of handguns;

(2) regularly instructs others in the use of handguns and has graduated from a handgun instructor school that uses a nationally accepted course designed to train persons as handgun instructors; or

(3) is certified by the National Rifle Association of America as a handgun instructor.

(b) In addition to the qualifications described by Subsection (a) of this section, a qualified handgun instructor must be qualified to instruct persons in:

(1) the laws that relate to weapons and to the use of deadly force;

(2) handgun use, proficiency, and safety;

(3) nonviolent dispute resolution; and

(4) proper storage practices for handguns, including storage practices that eliminate the possibility of accidental injury to a child.

(c) The department shall provide training to an individual who applies for certification as a qualified handgun instructor. An applicant shall pay a fee of $100 to the department for the training. An applicant must take and successfully complete the training offered by the department and pay the training fee before the department may certify the applicant as a qualified handgun instructor. The department shall waive the requirements regarding a handgun proficiency certification under Section 17 of this article for an applicant for a license to carry a concealed handgun who takes and successfully completes training under this subsection and pays the training fee. The department by rule may prorate or waive the training fee for an employee of another governmental entity.

(d) The certification of a qualified handgun instructor expires on the second anniversary after the date of certification. To renew a certification, the qualified handgun instructor must pay a fee of $100 and take and successfully complete the retraining courses required by rule of the department.

(e) After certification, a qualified handgun instructor may conduct training for applicants for a license under this article.

(f) If the department determines that a reason exists to revoke, suspend, or deny a license to carry a concealed handgun with respect to a person who is a qualified handgun instructor or an applicant for certification as a qualified handgun instructor, the department shall take that action against the person's certification as a qualified handgun instructor regardless of whether the person has a license issued under this article to carry a concealed handgun.

Sec. 19. REVIEW OF DENIAL, REVOCATION, OR SUSPENSION OF CERTIFICATION AS QUALIFIED HANDGUN INSTRUCTOR.

The procedures for the review of a denial, revocation, or suspension of a license under Section 7 of this article apply to the review of a denial, revocation, or suspension of certification as a qualified handgun instructor. The notice provisions of this article relating to denial, revocation, or suspension of handgun licenses apply to the proposed denial, revocation, or suspension of a certification of a qualified handgun instructor or applicant therefor.

Sec. 20. CONFIDENTIALITY OF RECORDS.

The department shall disclose to a criminal justice agency information contained in its files and records regarding whether a named individual or any individual named in a specified list is licensed under this article. The department shall, on written request and payment of a reasonable fee to cover costs of copying, disclose to any other individual whether a named individual or any individual whose full name is listed on a specified written list is licensed under this article. Information on an individual subject to disclosure under this section includes the individual's name, date of birth, gender, race, and zip code. Except as otherwise provided by this section and by Section 21 of this article, all other records maintained under this article are confidential and are not subject to mandatory disclosure under the open records law, Chapter 552, Government Code, except that the applicant or license holder may be furnished a copy of such disclosable records on request and the payment of a reasonable fee. The department shall notify a license holder of any request that is made for information relating to the license holder under this section and provide the name of the person or agency making the request. Nothing in this section shall prevent the department from making public and distributing to the public at no cost lists of individuals who are certified as qualified handgun instructors by the department.

Sec. 21. STATISTICAL REPORT.

The department shall make available, on request and payment of a reasonable fee to cover costs of copying, a statistical report that includes the number of licenses issued, denied, revoked, or suspended by the department during the preceding month, listed by age, gender, race, and zip code of the applicant or license holder.

Sec. 22. RULES.

The director shall adopt rules to administer this article.

Sec. 23. FUNDS.

The department shall forward the fees collected under this article to the comptroller of public accounts. The comptroller shall deposit the fees to the credit of an account in the general revenue fund to be known as the concealed handgun license account. The legislature may appropriate funds from the account only for the purpose of paying the costs of the department in implementing this article. At the end of each fiscal year, the comptroller shall transfer the excess funds in the account to the state treasury to the credit of the crime victims compensation fund.

Sec. 24. NOTICE.

(a) For the purpose of a notice required by this article, the department may assume that the address currently reported to the department by the applicant or license holder is the correct address.

(b) A written notice meets the requirements under this article if the notice is sent by certified mail to the current address reported by the applicant or license holder to the department.

(c) If a notice is returned to the department because the notice is not deliverable, the department may give notice by publication once in a newspaper of general interest in the county of the applicant's or license holder's last reported address. On the 31st day after the date the notice is published, the department may take the action proposed in the notice.

Sec. 25. METHOD OF PAYMENT.

A person may pay a fee required by this article only by cashier's check, money order made payable to the "Texas Department of Public Safety," or any other method approved by the department. A fee received by the department under this article is nonrefundable.

Sec. 26. LICENSE A BENEFIT.
The issuance of a license under this article is a benefit to the license holder for
  purposes of those sections of the Penal Code to which the definition of "benefit"
  under Section 1.07, Penal Code, apply.

Sec. 27. LAW ENFORCEMENT OFFICER ALIAS HANDGUN LICENSE.
(a) On written approval of the director, the department may issue to a law
  enforcement officer an alias license to carry a concealed handgun to be used in
  supervised activities involving criminal investigations.
(b) It is a defense to prosecution under Section 46.035, Initial Penal Code, that the
  actor, at the time of the commission of the offense, was the holder of an alias
  license issued under this section.

Sec. 28. HONORABLY RETIRED PEACE OFFICERS.
(a) A person who is licensed as a peace officer under Chapter 415, Government
  Code, and who has been employed full-time as a peace officer by a law
  enforcement agency may apply for a license under this article on retirement. The
  application must be made not later than the first anniversary after the date of
  retirement.
(b) The person shall submit two complete sets of legible and classifiable fingerprints
  and a sworn statement from the head of the law enforcement agency employing
  the applicant. The statement shall include:
(1) the name and rank of the applicant;
(2) the status of the applicant before retirement;
(3) whether or not the applicant was accused of misconduct at the time of the
  retirement;
(4) the physical and mental condition of the applicant;
(5) the type of weapons the applicant had demonstrated proficiency with during the
  last year of employment;
(6) whether the applicant would be eligible for reemployment with the agency, and if
  not, the reasons the applicant is not eligible; and
(7) a recommendation from the agency head regarding the issuance of a license
  under this article.
(c) The department may issue a license under this article to an applicant under this
  section if the applicant is honorably retired and physically and emotionally fit to
  possess a handgun. In this subsection, "honorably retired" means the applicant:
(1) did not retire in lieu of any disciplinary action;
(2) was employed as a full-time peace officer for not less than 10 years by one
  agency; and
(3) is entitled to receive a pension or annuity for service as a law enforcement
  officer.
(d) An applicant under this section shall pay a fee of $25 for a license issued under
  this article.
(e) A retired peace officer who obtains a license under this article must maintain, for
  the category of weapon licensed, the proficiency required for a peace officer
  under Section 415.035, Government Code. The department or a local law
  enforcement agency shall allow a retired peace officer of the department or
  agency an opportunity to annually demonstrate the required proficiency. The
  proficiency shall be reported to the department on application and renewal.
(f) A license issued under this section expires as provided by Section 9 of this
  article.
(g) A retired criminal investigator of the United States who is designated as a "special
  agent" is eligible for a license under this section. An applicant described by this
  subsection may submit the application at any time after retirement. The applicant
  shall submit with the application proper proof of retired status by presenting the
  following documents prepared by the agency from which the applicant retired:
(1) retirement credentials; and
(2) a letter from the agency head stating the applicant retired in good standing.

Sec. 29. APPLICATION TO LICENSED SECURITY OFFICERS.
This article does not exempt a license holder who is also employed as a security
  officer and licensed under the Private Investigators and Private Security Agencies
  Act (Article 4413(29bb), Vernon's Texas Civil Statutes) from the duty to comply
  with that Act or Section 46.02, Penal Code.

Sec. 30. ACTIVE AND RETIRED JUDICIAL OFFICERS.
(a) In this section:

(1) "Active judicial officer" means a person serving as a judge or justice of the supreme court, the court of criminal appeals, a court of appeals, a district court, a criminal district court, a constitutional county court, a statutory county court, a justice court, or a municipal court.

(2) "Retired judicial officer" means:

(A) a special judge appointed under Section 26.023 or 26.024, Government Code; or

(B) a senior judge designated under Section 75.001, Government Code, or a judicial officer as designated or defined by Section 75.001, 831.001, or 836.001, Government Code.

(b) Notwithstanding any other provision of this article, the department shall issue a license under this article to an active or retired judicial officer who meets the requirements of this section.

(c) An active judicial officer is eligible for a license to carry a concealed handgun under the authority of this article. A retired judicial officer is eligible for a license to carry a concealed handgun under the authority of this article if the officer:

(1) has not been convicted of a felony;

(2) has not, in the five years preceding the date of application, been convicted of a Class A or Class B misdemeanor;

(3) is not charged with the commission of a Class A or Class B misdemeanor or of a felony under an information or indictment;

(4) is not a chemically dependent person; and

(5) is not a person of unsound mind.

(d) An applicant for a license who is an active or retired judicial officer must submit to the department:

(1) a completed application on a form prescribed by the department;

(2) two recent color passport photographs of the applicant;

(3) a handgun proficiency certificate issued to the applicant as evidence that the applicant successfully completed the proficiency requirements of this article;

(4) a nonrefundable application and license fee set by the department in an amount reasonably designed to cover the administrative costs associated with issuance of a license to carry a concealed handgun under this article; and

(5) if the applicant is a retired judicial officer:

(A) two complete sets of legible and classifiable fingerprints of the applicant taken by a person employed by a law enforcement agency who is appropriately trained in recording fingerprints; and

(B) a form executed by the applicant that authorizes the department to make an inquiry into any noncriminal history records that are necessary to determine the applicant's eligibility for a license under this article.

(e) On receipt of all the application materials required by this section, the department shall:

(1) if the applicant is an active judicial officer, issue a license to carry a concealed handgun under the authority of this article; or

(2) if the applicant is a retired judicial officer, conduct an appropriate background investigation to determine the applicant's eligibility for the license and, if the applicant is eligible, issue a license to carry a concealed handgun under the authority of this article.

(f) Except as otherwise provided by this subsection, an applicant for a license under this section must satisfy the handgun proficiency requirements of Section 16 of this article. The classroom instruction part of the proficiency course for an active judicial officer is not subject to a minimum hour requirement. The instruction must include instruction only on:

(1) handgun use, proficiency, and safety; and

(2) proper storage practices for handguns with an emphasis on storage practices that eliminate the possibility of accidental injury to a child.

(g) A license issued under this section expires as provided by Section 9 of this article and, except as otherwise provided by this subsection, may be renewed in accordance with Section 11 of this article. An active judicial officer is not required to attend the classroom instruction part of the continuing education proficiency course to renew a license.

(h) The department shall issue a license to carry a concealed handgun under the authority of this article to an elected attorney representing the state in the prosecution of felony cases who meets the requirements of this section for an active judicial officer. The department shall waive any fee required for the issuance of an original, duplicate, or renewed license under this article for an applicant who is an attorney elected or employed to represent the state in the prosecution of felony cases.

Sec. 31. NOTICE REQUIRED ON CERTAIN PREMISES.

(a) A business that has a permit or license issued under Chapter 25, 28, 32, or 69, Alcoholic Beverage Code, and that derives 51 percent or more of its income from the sale of alcoholic beverages for on-premises consumption shall prominently display at each entrance to the business a sign that complies with the requirements of Subsection (c) of this section.

(b) A hospital licensed under Chapter 241, Health and Safety Code, or a nursing home licensed under Chapter 242, Health and Safety Code, shall prominently display at each entrance to the hospital or nursing home, as appropriate, a sign that complies with the requirements of Subsection (c) of this section.

(c) The sign required under Subsections (a) and (b) of this section must give notice in both English and Spanish that it is unlawful to carry a handgun on the premises. The sign must appear in contrasting colors with block letters at least one inch in height and shall be displayed in a conspicuous manner clearly visible to the public.

Sec. 32. RIGHTS OF EMPLOYERS.

This article does not prevent or otherwise limit the right of a public or private employer to prohibit persons who are licensed under this article from carrying a concealed handgun on the premises of the business.

Sec. 33. REDUCTION OF FEES DUE TO INDIGENCY.

(a) Notwithstanding any other provision of this article, the department shall reduce by 50 percent any fee required for the issuance of an original, duplicate, modified, or renewed license under this article if the department determines that the applicant is indigent.

(b) The department shall require an applicant requesting a reduction of a fee to submit proof of indigency with the application materials.

(c) For purposes of this section, an applicant is indigent if the applicant's income is not more than 100 percent of the applicable income level established by the federal poverty guidelines.

Sec. 34. REDUCTION OF FEES FOR SENIOR CITIZENS.

Notwithstanding any other provision of this article, the department shall reduce by 50 percent any fee required for the issuance of an original, duplicate, or modified license under this article if the applicant for the license is 60 years of age or older.

Sec. 35. RECIPROCAL LICENSE.

On application by a person who has a valid license to carry a concealed handgun issued by another state, the department may issue to the person a license under this article without requiring that the person meet eligibility requirements or pay fees otherwise imposed under this article, but only if the department determines that:

(1) the eligibility requirements imposed by the other state are at least as rigorous as the requirements imposed by this article; and

(2) the other state provides reciprocal licensing privileges to a person who holds a license issued under this article and applies for a license in the other state.

Sec. 36. AUTHORITY OF A PEACE OFFICER TO DISARM.

A peace officer who is acting in the lawful discharge of the officer's official duties is authorized to disarm a license holder at any time when the peace officer reasonably believes it is necessary for the protection of the license holder, peace officer, or other individuals. The peace officer shall return the handgun to the license holder before discharging the license holder from the scene when the peace officer has determined that the license holder is not a threat to the peace officer, license holder, or other individuals, and providing that the license holder has not violated any provision of this Act, or has not committed any other violation that results in the arrest of the license holder.

SECTION 2. Subsection (b), Section 46.02, Penal Code, is amended to read as follows:

(b) It is a defense to prosecution under this section that the actor was, at the time of the commission of the offense:

(1) in the actual discharge of his official duties as a member of the armed forces or state military forces as defined by Section 431.001, Government Code, or as a guard employed by a penal institution;

(2) on his own premises or premises under his control unless he is an employee or agent of the owner of the premises and his primary responsibility is to act in the capacity of a security guard to protect persons or property, in which event he must comply with Subdivision (5);

(3) traveling;

(4) engaging in lawful hunting, fishing, or other sporting activity on the immediate premises where the activity is conducted, or was directly en route between the premises and the actor's residence, if the weapon is a type commonly used in the activity;

(5) a person who holds a security officer commission issued by the Texas Board of Private Investigators and Private Security Agencies, if:

(A) he is engaged in the performance of his duties as a security officer or traveling to and from his place of assignment;

(B) he is wearing a distinctive uniform; and

(C) the weapon is in plain view; [or]

(6) a peace officer, other than a person commissioned by the Texas State Board of Pharmacy; or

(7) carrying a concealed handgun and a valid license issued under Article 4413 (29ee), Revised Statutes, to carry a concealed handgun of the same category as the handgun the person is carrying.

SECTION 3. Subsection (f), Section 46.03, Penal Code, is amended to read as follows:

(f) It is not a defense to prosecution under this section that the actor possessed a handgun and was licensed to carry a concealed handgun under Article 4413 (29ee), Revised Statutes.

(g) An offense under this section is a third degree felony.

SECTION 4. Chapter 46, Penal Code, is amended by adding Section 46.035 to read as follows:

Sec. 46.035. UNLAWFUL CARRYING OF HANDGUN BY LICENSE HOLDER.

(a) A license holder commits an offense if the license holder carries a handgun on or about the license holder's person under the authority of Article 4413 (29ee), Revised Statutes, and intentionally fails to conceal the handgun.

(b) A license holder commits an offense if the license holder intentionally, knowingly, or recklessly carries a handgun under the authority of Article 4413 (29ee), Revised Statutes, regardless of whether the handgun is concealed, on or about the license holder's person:

(1) on the premises of a business that has a permit or license issued under Chapter 25, 28, 32, or 69, Alcoholic Beverage Code, if the business derives 51 percent or more of its income from the sale of alcoholic beverages for on-premises consumption;

(2) on the premises where a high school, collegiate, or professional sporting event or interscholastic event is taking place, unless the license holder is a participant in the event and a handgun is used in the event;

(3) on the premises of a correctional facility;

(4) on the premises of a hospital licensed under Chapter 241, Health and Safety Code, or on the premises of a nursing home licensed under Chapter 242, Health and Safety Code, unless the license holder has written authorization of the hospital or nursing home administration, as appropriate;

(5) in an amusement park; or

(6) on the premises of a church, synagogue, or other established place of religious worship.

(c) A license holder commits an offense if the license holder intentionally, knowingly, or recklessly carries a handgun under the authority of Article 4413 (29ee), Revised Statutes, regardless of whether the handgun is concealed, at any meeting of a governmental entity.

(d) A license holder commits an offense if, while intoxicated, the license holder carries a handgun under the authority of Article 4413 (29ee), Revised Statutes, regardless of whether the handgun is concealed.

(e) A license holder who is licensed as a security officer under the Private
     Investigators and Private Security Agencies Act (Article 4413 (29bb), Vernon's
     Texas Civil Statutes) and employed as a security officer commits an offense if,
     while in the course and scope of the security officer's employment, the security
     officer violates a provision of Article 4413 (29ee), Revised Statutes.
(f) In this section:
(1) "Amusement park" means a permanent indoor or outdoor facility or park where
     amusement rides are available for use by the public that is located in a county
     with a population of more than 1 million, encompasses at least 75 acres in
     surface area, is enclosed with access only through controlled entries, is open for
     operation more than 120 days in each calendar year, and has security guards on
     the premises at all times. The term does not include any public or private
     driveway, street, sidewalk or walkway, parking lot, parking garage, or other
     parking area.
(2) "License holder" means a person licensed to carry a handgun under Article
     4413 (29ee), Revised Statutes.
(3) "Premises" means a building or a portion of a building. The term does not
     include any public or private driveway, street, sidewalk or walkway, parking lot,
     parking garage, or other parking area.
(g) An offense under Subsection (a), (b), (c), (d), or (e) is a Class A misdemeanor,
     unless the offense is committed under Subsection (b) (1) or (b) (3), in which
     event the offense is a felony of the third degree.
(h) It is a defense to prosecution under Subsection (a) that the actor, at the time of
     the commission of the offense, displayed the handgun under circumstances in
     which the actor would have been justified in the use of deadly force under
     Chapter 9.

SECTION 5. Section 51.16, Family Code, is amended by adding Subsection (m) to
     read as follows:
(m) On request of the Department of Public Safety, a juvenile court shall reopen and
     allow the department to inspect the files and records of the juvenile court relating
     to an applicant for a license to carry a concealed handgun under Article 4413
     (29ee), Revised Statutes.

SECTION 6. Subchapter D, Chapter 411, Government Code, is amended by adding
     Section 411.047 to read as follows:
Sec. 411.0747. REPORTING RELATED TO CONCEALED HANDGUN INCIDENTS.
(a) The department shall maintain statistics related to responses by law enforcement
     agencies to incidents in which a person licensed to carry a handgun under Article
     4413 (29ee), Revised Statutes, is arrested for an offense under Section 46.035,
     Penal Code, or discharges a handgun.
(b) The department by rule shall adopt procedures for local law enforcement to
     make reports to the department described by Subsection (a).

SECTION 7. Section 215.001 (b), Local Government Code, is amended to read as
     follows:
(b) Subsection (a) does not affect the authority a municipality has under another law
     to:
(1) require residents or public employees to be armed for personal or national
     defense, law enforcement, or other lawful purpose;
(2) regulate the discharge of firearms within the limits of the municipality;
(3) regulate the use of property, the location of a business, or uses at a business
     under the municipality's fire code, zoning ordinance, or land-use regulations as
     long as the code, ordinance, or regulations are not used to circumvent the intent
     of Subsection (a) or Subdivision (5) of this subsection;
(4) regulate the use of firearms in the case of an insurrection, riot, or natural disaster
     if the municipality finds the regulations necessary to protect public health and
     safety;
(5) regulate the storage or transportation of explosives to protect public health and
     safety, except that 25 pounds or less of black powder for each private residence
     and 50 pounds or less of black powder for each retail dealer are not subject to
     regulation; or

(6) regulate the carrying of a firearm by a person other than a person licensed to carry a concealed handgun under Article 4413 (29ee), Revised Statutes, at a:
(A) public park;
(B) public meeting of a municipality, county, or other governmental body;
(C) political rally, parade, or official political meeting; or
(D) nonfirearms-related school, college, or professional athletic event.

SECTION 8.

(a) This Act takes effect September 1, 1995, except that a license issued under this Act before January 1, 1996, is not effective until January 1, 1996. A license issued before January 1, 1996, shall be clearly marked to reflect the date on which it becomes effective, and the director of the Department of Public Safety shall inform each recipient of a license before that date that the license is not effective until that date.

(b) Notwithstanding Subsection (a), Section 9, Article 4413 (29ee), Revised Statutes, as added by this Act, the Department of Public Safety by rule may adopt a system to implement staggered and evenly distributed license expiration dates over the four-year period beginning January 1, 1996. The department may not issue a license that is effective for less than two years. A license that is effective for less than four years and is renewed expires as provided by Subsection (b), Section 9, Article 4413 (29ee), Revised Statutes, as added by this Act. Notwithstanding Subdivision (6), Subsection (a), Section 3, Article 4413 (29ee), Revised Statutes, as added by this Act, the department by rule shall prorate the nonrefundable application and license fee for applicants who receive licenses that are effective for less than four years under this subsection.

SECTION 9. The Department of Public Safety shall adopt the rules and establish the procedures required by Section 411.047, Government Code, as added by Section 6 of this Act, not later than January 1, 1996.

SECTION 10. An offense committed before January 1, 1996, is covered by the law in effect when the offense is committed, and the former law is continued in effect for this purpose.

SECTION 11. The importance of this legislation and the crowded condition of the calendars in both houses create an emergency and an imperative public necessity that the constitutional rule requiring bills to be read on three several days in each house be suspended, and this rule is hereby suspended.

About Alan Korwin

Alan Korwin is a professional writer and management consultant with two decades of experience in business, technical, news and promotional communication. He is a founder and two-term past president of the Arizona Book Publishing Association, on the national publicity committee of the Society for Technical Communication, and a former board member of the Society of Professional Journalists, Valley of the Sun Chapter.

Mr. Korwin helped forge the largest enclave of technologists in the state, as steering committee chair for the Arizona Coalition for Computer Technologies; he did the publicity for Pulitzer Prize cartoonist Steve Benson's 4th book; he wrote a business plan which raised $5 million in venture capital and launched SkyMall; in an executive-level strategic plan he helped American Express define its worldwide telecommunications strategy for the 1990s; and he had a hand in developing ASPED, Arizona's economic strategic plan. Korwin's writing appears regularly in local and national publications, and he serves an extensive business client base.

In 1990 Mr. Korwin introduced a unique seminar entitled, *Instant Expertise—How To Find Out Practically Anything, Fast.* The 4-hour course reveals the trade secrets he uses to gather any information short of espionage—and this is not about databases. He also teaches writing (How To Get Yourself Published At Last), publishing (The Secret of Self-Publishing), phone power (How to Supercharge Your Telephones) and publicity (The Secret of Free Publicity), at colleges, for businesses and privately. His talk on Constitutional issues (The Pen and The Sword, Constitutional Rights Under Attack) is a real eye opener.

Alan Korwin is originally from New York City, where his clients included IBM, AT&T, NYNEX and others, many with real names. In 1986, finally married, he moved to the Valley of the Sun. It was a joyful and successful move.

About Georgene Lockwood

Georgene Lockwood has written about everything from car racing and computers to weddings and comic books, in a 20-year writing career. After a stint as a newspaper reporter, she worked for high-tech and industrial companies as a marketing communications specialist and public relations counselor, both on-staff and as president of her own communications company.

Lockwood has covered auto racing for the Associated Press and has written for the Skip Barber Racing School. She is a member of the International Motor Press Association and the Madison Avenue Sports Car Driving and Chowder Society.

An interest in American social history and handcrafts is reflected in much of Georgene Lockwood's recent work. She's the author of *Your Victorian Wedding: A Modern Guide for the Romantic Bride* (Prentice-Hall), and her work has appeared in *Working Woman*, *Modern Bride*, *Victorian Decorating and Lifestyles*, *Country Decorator* and *Lady's Circle Patchwork Quilts*.

Lockwood writes about computers, specializing in hardware and telecommunications, and has written for such technical publications as *Computerworld*, *Computer Graphics World* and *Computer Decisions*. She is a CompuServe sysop, has lectured widely on the use of online services, and has taught journalism at the university level.

An avid target shooter, Lockwood is working on *Pistol Packin' Mamas*, a book about the history of women and firearms in America. Lockwood is the founder and current president of the Arizona chapter of the American Society of Journalists and Authors, and is a member of the Authors Guild and the American History Association.

Originally from New York City, Lockwood resides with her husband Jim, a well known Hollywood-gun-leather maker, in Prescott, Arizona.

About The Pensus Group

This book has been produced in cooperation with The Pensus Group. Pensus is an eclectic firm, comprised of individuals and companies active in diversified businesses. These range from commercial real estate development and public-private partnerships to marinas and an all-purpose outdoor western theme town, Cowtown. One division of the firm helps equip law enforcement agencies in 14 states, and Pensus owns Shooter's World, in Phoenix, Ariz., one of the largest retail gun ranges in America.

With the exception of a number of professional and scholarly papers (the principals all hold advanced degrees) *The Texas Gun Owner's Guide* represents their initial venture in the book publishing field.

Also by *Alan Korwin*

THE ARIZONA GUN OWNER'S GUIDE

Bloomfield Press (Phoenix) $10.95
ISBN: 0-9621958-3-9 160pp., illus., softcover

The one book every gun owner in Arizona should have. Plain English descriptions of the gun laws for private citizens, complete text of the state gun laws, training material for concealed-weapon-permit applicants, more than 150 self-test questions, 22 lethal-encounter scenarios with commentary for study and discussion and much more. The most complete treatment available anywhere of one state's handling of the 2nd Amendment to the Constitution. Used and endorsed statewide, now in its *15th* edition.

"Indispensable" *–Arizona Highways*

WICKENBURG!
The ultimate guide to the ultimate western town.

Bloomfield Press (Phoenix) $9.95
ISBN: 0-9621958-1-2 176pp., illus., photo, softcover

If you have any love at all for the American West then this book—and this incredible little town—is for you! Everything imaginable about Wickenburg, a 130-year-old pioneer city spawned by gold. Dig into its history and folklore, what to see when you visit, where to eat, the world-famous Dude and Guest Ranches, the original Vulture Mine that started it all, the great dam disaster that inspired countless books and movies, horseback events, golf, rockhounding, the town's famous museum, the historic downtown tour, more!

SCOTTSDALE

by Alan Korwin and William Franklin
American and World Geographic Publishing, Helena, Montana
*ISBN: 1-56037-019-X, **96 full-color photos**, 104 pp., softcover, $15.95*

A glorious full-color table-top book about one of America's most scenic cities. Covers the history from before people walked the land through the nightlife in downtown today. Be careful reading the lush prose in these pages—you'll want to move to Scottsdale.

IT'S NOT JUST A BOOK, IT'S AN EVENT

Produced by *Alan Korwin*
with Attorney Michael P. Anthony

ISBN: 0-9621958-6-3, 336 pp., illus., $19.95 (+$3 S&H)

Brand new and very hot! Takes all the guesswork out of federal gun law, explains clearly how the whole thing works. Covers citizens, dealers, manufacturers, importers, collectors, the "proper" authorities, the Militia, the National Guard, global disarmament, explosives, great laws, bad laws, 70 pages of juicy intro material, the lost National Right to Carry; without a doubt it is *the* fundamental firearm reference book.

America's gun laws are generally excellent and quite clear—they protect the right of the people to bear arms for all lawful purposes, carefully regulate government involvement, and severely punish any criminal activity. The gun laws are such a mystery, basically, because very few people have ever seen them all.

"Replaces the black whole of ignorance with the bright white light of knowledge."

"Outstanding" –Bob Corbin
"Unique" –Stephen P. Halbrook, Ph.D.
"A whale of a good job" –Joe Foss

For retail or wholesale orders, just turn the page. Easy.